Of Straw And Stripes

Of Straw And Stripes

William Lawrenson

The Pentland Press Limited
Edinburgh • Cambridge • Durham • USA

© William Lawrenson 1998

First published in 1998 by
The Pentland Press Ltd.
1 Hutton Close
South Church
Bishop Auckland
Durham

All rights reserved.
Unauthorised duplication
contravenes existing laws.

British Library Cataloguing in Publication Data.
A Catalogue record for this book is available
from the British Library.

ISBN 1 85821 579 X

Typeset by CBS, Felixstowe, Suffolk
Printed and bound by Antony Rowe Ltd, Chippenham

To Vivien, who was the first
to baptise this book with
readership.

Chapter 1

It was, I recall, a terrible winter that year. Mind you, it all depended on the viewpoint. From the attitude of winters generally – the qualities for other winters to envy, so to speak – you might say that it was in the way of being a truly glorious one. Certainly, it was providing the most biting cold we had felt for some time – an absolute misery of cold; cold that went well with the general atmosphere of gloom and depression and near despair which pervaded our part of the world; cold, indeed, that is hard to credit now, when central heating would have been stepping in as an effective muffler against its harshness. As it was, however, I have to admit to its being a winter fit to be properly proud of itself. Argue as you may about its lack of snow, it had been lacking in nothing else whatsoever so far as bleakness was concerned – and snow might in any event have broken the sheer grip of the cold and demeaned the whole season within its peculiar hierarchy.

1942! January of 1942. *That* January, indeed – a January which at once seems only hours ago, and, on reflection, veritable light-years behind me. A month of the very long ago; securely and deeply etched into History – into mine, at any rate.

For it marked, after all, the end of my particular variety of the universal 'waiting' which had been with us, on and off, for years; at first, the waiting for an increasingly inevitable outbreak of war, and, when that had become a reality, for sight of the prolonged, unspeakable, night-by-night devastation which was undoubtedly destined for us.

I have to remind myself that not everyone had had the privilege of continuing to wait so long. Books galore are now with us, in any event, to record the facts as examples, they say, of glorious triumphs of the 'British spirit'. Dunkirk, the London Blitz, the Battle of Britain – each of them rolls proudly off the tongue, in hindsight. But I was very young, and far away from them; and, at the time, they seemed more like continuing disasters of the kind which, as long as I could remember, had stacked themselves one on top of the other from the outbreak of the War and even before.

Not, of course, that we hadn't had our own samples of the horror. For a time, admittedly, the wailing of air-raid sirens continued to be nothing more than a commonplace abstraction – far separated from any real war – since it was seldom that anything more extraordinary than the eventual 'all-clear' ever happened. Once or twice, there would be the unfriendly overhead droning of a suspect aeroplane, and the probing of searchlights, and the briefest of salvos from defending guns – even, more rarely, an isolated explosion somewhere in the distance. Nothing, on the other hand, so near to us, or so concentrated or smacking at all of 'real warfare', as to worry any one of us. Becoming inured, indeed, we got to brazening it out in the cinema to the end of the main feature; fearlessly lounging home in the dusk; disdaining the precaution of our 'Anderson shelter' in favour of bedwarmth; and even – lunatic-like – believing that nothing substantial would *ever* happen. How innocent a relic of peacetime! But the viciousness of war was still not comprehensible; a bomb still a thing to be read of in books and newspapers, not at all connectable with close-quarters reality.

And then there came that particular night when it was again my turn to 'fire-watch' at my place of work, on the north side of the river. There was nothing special about fire-watching, of course. It came round about once a week, and had become every bit as uneventful as the air-raid sirens. All business premises – or sometimes small groups of them – had to ensure that at least a couple of watchers were 'watching' at any one time.

I suppose that is the obvious way of describing what we were doing during those dark, dead hours of the night. How like the bleak, soul-less trampings up and down which I was later to endure under the compulsion of 'guard duty'. But that is a later part of this story; and, by comparison, we had the luxury of sitting around and talking and drinking tea, before taking our turn to doze off. There wasn't the loneliness of the later, Army chore; but there was the same blank boredom of it all, and the same petrification of time. I came to think of it as merely keeping the building company, as it were. Fiction said that something, some day, might descend upon it from the skies – a dramatic fantasy of incendiary bombs or ill-intended high explosive. A far-fetched idea, indeed. More often than not, there was nothing to interest us in the darkness outside but silence.

I am not sure, now, whether I was the one scheduled for dozing when it was that the world around us changed for ever. I was certainly awake when it happened: it seemed nonsense to imagine I had ever slept at all, at any time. There had been the siren, and, casually peeping through the black-out curtains, we had seen searchlights and heard gun-fire. But that had happened before, and the skies had cleared quickly and uneventfully. This time, however, we sensed strange noises in the near distance. Sounding suspiciously like explosions, they continued in spasms for some time; yet they were too remote to bode danger. Nothing at all of a proper warning for what came next; of a sudden, that great, thudding, terrifying, sheer calamity of an earthquake which shook us and the building to our very foundations. More spasmodic explosions followed; and then – complete silence again, to emphasise how loud had been the noise of the guns and the planes and the bombs (what else?). There followed the sounds of excited outdoor confusion, but this time from the frantic activities around a nearby gas-mains, hit by one of the bombs.

The archives tell us that the bombing – still labelled as 'indiscriminate' (though, with bad navigation by the Germans, we were probably the wrong target altogether) – lasted that night for over an hour. Certainly, this had never been fiction. Evidently, bombs were real enough, particularly when there was the effrontery to drop them on the North-East; and from then on, the War was with us all the time, far-off happenings seeming not nearly so distant as before. Ramming home the message, a scene of complete devastation awaited me the following morning when I returned home, after crossing the river as normal by ferry. The whole of my town's market-place, together with its two principal department stores, appeared to have degenerated into piles of broken bricks and concrete. And, travelling by tramcar up to what was now my home, on the fringe of the town, I was unable to gain access to the district around it. All the streets were roped off, following the nearby dropping of a land-mine! It was only after two full hours of useless frustration that I could reassure myself that my parents were safe and our house untouched.

Normality took some time to re-assert itself. Or did it ever, after that? Admittedly, matters did settle down after a fashion; though nothing, clearly, could ever resurrect the heaps of rubbish which had been Crofton's and Woolworth's Threepenny and Sixpenny Stores; the very heart of what I had always taken for granted as completely stable and permanent. Yet that was the 'end of the performance', for the time being. One startling occurrence, and nothing more.

It was, therefore, amid this re-established and artificial peace which lingered on so tantalisingly over the next month or so, that there thrived the anxious uncertainty, all my own, as to the timing of the official summons which would be for sucking me into the armed chaos, with all the rest of them. In secret, I was dreading the unfathomability of what was to follow when those call-up papers (as inevitable now as the War itself had previously been) finally came. If landmines and bombed gas-mains went with civilian life, what could I expect when I was among the real 'fighting'?

Yet I wasn't about to leave behind me Paradise. Even thus far, I had been having a sad time of it altogether. By now, I had laboured away at that first 'proper job' of mine (a clerkship, in what I had found a denigratingly-routine Civil Service) for almost two and a half very long years; a couple of months longer, indeed, than that far-away War had been pursuing its interminable futilities of destruction. Never minding the mysterious delay in the resumption of the bombing, and the absence of any sign of the gas attacks and the great German invasion which we had been promised, the prevailing War septicaemia had already seeped into me and mine – the hitherto permanent domesticity amongst which I had been raised – long since.

Since I was nothing if not a child of my family – having always taken the unseen strength of it, clustered around me, for granted – it had been disorientating, at the very start of the War, when I found my accustomed régime descending into such strange instability. The departure from our home of people was to lead, indeed, to departure by sale of the house itself; the War dealing a cold, psychopathic *coup de grâce* to a somewhat fragile family circle. Sadly, my parents were already, increasingly, its weak link, each of the two who had created it and held it together over the bad times. When we moved out of the old place, neither was to have more than a couple of years still to live, and those only in pathetic mockery of past healthier resilience.

This remaining ration had been reduced to a mere three months by that dismal January morning, when I was leaving our 'new place' – the smart, newly-built, exclusive bungalow of my eldest brother – for what was to prove my complete regeneration. I had no idea of what lay in front of me, or whether, in fact, very much of anything did. I knew, of course, that most of the others in most of the other families were similarly being uprooted into an uncertain future; but there was an undefined, additional loneliness within me, from the sense that I had no longer any roots from which to be separated. This feeling lingered throughout my Forces experience; the lack of an excuse for feeling properly homesick; an emptiness of that background to which I should have been longing to return when the world returned to sanity. I was in limbo.

There was the irony of it, after all. Our break-up wasn't really to do with anyone being called up – not *en masse*, at any rate. In fact, I was the only one of the five of us (even the two who had already left home) not to have shelter from the umbrella of being too old, or medically or occupationally exempt; the only one ever to feel the coarseness of a Services uniform or of a Sergeant-Major's tongue. But my brother and sister, both schoolteachers, had been torn away, urgently, to be with their evacuated children in the safer reaches of the Lake District, far off on the other side of the country – and that had been that. At a stroke, the old house, losing its *raison d'être*, had become little more than an exhausted hulk, waiting for the local estate agent's funeral arrangements.

Chapter 2

At last, the waiting was over. I was wandering uncertainly down our front path, and through the gate, and away into the unknown. Was it really so foggy as all that? Come to think of it, there wasn't any – fog, I mean. Not a wisp of it around. Not even a suspicion of mist, either; just the crackle of the frost under my feet, and the bite of the cold on my ears and on fingers clutching the small case holding my belongings.

Yet there might just as well have been an invasion from the South of one of the London 'pea-soupers' for all that remains with me of that fateful journey down to Yorkshire. I knew that I had to get to Richmond (which was to be the starting-off point for what I thought of as my personal career of violence), and I know that I got there all right; but what came between that garden gate and the Richmond railway station remains clothed in dense and obstinate obscurity. Certainly, by all the laws of Nature, every inch of the journey should have heat-branded itself on my brain, for this was only the second time that I had been any distance outside my home town. In any event, I had been only small, with no more than a blur of memory, at the time of my first expedition – to that little anonymous Northumbrian cottage, barely twenty miles away, where we had spent our one and only family holiday (ever) in a constant condition of uncomfortable strangeness. You can safely say, therefore, that the outside world was still virgin wasteland where I was concerned.

I suppose that the confusion was to blame; the confusion in my mind. It must surely have haunted me all the way, first in the creaking tramcar which jolted and swayed me along to the town centre, and then in that puff-puff-puffing steam train, chugging ponderously down to the Yorkshire Dales. I couldn't possibly have had thoughts to spare – none, certainly, for any part of the scene that was moving backwards from me, irrevocably and for ever (it must have seemed), just outside my window; for I sensed that it was not just one landscape merging into another, but a complete outlook on life which was moving to lodgings in an alien set of values – with an absence of most of the things which I held most important. That is what must have obsessed me and stupefied me.

At any rate, out of doubts and uncertainties there was surfacing a strong feeling of relief. I was by way of returning to the herd. My finger-tip hold on the past had finally slipped; or, rather, it was a case of the War finally having trodden on my knuckles to make me let go. Obstinately – illogically, too: what indeed could be more irrelevant to reality? – I had recently been catching up on my deficiencies of education in the realms of music. Paying now, myself, for the piano-playing lessons which more appropriately should have been bought for me years before, I had conquered two of those rigid mid-grade examinations in fine style, the one within only months of the other. Neither of these inquisitions had caused me any real concern, but a potential third of them had been a different matter, looming up as it did for the very month when I was expecting my call-up papers to be arriving.

Apart from anything else, it had bred in me a sense of treachery. Perhaps that is putting it strongly, but certainly I was beginning to think of myself as some sort of 'conscientious objector'. A hypocritical sort, at that, which, in wartime, is the very worst of creeds. Despicable to others, and despicable to oneself.

How frequently are nightmares dismissed as unwarranted and needless by Time! Today, the delay to that dressing up of me in khaki appears paltry – an unimportant few weeks; nothing more than a drop in the ocean, you might say, of the five long years which I was to serve. Then, however, the very notion of applying for deferment of my call-up savoured of guilt and stealth, even of cowardice; qualities confirmed only too firmly within me when stubbornness finally made me post the letter.

Not, mind you, that it was my idea in the first place. Nor, strangely enough, was it anything to do with my family. (For that matter, neither had the concept of seeking out a music teacher; which had, indeed, originated with me, but in complete secrecy from all of them.) This later extension of the whole affair had, however, been sown in me – admittedly on fertile ground – by a certain Miss Gertrude Ockleford. This was the particular individual to whom, after seriously prolonged porings over the advertisement columns of the local evening newspaper, I had finally delivered myself for musical wellbeing.

Exactly how strongly her very name – surely an escaper from some glorious Victorian literary romance? – may have influenced my decision, is now blurred by the years; but it was certainly a factor. In any event, however, she was reputed to be a tower of strength among the myriad of piano teachers who practised their rather mechanical craft in the town; and when, my heart in my stomach, I first knocked at the door of her nondescript terrace house one dusky evening, I felt entirely trustful that I had chosen well – though I was not nearly so sure, by that time, that what I was intent on doing was sensible in itself. For the distance of the actual War had lent very little enchantment to the 'civvy street' left behind by all the fast-departing conscripts of the area. Everything remaining was redolent of it; its philosophy obsessed us; it had become the compelling fashion which overwhelmed our thoughts.

Having said that, to enter the Ockleford ménage was temporarily to forget; as I found its neat, cosy, well-worn interior (decorated dingily in faded fawns and reds and browns) smacking more of the First World War than the Second. The piano which rested wearily in her sitting room looked every bit as ancient as that upon which I had struggled to teach myself its basics in my own home of earlier years. Its keys, roughly trodden for so long by so many fingers, were now well past the whiteness of their youth, having by this time assumed the semblance of a set of oversized, tobacco-stained teeth, badly in need of the vigour of a stout toothbrush for the avoidance of a visit to the dentist's.

Whilst this familiar vignette of the past may not quite have matched up to my expectations, it is certain that the sight of Miss Ockleford herself fell well short of them. I had envisaged a slender, attractive, intellectual (and very possibly, for some unknown reason, bespectacled) young lady – gentle and persuasive, as all artistic creatures were bound to be. I was to have been swirled along, not only by her last word in teaching methods but by her own examples of what could only be pianistic witchery. Perhaps even approaching the keyboard acrobatics which I had heard from that Grammar School music master of ours, and within close-quarter, magnifying-glass, analytical range, into the bargain. In reality, she materialised from the recesses of her back room as a strongly-built, strongly-motivated and well-middle-aged woman; pleasant enough, in all honesty, yet clearly steeled in the whirlpool of Life against obstruction from absolutely anyone, pupils or music examiners alike.

Since (at the worst of times) I was never an obstructor, she must have viewed me from the start as something of an original. Even, perhaps, within the long succession of youngsters pushed unrelentingly in front of her by their parents, altogether unique. Evidently, no-one whosoever had pushed this one, and, in any event, a young man of all of seventeen and a half hardly qualified as a 'youngster' in the first place. Surely, manna from Heaven!

After all, nothing more than 'finishing school' was called for, if she could trust her senses. Already, somehow or other, I had evidently solved the secret of getting notes to jump from paper to keys into the reality of sound, and she gathered, indeed, that I had been able to play the instrument of a fashion long since. Probably, too, of a more reasonable fashion than I then imagined; for those untrained fingers of mine, stumbling so often from lack of technique, may have masked the many musical truths which I had profitably been absorbing into my system amidst the clumsiness of my labours. At any rate – unlike the very many who are content only to dabble – I had by now the surest of instincts as to how I wanted the music itself to speak at the end of the affair; a finished product rightly as stimulating as the mere mechanics of it may have been boring. Simply pressing down the correct keys had never held much interest for me, once I had first heard (on the wireless) real musicians really performing, more often than not with the most exquisite subtleties of expression.

What I got, as it turned out, was not what I wanted but what I needed. I had looked forward to hearing, by example, the very best that a piano could provide. I was to have been dazzled and bemused by the blur of fingers speeding over the keys, and then to have drooled over the seamlessness of singing tones apparently unrelated to any fingers whatsoever. Without doubt, I would be titillated by the sheer magnificence of a good instrument's sonorities, when played properly. Instead of such heady excitement, however, I was launched into hours upon hours of all the mind-stupefying, mechanical stuff you could imagine. Scales, mostly, as I recall, in all sorts of direction; up and down, down and up; both hands agreeing which way to go; then, in the cause of stubbornness, one galloping upwards while the other insisted 'down!'. And then there were the arpeggios and the octaves and, sometimes, the annoying eccentricity of having to travel in 'thirds' or 'sixths' or what have you – until my fingers and my very arms ached for a rest.

Now, I could easily have been persuaded that this universal purgatory was the cause of the weary look on the face of the piano in Miss

Ockleford's sitting room – for assuredly it did have a face of sorts (a hard, weatherbeaten, walnut face) to complement its grinning teeth – were it not that nearly everything had to be pounded out at home, never minding its numbing effect on neighbours, or, for that matter, the lack of anything like sufficient time. Certainly, I had little enough to spare of an evening, since closure of business in that office of ours, on the far side of the river, always teetered on the whim of our supervising clerk. Until he had personally pored over the day's cashbook entries, checking each one (with his ever so precise red inverted tick) against its twin in one of the hugely ponderous County Court ledgers, no-one would dare to leave the premises. Most days, he didn't get round to this closing ceremony until almost seven o'clock, which left my long journey home delayed for a further half hour, and, many weeks, nothing more substantial than Saturday afternoon and Sunday to call my 'free time' (if properly that was the name for it!).

Small wonder, then, that my weekly schedule of 'musical jerks', as I came to think of them, was sometimes given short shrift; even, on one occasion, no shrift at all, as it were. I stagger even now under the weight of the guilt which I remember dragging with me into that particular one of her sessions. I knew that I hadn't touched a piano since the last time round, and that, constant repetition being the elixir of any degree of finger dexterity, I would surely sound like some sort of artistic cripple, as soon as I sat down to demonstrate what should have been progress.

And, of course, that piano knew all about it – without any question it did. There was now around it such an aura of stern, cold disapproval that I was evidently to perform not just on its teeth but on its clenched teeth. As my fingers joined battle, I sensed the two joint proprietors, Miss Ockleford herself and her ancient widowed mother (the 'sleeping partner', I suppose, in the concern), to be in their usual places; the latter in her armchair to the left of me, her daughter stationed sturdily behind my right shoulder and radiating her usual brand of resolute, critical benevolence.

If I had needed a second opinion on the piano's outright condemnation of me, it would presumably have come from the facial expression of Ockleford major. Hers, after all, was the only face I could see, and there I would recognise even the slightest of distaste or disappointment, since it so rarely displayed anything less than a bubbling-over of pleasure. To be fair, she never actually fell asleep in front of me –

though so often she would appear to be well on the way, with her constant mannerism of swaying slightly forward in the chair, coincidental with nods of her head in apparent benign approval of everything around. 'Doesn't this sound glorious?' she seemed to beam. 'Sole credit to me, if you did but know!' Each subsequent nod merely reinforced this conviction as to the true state of affairs; and her chubby features would glow with the accumulated wisdom of a bespectacled, grandmotherly owl.

I doubt that the minor member of the clan – no-one could be less subservient than Miss Ockleford – would have agreed to serve as proxy for anyone, ever, and least of all for her mother. Uncomfortably, I could almost feel her breath down my collar as I went through the motions of the scales, the set pieces, even the tests in sight-reading; and *her* disapproval would probably have stung my ears long before my eyes focused on anything at all. So that, when I sensed that nods were still coming my way (together with the odd sway or two), I could have rested content even then that the sun was still shining. At any rate, when – from behind – there came only slight suggestions for the honing of fine detail in my performance, the incredible became certainty. I had managed to crawl around the barbed wire and escape, after all, for another week!

If this proved anything, it was that I had no talent for the activities of a 'con-man'. True, I had evidently done the 'conning' bit of it with some flair and skill – might it, indeed, even have approached the status of bare-faced fraud? – but I was powerless to disperse the pressure of the remorse which came with it. (As a full-timer in the profession, I would likely have turned to the Catholic faith and spent half of my life in the confessional box.) Of course, there was that flash of a notion of comparative blamelessness. If – a suspicion hitherto unrecognised within me – I was some embryo genius of a musician, the perpetual grind might be unnecessary, after all. Was this, then, to inform me of an inner brilliance which could get by with almost anything? If not, the level of someone else's standards must be distinctly lower than my own. Or else – more likely – had I merely been lucky to negotiate all that barbed wire? Coming quickly down on the side of this last solution, I never again skimped the hard work, or, at any rate, not nearly so savagely.

Mind you, the results of the first two of the examinations into which I was quickly shoved by the enthusiasm of Ockleford minor – those obstacle courses which are seemingly inseparable, like them or lump them, from any musical apprenticeship whatsoever – might easily have jogged conceit into a rethink about my natural talent. I emerged, trembling, from each of them with a percentage marking in the mid-nineties, and a proud little bronze medal with my name engraved in gilt upon it boastfully and indelibly. Strangely, it was only after the first of these successes that anyone at home even recognised anything unusual in my recent efforts at pianism! A dampening revelation, if indeed I had needed one, of the negligible effect they had been having on surrounding ears.

It was an early education for me of the power of 'paper' over attitudes and judgements. All of a sudden I found myself regarded as a good pianist (perhaps even as a 'brilliant' one?), by many whose sensitivities had hitherto heard nothing even worthy of attention. Evidently, that first certificate of mine, by a flash of its own particular brand of lightning, had perfected my fingers into miracles of dexterity – quite unrecognisable from their everyday selves of previous weeks, or from my own continuing knowledge of them.

This didn't so much distress me as unsettle my mind. Perhaps I should be honest and admit that it only served to increase the turmoil which was already there; a constant state of unsettlement being, after all, just another definition of adolescence itself, when absolute certainties of one's rightful destiny fight ceaselessly against more realistic suspicions. In turn, of course, a positive surfeit of the certainties (all equally absolute) arrive and depart so frequently and embarrassingly as to let doubts squeeze in – for mixing with the suspicions into a rare old broth of confusion in one's head. Despair can sometimes be close by.

In my case, there was always the difficulty of the avenue of all my ambitions, and of the vague nature of most of them. They were all on the artistic side; which is regarded as strange and not really understandable or even desirable by most people. I was later to sense that the near relatives of almost every outstanding creative artist throughout history seem to have insisted from the start on a proper subjugation to a properly understandable, properly solid kind of job; in Law, or Medicine, or Accountancy, or any of the other professions in which it is possible to earn respectable amounts of money, or (just as important) respectable amounts of respect itself. Actor, musician, writer, composer, painter in watercolours or oils; it has made no difference to the initial damnation by the family. Except, perhaps, where the family itself is prospering in one of these outlawed ways of life – success having seemingly merited a Royal pardon. Even then, how loudly echoes its first horror, at the very idea of the hardships of close-memory being for the newcomer, too, on the way up! (No-one, it may be said, dwells upon the fog of boredom to be found on the lower of the more respectable slopes, or, for that matter, upon the strong possibility of never being able to climb above it.)

Far be it from me to accuse anyone of shoving. I have never had much of a sense of direction, particularly in fog, and – with no recollection of having dwelt upon anything at all, or, indeed, of having had the slightest of advice on the differing quality or location of habitable dwellings – I probably just stumbled into it, with not much hope of finding my way. Were it not for the 'scrambling' effect, as it were, of the War, I suppose that I might well be immersed in it still. But I cannot fairly complain of others' lack of interest. That would ignore my family's persistent probings and proddings. 'Come on, now, what do you *really* want to do with yourself?' came the most prevalent of their worries (strangely suggestive of the disposal activities of an abattoir). And – 'Haven't you *yet* made up your mind?', together with that traditional doom-ridden caution of time 'getting on, you know!' (the latter ramming home the seeming tragedy of Time sinking fast into the senility of extreme old age). Amidst all this concern, I can now see that the problem was not the answer but the question. If I seemed indecisive, what was there for me to decide?

There accumulated within me a certainty that almost all of the workers of the world (those, that is, wearing smart, gleamingly-white collars – for I had even less inclination than muscles for any of the manual jobs) must either be instinctive schoolteachers or instinctive civil servants. Since the former evidently needed brainwashing by some sort of university, and I had no taste for stretching my education into the probable entwinement with a World War, this left no choice at all. Despite my never discovering the slightest instinct for it, I could offer no worthwhile resistance, therefore, to the safety and security of the Civil Service, which duly overwhelmed me into its rigid régime. My dream-paradise of Art was no longer in view. Had it ever existed? No-one around me seemed to know, or to care.

Nevertheless, this apparently predestined 'job-slot', as it were, never felt right. Regarding it at first as just a stopgap on the way to better things, I came gradually to recognise its inescapability and permanence. In any event, with the crippling hours which I had to work (or, during so many, to hang around waiting for other people's inverted red ticks), there was little overspill, even for thoughts of what I really wanted. Yet I knew what I didn't want; and the mists swirling around on these, the very lowest slopes of the Civil Service, could not disguise the absurdity of some of my daily tasks. The stamping and posting of mail, the painstaking updatings of leaden-footed ledgers from front-running cashbook entries, the long-windedness of Court days, when I sat in the midst of boredom learning fee-collection; these were not, I thought, subtleties which merited a grammar school education, or, more surprisingly, the harshness of an entrance examination specifically designed to obliterate half the candidates. Pacing impatiently around the deck of the Tyne ferry – amid an evening's indisputably *real* sea-mist – as we floated gingerly towards my home jetty on the south riverbank, I would bemoan the void which separated my sheer grind of a job from any vestige of creative activity – artistic or not.

And that, of course, was the nub of it. Nothing could disperse a gnawing obsession that I had it in me to 'make a name for myself', as they say. Strangely, the 'name' bit of it was the vital ingredient. Having to earn comfortable amounts of money seemed, on the other hand, an unimportant (if unavoidable) nuisance – an attitude which now seems peculiar, since most of the hardships around were obvious descendants of a constant lack of it. No matter; there was still this stubbornness – which had spluttered on and off even during my schooldays – for getting into print as a writer, or into painting or sketching as an artist (even if just as a black-and-white cartoonist). Stretching imagination indeed to its limit, into composing classical music, too. Whatever else, however, I sought originality – the creation of something with my name upon it, indelible, for the far future. As a long-term horror, I had the constant nightmare of settling down to a mediocre performance in a mediocre job.

In the glare of this philosophy, my life-style showed up as mere existence: at worst, bereft of all hope and quite meaningless; at best, dream-like, with no confident purpose. If really put to it, I would have chosen music as the best dream of the lot of them, but not, I realised, one that was ever likely to withstand the fresh air of actuality. I could learn to read it, and to play it, and to write down my ideas of it on paper; but, in the absence of my *bête-noir* of 'brainwashing' at a university – and much more of that was needed than for school-teaching – the crafting of it, the harmonies, the key modulations, counterpoints, cross rhythms and the like, were out of my reach and unlearnable with only books as my teachers. Not a glimmer of brilliance, not a shadow of it, was in me, I conceded; a fact of life which was reinforced when I compelled myself into a correspondence course (cold, and clinically unsympathetic) in search of four-part harmony. Though this did reveal a few of the basics, I was left with a vague sense of having failed some dreary test in arithmetic. Come to that, even if I had reconciled myself to the more realistic hard slog of full-time tuition, where could I have found it? I knew neither whom to contact, nor, for that matter, what to ask for. Certainly, I got no pointing finger from the school's careers office; other, of course, than to those same proper avenues for proper respectability.

I have to admit that, ever since, I have suspected all these careers 'specialists', not so much of being ignorant of what is available in the wide world outside, but of lacking the recognition of artistic talents, so easily suffocated in the crush of the run-of-the-mill. These need rescuing with vigorous shoves of enthusiasm – above all, too, with the encouragement which is in such short supply for those striving to find their best first direction. In all fairness, however, nothing short of telepathy by the school could have revealed any potential I might have had for composing music. Come to that, for performing it, either. My obscure position among the 'seconds' of its choir hardly had the right acoustics for revealing even a budding Caruso (and I was anything but that), while my secret efforts, back home, at writing a piano sonata of horrendously amateur quality, together with a smattering of smaller offerings, were obviously unknown to anyone but myself and the music publishers whom I had had the extreme effrontery to approach.

In the normal 'Art' sessions of the school, however, I had worn no such disguise, and from start to finish had outclassed all the others. Strangely, therefore, it was the absence of *dis*couragement which now seems so heinous. What I am talking about is my hasty decision to drop the subject altogether in the year of that first, all-important obstacle course of the matriculation examination. That, at any rate, is how we generally knew it. It wasn't, we realised, the final gateway to one of the Universities, but it was the essential first standard which needed to be proved, and one of the prime reasons, in any event, for going to a grammar school. (Ordinary, elementary school, pupils merely progressed unceremoniously to 'secondary' education, in which a university was a commodity largely unheard-of.) I was, of course, every bit as anxious as the rest of them to master this particular brand of barbed wire. When I discovered, therefore, that 'Art', within the oddities of the system, was squeezed into a group of subjects of no overall benefit to me, I simply ditched it – coldly, without sentiment or much consideration.

It had been my strong, natural talent from as far back as I could remember, and I was throwing it recklessly aside. Yet no-one paid any attention; no-one asked me why I was seemingly committing artistic suicide; no-one even suggested that I should think afresh. No-one, that is, thought it at all important. Respectability wasn't at stake, after all.

Unpleasant, or unwelcome, situations mostly take some time to ferment to the full strength of their position; in this case, a question of years. In the end, however, I succumbed to a nasty realisation of the irony which had gradually enveloped me. Here was I, staggering around by instinct rather than knowledge or advice in most of my chosen directions, and yet only submitting to a proper apprenticeship in a craft which could never make a name for me. I had first wanted to become a respectable pianist, I suppose, as a social asset. But the fashion of the day had changed: the age of easier music, from the wireless, was already with us, and the final belt-entertainment of television itself not so far ahead. Throw into this mixture the threatening scenario of War, and what I was undertaking seemed even more meaningless. Would that I could simply have cast it all aside, and forgotten it.

In one way, the War was there to rescue me; but it could only be rescue by destruction, and, since I felt that most of the rest of my life was already being destroyed, it became a question of two evils. Certainly, after the second of my medal awards, I was tempted indeed to call a halt and just wait for my 'call to arms'. On the one hand, however, there was a triumphant Miss Ockleford waving her substantial arms and enthusing that I was most definitely on course 'for my letters' – which was her way of forecasting an eventual diploma which would be a permanent parasite to my surname. On the other, whilst I had no ambition – or even liking – for the idea, there was an ache in my stomach which told me of the 'once and for all' nature of this opportunity, for achieving *something* before I went into the War's melting-pot of total change. When it was all over, I sensed, I would never again attempt further progress. By that time, my fingers would be 'over-the-hill' for learning – maybe disabled (thinking gloomily).

In the end, as you may guess, I was swirled along with the tide. There wasn't much decision about it, coming to a dead stop being so much more difficult than continuing to move. Yet taking this easier course forced an unwelcome compulsion into me for stifling my guilt and putting in for that deferment, after all. Nevertheless, a couple of months of the latter, when it eventually dropped on the hall mat without fuss or bother, enabled me to get down to some really hard work, this time without the likelihood of wasted effort. The grade I was assaulting was on the doorstep of the 'letters' so revered by Ockleford minor, and though I knew that those would remain a permanent, mythical 'what-might-have-been' after the War, I was determined that any present slip-up wouldn't make them a 'couldn't-possibly-have-been'. In fact, I went at my new imposition of keyboard acrobatics more like a madman, at times, than a musician; though, in reality, I may simply have had the conceit to be aping the antics of a full-blooded concert pianist, to whom full eight hours practice is a common day's penance for seeming effortless brilliance. True, I was never quite as frenetic as that, but three unbroken hours of scales and the like were well within my stamina. Moreover, in the course of this determined (as it were) self-flagellation, which possibly threatened the aural pain-thresholds of the neighbours, I got very near to enjoying it. At any rate, I started to believe in miracles – those which flesh-and-blood fingers can be brought to perform, almost automatically, out of constant repetition of first difficulties.

It was just as well that mine had, in fact, been thus brain-washed, for the state of my own brain, as I climbed the stairs to the first floor of the town's largest restaurant (where the examiner was in session), was one of increasing fragility with every step I took. I was too pent-up, too anxious, too taut. Too desperate to succeed. Much too much fearful of failure. And all of this a dangerous block to any degree of relaxation, the life-blood of convincing pianism. How peculiar! If anything, I was in worse mental turmoil than on that previous occasion when, without an iota of practice, I had effortlessly performed my confidence trick on the Ocklefords. Having presently been slaving away in the opposite direction to the innermost capacity of my very soul, I should surely have been cock-a-hoop by now, confidently 'raring to go', as they say! Instead, I was something of a nervous wreck.

I may say that, ever since, I've been chary of conjuring up the worst outcome of any particular scenario. Many swear by it, of course. Plunge into imagined doom, they say, and reality will turn up contrastingly pleasant. None of that mumbo-jumbo for me, however – not after that near disaster. I had brooded over it, and accordingly it came to pass. It wasn't as if I even got past first base, as they say. More factually, I suppose, past the first couple of octaves of my opening scales, taken at speed; for those fingers of mine, supposedly automated, were operating very much like a modern-day computer when the electronics in its stomach have gone inexplicably haywire. Certainly, I was never in any sort of control. Mercifully soon, at any rate, my hands slid gracelessly off the keyboard in a state of confused entanglement; for a moment, indeed, seeming resigned to hanging uselessly at the end of my arms. But the noise they had engendered before giving up the ghost had been similarly confused, and I panicked at the mere recollection of it.

Never mind my fingers, the whole of the rest of me, too, was very close to giving the whole business up for lost and skulking home in shame. The stumbling manner of my brief apologies to the examiner gave every prospect of my doing so. What a stupid charade! All that commotion of deferment – and only for an anticlimax like this! And then it was that logicality gave way to the unexpected. I stayed still for quite a few moments, took a deep gulp of air into my lungs, and started again. And, against all the odds, I was suddenly relaxed and renewedly proficient. My fingers had become sensibly obedient, and I began to enjoy the sounds, now, that I was producing. Everything was going like a dream: doom was no longer around the corner. Scales of all varieties, arpeggios, set pieces, even the tripwire of sightreading – I heard all of these cascading spiritedly out of me. At the end of it all, I walked away in a state of dazed bewilderment.

During the next week or so, I found it hard to decide what it was that I most awaited, the result or my call-up. Most probably the latter, for nothing could entirely rescue me from the memory of that initial musical catastrophe. Whilst I had doubtless passed muster overall, it was, this time, to be a final douche of cold water in my face – after those two tantalising little bronze medals – merely not to have failed. Moreover, working flat out (for the first time) had left me no excuse against what would be stark confirmation of my true worth – 'only average', after all. Even in advance of publication, then, I began to feel disillusioned. Mind you, one half of me counselled unconcern about the whole affair (surely, in wartime, an artificial triviality). But the other, incurably downcast, knew that nothing but a prompt Army directive could now save me from the full shame of it. Certainly, hearing the news from afar might put it into more soothing perspective. Didn't they always say 'Out of sight, out of mind'?

All the while, I was continuing my visits to the Ocklefords; more by habit, now, than anything else, since they could only serve some highly improbable renewal of my progress, unknown years ahead. Very soon, however, at one of these sessions, I suddenly had the feeling that something was up; rather, that something had *come* up – had arrived. Those matriarchal nods were coming from the direction of the armchair even before I had a chance to seat myself at the piano. A bevy of enthusiastic sways, too, into the bargain. And when Miss Ockleford herself put in an appearance, her eyes were simply glittering with pride, as she informed me of the unbelievable. It seemed that I had achieved the absolute top accolade for the grade, a 'first-class' silver medal! Nothing small, either, about this one; the very best piece of ostentation that the Music Board had thought up – instantly reducing my little bronze decorations to very small beer indeed, at best to far-distant cousins. Nor was there anything wrong with the marks I had been awarded – anything, that is, except their apparent unreality. For, of the hundred percentage points on offer, I was being asked to believe that I had collected all of them save one! An incredible verdict of near perfection, you might say, and one which took some time for me to accept as established fact.

When comprehension had finally blossomed into actual belief, however, the completeness of my success continued to stagger me. Intellectually, I should have been boosted almost as thoroughly as that earthquake of a bombed gas-main had previously demoralised me. Surely, this was for savouring to the full while the flavour lasted. I was duty bound to relish it – now or never, for all it was worth. Yet, just as a spell of nothingness had followed the air attack, so a restless, disturbed, vacuum-like existence seemed to enter into me after this benign explosion of supreme triumph.

What, really, *was* there to relish, after all? Relaxation, freedom from further effort, a vague feeling of it not having been a waste of time; but what else? I had climbed my mountain, only to find myself standing at the top, wondering why.

It was a strange feeling – unexpectedly strange, for I had already known the adrenalin of artistic success, albeit at schoolboy level, in that profusion of painting competitions run by the newspapers and children's magazines of the day. Certainly, I had won first prize in each one of those, and none had produced even a snatch of this present sense of emptiness. I had simply rejoiced to the very skies at having bettered the rest of them. Not one query as to worthwhileness or anything of that sort. Just sheer uninhibited enjoyment.

But they had been straightforward competitions, after all; everything pure and simple; coming first leaving nothing else to be desired. Comparing degrees of excellence hadn't entered into it at all, and I had never doubted my right to gloat unrestrainedly over the 'prize' of the moment. Right in front of my eyes, this had almost always been a thing of obvious desirability – something with days, even weeks, of play-value or reading-value. It was only the last of my acquisitions which had had anything of the abstract about it, but that one, from possibly the most prestigious contest of the lot – involving no less than cumulative entries for a whole week of daily paintings in advertisement of a current film 'blockbuster' – had been at any rate *spendable*. A cheque for the princely sum of two guineas, presented, in solemn ceremony and in full, gold-chained panoply, by the town's mayor, no less, on the stage of our principal cinema, had certainly seemed so at first. Irritatingly, because of family insistence on the purchase of National Savings certificates 'for my future' (as strange and unbelievable an abstraction as ever I had heard), the spending part of it had soon become soured with the intangibility of 'potential'. Yet it had still been vaguely credible that this elusive windfall, too, might have some (eventual) coldly-mysterious value and worthwhileness.

But how different, now! I was older, of course, and increasingly self-critical. Moreover, that silver medallion of mine wasn't anything like as soothing as the Meccano set had been, or the boxes of games, the books – or that ephemeral cheque, for that matter. My present adornment, never minding its undoubted 'class' and resemblance to an oversized, newly-minted halfcrown, had amongst its attributes no spendability whatsoever. Not an iota of morale to it, either; nothing of reassurance that I could see, not a gleam or glitter from it of my ever having come in first, anywhere or at any time. It simply boasted of a very high standard; and, whilst others were only too pleased to dance to its tune – the local newspaper quickly concocting as a minor headline 'Boy Pianist's Triple Success' (an effective damper, indeed, to the fondly imagined maturity of a raw nineteen-year-old) – I remained unconvinced of any of my supposed prowess.

Nothing really mattered, come to that. The everyday existence around me was matching my emptiness of spirit, to make me feel not only alone but positively lonely. Of my dispersed family, I was now living only with my eldest brother – so old, by comparison, as to seem nothing closer than a substitute father-figure – and what remained of parents degenerating swiftly into their final decay; my adored Mother, by this time, lacking any clear recognition either of me or of anyone else in the house. None of the superficial friendships of schooldays having survived emergence into the real world, I hadn't found anyone of even the remotest affinity at my workplace to make up for the loss of them. In point of fact, only two others were employed there, and one of those, indeed, was that 'inverted-red-ticker' of a senior clerk, so often the bane of my very life.

Circumstances were evidently conspiring towards permanence for me as an out-and-out 'loner', despite all my continued longings to be a normal individual. My past seemed vague and unimportant, my present directionless, and my future incomprehensible – yet doubtlessly just as dispiriting when it decided to arrive. I was, you will gather, very, very low. 'Properly down in the dumps', as Mother would have put it, more comfortingly, in her cognitive days.

Even my occasional visit to one of the local cinemas (of which there were up to a dozen, mostly playing to full houses every day of the week) could no longer counteract the prevailing drabness. Sitting there inside, mind you, I continued to be reassured by the sight of others so much better off than us (proving that hope *was* still hanging around, if only one could find it!); people, War or no War, evidently still living in the same luxury as had surrounded them from birth onwards – taken for granted by them just as much as we did the 'happy ending' to each of their stories.

Now and again, of course, a film might centre around ordinary, working-class folk, albeit more attractive samples than any of us, but few remembered it for long, compared with the ambitious, frothy, 'top-hat-and-tails' entertainments which were mostly on demand; advertising sophistication the like of which had never been seen or heard of in the district – and all the more entrancing for that. Coming out of the hall, however, through the swing doors and into the evening's cold, it was increasingly obvious that neither the top hats *nor* the tails could possibly have survived the North-East, even if shipped compulsorily up here in great numbers complete with trousers and occupants. Neither could I now retain more than a flash of belief in the sumptuous, fairy-tale, American life-style which only just now I had been worshipping. As I tramped resignedly back home, the air-raid siren would often be confirming my return to basics.

And these were worsening by the day, I thought. Certainly, by the week; for fresh doubt was breeding fresh guilt, that plea of mine for deferment having a lot to answer for. Riddled with shame from the start, I had felt firmly rubber-stamped as 'guilty on all counts' by the very fact of the grant of it. Yet, now, you could say there was a further count against me; an insidious one, too, with a possible heinous indictment – for the crime, this time, of *hope*! As one week followed the other, my deferment finished and done with, nothing whatsoever was transpiring. Had they lost my records, I wondered? Had the Army forgotten me? Put alongside the universal public jingoism of the day, such Utopian daydreams were unquestionably criminal.

Muddle! That was what it was – thorough confusion, everywhere and at all times. By now, lacking conviction even of what I would like to do, given the chance, confidence in my ability to do *anything* worthwhile was draining away. Worse still, wartime vetoed even the imagining of better times: untold years of cold abnormality evidently lay ahead of me. I dreaded the nearness of my Army service; yet not to be summoned threatened an abyss of dismal and meaningless and endless despondency. My parents were nearing their final departure; close-knit family life had already snuffed itself out; and I had absolutely no friends. Without a choice, I was solitary in the prison of my own particular muddle.

* * *

Was I right? *Were* we slowing down? That steam-engine, at any rate, must have known for certain; for it had started to judder in vigorous protest, before resigning itself (with its usual paroxysm of screeches, and hisses, and grating noises) to the fact that it had no option. No doubt of it now, in any event. The blurred greens of the scrub-growth passing the window were merging relentlessly into the dirty grey of a country town's railway station; and a more violent rattling and shaking of the carriage finally confirmed the whole business. We had most definitely arrived. Or perhaps I should have said that *it* had arrived? My fate, that is, in the shape of Richmond in Yorkshire.

Chapter 3

The immensity of the change in my fortunes was overwhelming me even as I stepped down on to the platform. Not so long ago, the boundary of my life had been a paltry half dozen well-worn streets. True, it had latterly stretched out to the slender border of modern bungalows on the countryfied fringe of the town, but this addition had merely served as the permanent staging post, as it were, for those obligatory sallies to and from the penance of my work. Now, it seemed, my confines were no longer to be of bricks or concrete, but of human beings, simply hundreds (or was it thousands?) of them; milling around me on all sides; pressing me so closely as to squeeze out any considered thought of past, present, or future alike.

While the packed state of the train's capacity had been obvious (almost entirely men, too, come to think of it), none of the passengers had looked interesting to me. Any one of them might have been going anywhere at all – nowhere, for that matter, or even some indistinct mixture of the two – for all I was concerned. Neither had the fact that so few were alighting at any of the intermediate stations generated even a flicker of curiosity. After all, in sum total, what were they? Evidently, just a mundane cross-section of anonymity. Each with little relevance to their neighbour. None whatsoever to me. Feeling so cut-off, you see, from everybody and everything I had ever known, I was relevant only to myself.

Outside, however, in the bitter-crisp cold of Richmond's winter – or as much of it as could reach me through the jostling figures making their way towards the exit gate – opinions quickly turned topsy-turvy. *Everyone* was now relevant. Relevance was seemingly to be found, indeed, in the station's every nook and cranny. And the main relevance of all (confounding my previous apathy) was in fact revealed as the destination of these self-same people, since almost all were evidently heading for mine. Or, that is, hoping like me to find the compass bearings for it at the other side of the exit.

Of Straw And Stripes

I have no recollection of ever discovering anything of the sort. Not a whisper of voiced instructions; not a glimpse of a pointing finger, or of any official-looking busybody, in any event, who might possess such an informed digit. Yet, in the course of a confused ten minutes or so, we had instinctively huddled ourselves together in rough formation in the centre of the main thoroughfare and, as if suddenly granted Divine intuition, were starting to shuffle forward. A thorough rag-tag-and-bobtail of a mob we must have appeared, each encumbered with some bulging bag or case holding his last remnants of the world being left behind, and none with any concept as yet of keeping 'in step'. We might have been in any town at all for what we saw, apart from the road ahead; there being only the sensation (and effort) of mounting a gentle hill-slope to convince us that we were indeed going somewhere or other, and would presumably 'arrive' before too long. But, surely enough (this time with the aid of a flurry of screamed commands), we soon found ourselves hustled on to the foreboding barrack square of a rather dismal-looking Army camp. Ringed around were the Nissen huts which were to be our barrack-room refuges for the foreseeable future.

These prime specimens of military architecture were, on first acquaintance, just as unsavoury inside as out, their curved corrugated-iron simulating huge loaves of bread, long since stale yet still awaiting slicing along their surface grooves. Certainly, to enter was to find not a crumb of comfort for body or soul alike; the roughly concreted floor setting a pattern for those stark rows of wooden double-bunks and the black misery of the inevitable coke stove – its leaky flue-pipe crudely impaling the roof – all of which, you could say, amounted to a scenario of pure desolation.

Most first impressions are indelible in their importance, but, to be fair, this set had only moments in which to arbitrate; nothing more than the time on offer for the dumping of our baggage on any reachable vacant bunk, after which we found ourselves again being bustled and browbeaten over to the barrack square, this time en route for the Quartermaster's Store. And by the time he (or, rather, his minions) had finished with us, I was well and truly encrusted with most of a conscript's obligatory veneer; the battledress, the denims, the boots and socks, the 'Long-John' underpants, the mess-tins, the four grey blankets, and, just as a reminder that none of this was part of a game, that worn, clumsy-looking Lee-Enfield rifle – which was, however, to prove more of a top heavy juggling club for the Drill Sergeant's 'shouldering' and 'presenting' rituals than any source of harm or violence.

But the impact of the whole of this munificence was as nothing to that produced, in all senses, by the shapeless, dark-blue receptacle slung disparagingly at me as the end of my part in the proceedings. This, I thought, must indeed be the legendary 'kit bag' of First World War renown! I vaguely remembered songs about it. Wasn't I supposed to stuff my troubles into it, amongst other things? But why had it to be blue, of all colours? I wasn't joining the Royal Navy, after all: what was wrong with khaki? Even so, I seemed to sense that, for better or worse, it would become my most personal possession, a continuing link with me which could only be broken by the end of the War, or the end of me. Overly dramatic, you will say, for a nineteen-year-old's philosophy; yet – so strange, now, from so far off – wartime produces torrents of emotion and sentiment, even of religious beliefs, hidden and unrecognised in more normal times.

Even at this stage, I was experiencing what you might call 'cattle syndrome'. No longer in control of what I did, I felt driven – driven here, driven there; not exactly whipped, but cursed and sworn at, all the same; ordered all over the place at the whim of this one or that. Herded closely with the others, I was never again to be allowed the privilege of straying.

In my most extravagant imagination, I had never met authority of this extent. However unimpressive otherwise, the display of one of those strange, V-shaped signs on each arm of a battledress jacket – even more frighteningly, a couple of them, or a full set of three – turned a mortal into a god. Whenever he spoke (a most frequent occurrence), woe betide any who didn't immediately listen and 'jump to it' to obey. That is to say, every little edict of his; anything at all which he might have conjured up for us – often, seemingly, just for the pleasure of the moment, relieving him of the anathema produced by others' relaxation.

Nor was it usually sufficient merely to carry out instructions. Most of them, particularly those of the barrack square variety, needed style; a peculiar style which I still think of as 'spiky'. There had to be absolutely nothing around which was curved or indirect. Straight lines, and right angles, and sharp hundred-and-eighty-degree contortions formed the compulsory religion out there. One's rifle, too, had similarly to be conditioned. Straight up, straight down, straight horizontal, straight perpendicular. Even when angled on my shoulder, I still felt that it must (to something) be having pretensions to ninety degrees. Certainly, it always managed to get by with its own undoubted straightness.

If these humiliations in themselves were insufficient to kill all of our morale, there was always, to finish the job, the knowledge that we were in a cul-de-sac. Generally speaking, we were never going to succeed; most probably, never even survive. And if we did scrape through, standards were unlikely to have much resemblance to respectability. Others before us – all of them, in fact – had evidently surmounted the pitfalls, many with ease and some quite brilliantly. We, on the other hand, must surely be the worst mob of 'rookies' the camp had ever seen. This, mind you, was not just our view of matters. Daily, the Drill Sergeant was only too pleased to give us his 'second opinion', constantly reinforcing it to us with a choice variety of oaths and comments on the illegitimacy of our parentage.

How innocent we must have been! – though not unusually for those times. Civilian life – certainly, in mixed company – was quite mannered and gentle, even if, with none of the present widespread coarseness of speech and behaviour for comparison, we would never have considered it so. But the Army proved it for us, I suppose (even at the time), by the shock which its streams of vocal obscenities administered to many of our systems. I never once suspected that any of the foul temper or positive vilification which was flung in our direction could possibly be part of a deliberate pattern. Theories never seriously occurred to me. Breaking down individualistic pride into interdependence and instant obedience – if this had indeed been planned, it would have called for higher intellect than the brawny, lumbering manhandling of us suggested. Nothing was explained and nothing comprehended. In retrospect, probably just as intended.

I would like to believe that the invective against us was as well-meaningly fraudulent as that directed at other typical squads. Realistically, however, I have my doubts. We were, you must know, as motley a gathering of odds and ends as ever could have been devised by the Army Posting Panel. The training, a full schedule of infantry requirements, was being conducted by seasoned Regular Army soldiers. We, on the other hand, were for eventual utilisation only by the Royal Army Ordnance Corps, a title which at any rate sounded impressive, even if quite unintelligible. All we knew was that it formed part of the front line's main 'back-up troops', and that there were amongst us those who had been designated as specialist drivers, and others destined to be driver-mechanics, 'storemen', clerks technical or clerks regimental. I was one of the latter, a terminology which didn't suggest much of a close relationship with poison gas or machine-gun fire – even less, somehow, with grenades. With the apparent necessity for this kind of training, however, it was already becoming clear that the Civil Service's idea of a clerk and that of the Army must be somewhat different. I would certainly have to wait and see: I could hardly do any other.

Come to that, what choice had we left to us on any subject under the sun? Choice had suddenly become a commodity which, of necessity, always descended upon us – already decided – from somewhere up above; mostly from such a height as to make its origin masked by the clouds. And the quantity of luck which had become involved by the time it got down to us was unfathomable; together with the proportion of the outcome which had been arrived at with the assistance of a pin. Later on, the region of the War in which I was to be most involved – not just a question of miles this way or that, but which side of the very earth itself – was to teeter on the scales of chance alone. Even at the beginning, I might just as easily have been tossed into the Commandos or one of the Armoured Brigades, or (more down to earth) the toilings of the Pioneer Corps. I now see those 'choices' made for me as nothing more sophisticated than lotteries. As it turned out, they were to leave me alive and unscathed, and sitting happily now at my typewriter. It could so easily have been different: at the time, we were only too aware of the fragility of the future.

The present, however, was more than sufficient to restrict our long-sight, as well as the depth of our philosophy. For the next month or so, the future was largely to consist of nothing more than the following day; 'today' itself being one continuing series of apprehensions as to the next item on the agenda to be thrown at us. 'Square-bashing' was the staple diet, of course, but there were untasty condiments galore to complement it; early morning physical jerks (little later than dawn); bayonet practice against long-suffering stuffed enemy effigies; paroxysms of simulated savagery in bouts of 'unarmed combat'; testing of gas-masks (when, discouragingly, wisps of the gas would seem to penetrate mine!); untold 'kit inspections' back in the barrack room; a dispiritingly-impossible assault course; a full day's route march (in full battledress baggage) reputedly all of twenty miles; and, when ideas were in any way flagging against the *bête-noir* of relaxation, any haphazard assignment whatsoever which came to mind – chores such as peeling mountainous accumulations of potatoes, or washing grease-drenched crockery in luke-warm water, or shovelling unending coal into unending bunkers.

    A gang of determined, muscle-bound navvies might, of course, have been quite at home in all of this. I say 'might', however, as I was thinking only of the strength bit of it – the stamina bit. Whether they would have matched up to the split-second reflex action seemingly vital at any minute of night or day, is more debatable. Commonly, the raucous bellow of 'C'me on, now – should've been there b'now!' would be rattling around our eardrums only half a second after the particular order of the moment. These verbal whiplashes produced, indeed, little more than a permanent resignation to the obviously unimprovable nature of our failings. Only an instant soothsayer, we thought – sensing instructions seconds before their communication – could have hoped to reach this requirement for exceeding perfection.

    Most especially was it depressing to be falling short on agility of mind. After all, if we couldn't suffice there, what chance had we in the beefier part of the Military's essentials? It so happened, you see, that most of us had benefited, in civilian clothes, from brain rather than brawn, of which latter quality Nature had rationed us ungenerously. Clerks, legal executives, accountants, schoolteachers, bank cashiers; there were examples of all these amongst us. We were, you could say, a uselessly over-educated assortment; as awkward on Army soil as any bunch of penguins waddling around on dry land.

    It was hard, therefore, to imagine any further difficulties which could have been thought up, to those already surrounding us; but, barely a day or so into our settling-in period at the Camp, the elements themselves decided to make an entrance. Before we knew it, the sky was almost solid with slowly drifting snowflakes, and, as if to atone for its recent omission of a 'white Christmas' (surely an obligatory going-away present?), it continued relentlessly in the same condition, until the ground had disappeared under feet-deep snowdrifts and we were slithering around, largely out of control of both the Drill Sergeant and ourselves.

    The immediate effect of this white cataclysm was to anchor each of our feet to a kind of soggy millstone, designed to slow down the regulated strutting which we were still attempting, on what was now a glistening wasteland of a parade ground. At any rate, it brought a measure of variety to our shovelling activities; coal, without quibble, giving way to snow as first call on our sweated toil. Moreover (unlike the loading of those bunkers), there was a clear reason for putting our backs into clearing the drifts: the more snow we shifted, the lighter seemed our millstones.

Despite all our labours, however, the wintry downfall was still persisting, and any lengthy period of drill was unusually sapping of strength. I well recall, one morning, a member of the squad suddenly heeling over on to the ground, and having to be removed, sack-like and unconscious, to the healing warmth of the sick-bay. It was an incident which, strangely, alarmed most of us not in the slightest. We felt resilient, in fact – if only by contrast. We were reassured not to have proved the weakest link in the chain. It was nice, if only for a moment, to be better than someone else.

Where I was concerned, cause for any degree of self-esteem was never again discovered; unlike the few, for example, who found the conquering of assault course obstacles easy with the help of instinct and lack of imagination, or whose tougher muscles never, like mine, felt wrenched when jerking up those infernal rifles for 'shouldering'. And then there were others who, whilst not obviously lauding their particular species of superiority, managed nevertheless to do so quietly and with dignity, and with daily demonstrations of it as a matter of routine emphasis. First thing in the morning, too – when I was at my most vulnerable. But that, of course, was the crux of it; the time of day when patently, since birth, I must always have been at my most second-rate of all.

Mind you, I had never recognised it until now. The very idea of crawling from a warm bed into the early cold of winter was bad enough in itself, and the whole theory of early rising quite heinous, whatever the season or weather. This was obvious. All without exception must agree, I had thought – the possibility of anyone being able to jump straight out, willingly and without regret, seeming such a warped eventuality as to joust with sanity.

Indeed, in all the winters I had known in childhood, getting into the bed in the first place had been almost as off-putting as getting out of it. The chill of the staircase would be sinking into my limbs before ever I reached the bedroom and those intimidatingly freezing white sheets, peeping out through the ultimate haven of the blankets. From experience, their pristine whiteness suggested frost itself – which was specifically the effect on my toes and feet and ankles, as I edged myself in, inch by inch. Nothing could have been more unfriendly than those sheets; not at first, that is. When fully inside the bedding, of course, it was possible (ever so gradually) to benefit from 'striking the heat', our name for the burgeoning of the heavenly, reassuring comfort.

The fact that the very existence of bedsheets was unknown to the Quartermaster proved, therefore, somewhat advantageous. In the event, our staple issue of drab-grey blankets, combined with the constant percolation of warmth (albeit slightly coke-flavoured) from the barrack-room stove, was more than sufficient to avoid a repetition of such temperature shocks.

After only a couple of days of outdoor training, indeed, it was extraordinary to return at dusk to our quarters, astonished by the metamorphosis which had taken place in the whole of the room. Had I really ever thought it desolate? It was positively cheery. Even the bunks looked inviting – especially the bunks, to be honest; and the blankets savoured of near luxury! With the bareness of the place now clothed in bawdy, irreverent talk, everyone – hush, keep it from the Sergeant! – was very close indeed to relaxation. Tired out, near to exhaustion, never was bed-time more welcome! And, climbing up to my straw palliasse on the top bunk (the better by far of the two, I had found), it was sheer glory to be snuggling into those blankets, with hours of blissful escapist sleep ahead of me.

But the splendours of Heaven are mostly illumined by the dread of Hell, and the 'reveille' trumpet call of early dawn was nothing if not hellish, through and through, with its strident reminder of the day to come. In case we might have missed it, there was the precaution of our Corporal – always in prospect of earning a further 'stripe' for good behaviour – running down the room bawling admonitions of 'Pronto! Get out of those bloody wanking pits!' – together with his peculiar shout of 'Jilldie!', for further emphasis. 'Jilldie, now!' he would bellow, 'Should have been there by now!' He clearly believed in total mimicry of the Sergeant, who also had the word in his vocabulary. To my knowledge, a slot has never been found for 'jilldie' in any dictionary, nor a proper spelling for it anywhere registered. Never since seen or heard of, it remains nevertheless raucously in my head as I write. If that Corporal were still about (perpetually unpromoted), he would undoubtedly be yelling his head off as always, very probably now ordering me – pronto! – to 'jilldie' this book. Most definitely (he would be telling me) it should already have been there by now!

However unwelcome the cacophony of these combined alarums, the barrack-room was still warm enough, from the embers of the evening stove, to soften this daily forced eviction from my 'nest of straw' (as I suppose I considered it). The outside wash-room, however, while roughly covered from the weather, was scarcely above freezing; as was the water in the taps and the metal washbowls, from which we not only had to splash our faces but shave every single hair from our chins. In my case, this only amounted to the Sergeant's description of 'bum-fluff', since the supreme moment of my producing bristles of any respectability had not yet arrived. The whole procedure amounted to a session of creeping refrigeration, as it were, the more quickly completed the better. How galling a sight, then, these minor deities finicking around, calmly and with such obvious pleasure; cream, razors, lotions, talcum and all. No hurrying, either, for them; that too, having effortlessly been assured, leaping instantly – joyously and wide awake – into an entertainment to which I would still be pushing myself.

I hadn't known that they even existed, these people whom early light seemed to endow with all the serenading instincts of a rooster. Of course, it might only be a charade, I reasoned, acted out to keep their spirits up and, by see-saw effect, mine down. Otherwise, this was a steeled moral determination, against all the odds, which was well beyond my capabilities. And certainly, no odds could ever have been greater than that igloo of a wash-house! Whilst I came to tolerate it, I never quite mastered its dismal effect on the rest of the morning.

It is clear enough, now, that had I been older, comparisons wouldn't have bothered me so much, even if the cold would have been feeling no less bitter. Like other youngsters, I had been pestered, over the years, with calls to imitate this individual or that (always someone whose worth had been merited, allegedly, by painstaking perseverance). A multitude of anxieties had arisen for rectification. Early on, for example, the state of my unruly hair – 'Now, why don't you brush it thoroughly, like your brother Andrew? That'll make it stay in place, just as his does!' Then it had been the turn of my teeth for attention, all of them evidently needing the most frequent and frenzied of scrubbings with toothpaste – 'In time, they'll turn gleaming white, you know!' By this time, my very posture was causing concern; considerable, apparently, as there developed a constant nagging for me to 'stand up straight', and to keep my 'head up, with shoulders straight' (the Army obviously not having the sole prerogative of this fetish for universal straightness). And, as a general underlying safeguard, the strictest of taboos had been pronounced on 'slouching'; a term which seemingly covered anything having the remotest resemblance to relaxation – another dogma shared, strangely, with my present régime.

Now, much of this had been reasonable. My hair would flop around at the whim of the slightest breeze; my teeth were visibly shades away from pure whiteness; and an instinct to slouch was as pleasurable for me as for anyone else in his right senses. But it was the determination supposedly possessed by others – each of the oft-quoted examples of it – which has since turned up as bogus. My hair, for example was always wilfully silk-soft, whereas my brother's was obediently wiry. As a scientific fact, my cream-shaded tooth enamel could never have lightened (however many the brushings) to the virgin-white of the few who possessed it by birthright. And of those easily conforming to that rigidly 'straight' doctrine, I suspect many to have had the irony of a backbone curved slightly backwards from true, making the least suspicion of a slouch difficult to manoeuvre, in the first place.

In more than one sense, this had been a series of confidence tricks; but, with all of them concerning my outward appearance, the visual truth was bound to have dawned sooner, rather than later. The strangeness of that wash-house 'rooster' behaviour, on the other hand, touched on subtleties of human resolve; the reason, no doubt, that I surrounded it for so long with a complex web of frustrated admiration which it hadn't deservedly spun. Eventually, of course, I was able to recognise it as nothing more than a compulsive instinct. Some – with wrongly curved spines – are condemned to 'stand up straight' all their lives; others to jump robot-like from their bed at an ungodly hour, quite unable to remain there even if they wish. Amidst such moral confusion (I now ask myself), where was all that grit and determination which I thought I should have been emulating?

If, while still at Richmond, I had possessed the time, or (in the rawness of my youth) the premature acumen for making earlier diagnoses of these worries, it might have boosted my own grit, at any rate for basic survival. Yet discovering the superficiality of the Sergeant's viewpoint (and of the Corporal's cloned copy of it) would have done nothing to calm his pursuance of it by way of our eardrums. Plugs for them might have been a defence, but even they couldn't wholly have dampened such a volcano of a voice.

Giving that snow its proper due, however, it did have redeeming features. Plaguing us throughout with numbingly frosted dampness and dispiriting exhaustion, it nevertheless revealed a delicate, soft side to its character; insulating hard concrete against the stamp of our Army boots, and preventing, at any rate, the bark of the drill commands from echoing – humanising it, you might say, for the time being.

No doubt convinced that it was thus atoning for its undoubted sins, the snow must have felt free to proceed on its way entirely unchecked. Certainly, thick masses of snowflakes continued to waft silently down on us. There was no sign at all that the Heavens were yet running short of supplies . . .

Chapter 4

Throughout, my acquaintanceship with the ways of the British Army was a wholly negative affair. How long was it likely to last? This unsolvable enigma stifled the idea that good could ever come from it; but in fact it was the most successful and wide-ranging finishing education I could possibly have had, filling the several lamentable gaps in my knowledge of the human race. Surrounded by people of all classes and temperaments, there was a continuous stream of fresh learning for me, simply for the taking; lessons from which the blinkered compartments of civilian life, left to themselves, would forever have shielded me.

Most of these potential revelations were heavy stuff, too heavy to interest me then. In any event, observations most often need the past to give them proper context and meaning, and as yet I hadn't any past to speak of. Fortunately, just as Life itself isn't always deadly serious, there was the occasional trivial discovery thrown to me as a lighter titbit. Such as the peculiar little matter of 'housie-housie'.

On reflection, mind you, there was nothing minimal about it in the way of importance – not, that is, when we learned what it really was, the name in itself conjuring up nothing more seductive than some discussion group for budding estate agents. Certainly, the unexpected message (a mere 'invitation' to an evening meeting over at the Cookhouse) was weird enough, if nothing else, because it came from the Sergeant-Major himself. Spurning the need for any stripes whatsoever in his emblems of authority, this colossus – with positively the loudest yell of the lot of them – exuded such omnipotence as to make anything so subdued as a request or a suggestion a development which was both startling and worrying. What on earth could he be up to (we were thinking)?

Nevertheless, almost without exception, we trudged along there quite willingly; making our way, in the dusk, between the man-made drifts of cleared snow. After all, by this time any variation whatsoever was

Of Straw And Stripes

preferable to the normal nightly ritual of the Camp Canteen, where, apart from the services of a battered old piano (long resigned to untold further batterings from cacophonous approximations of 'eight-in-the-bar' jazz), there was little on offer except stewed tea – that strong, unmistakeably NAAFI version of it; for all of us, surely the most long-lasting of our distastes following demobilisation. If only by contrast, this elevated the tea served with our Cookhouse meals – one bucketful per table, for rationing into mess-tins – to an apparent standard of delectable freshness which it can never properly have attained, since there was a universal certainty of its always being liberally laced with 'bromide' (the Army's sure antidote, we understood, to any sexual lusts which might otherwise have survived the exhaustions of the barrack square).

In any event, with barrenness of choice, we had already learned to accept what was put before us, and never to expect much in the first place. So it was that, coming through those Cookhouse doors into its welcome warmth, we were probably expecting nothing at all except, maybe, a further harangue – in authoritative overtime, as it were – about shortcomings which might somehow have eluded the day's routine bawlings. As a whole, perhaps we needed even further shavings off our 'short-back-and-sides' haircuts? Or had the interminable polishing of our boots still not turned them into mirrors? Possibly, the brass of our cap-badges and trenchcoat buttons was not yet properly challenging the glitter of gold? Or – worst nightmare of all! – were those tiny, theoretical specks of dirt, reputed on inspection to frequent the insides of our rifle-barrels, now breeding in greater numbers? (How many more times would that oily little 'four by two' cleaning rag of mine have to be pulled through?)

In point of fact, shuffling along to find a vacant seat behind one of the tables, I failed at first to grasp what was really going on. There, dominating the top end of the room, stood our Sergeant-Major, red-faced as ever from the force of his habitual invective, and evidently already in armed conflict with his audience, most of whom were staring fixedly downwards – possibly in embarrassment – at what seemed notesheets, set out individually before them. This momentarily amazed me. Surely, our misdemeanours hadn't been so profligate as to need listing? At any rate, authority must have been thoroughly infuriated by them, to judge by the vitriolic remarks apparently being hurled in our direction. Yet, what was I now hearing? Something or other about 'legs' – presumably a serious injury, since there was also a shout of 'doctor'. Needed urgently, too, it would seem, by the tone of the Sergeant-Major's screamed concern.

Of course, reality burst upon me quite quickly, but it was such an unbelievable reality that fiction itself wouldn't have tolerated it. The first hint came from the chuckles which were beginning to surface here and there amongst us. Little spasms, too, of lively conversation. (Nothing of that sort normally, with the SM at such full throttle.) Additionally, there was the text of what he was actually roaring at us. 'Clickety click!' came through as his initial advice. In evident elaboration, he then bellowed out a warning about 'Legs eleven!' (a message conveyed with passionate elocution, maybe in fond memory of pre-War chorus girls), and followed it up with an equally fiery broadside on the need to follow 'Doctor's orders!' Another couple of minutes of this random gibberish, and I was forced into comprehension. Astonishingly, he was playing a game! Not only that, but allowing us – expecting us, in fact – to play it with him!

As it happened, this somewhat undersized the truth. The aggressive determination which sparked from every inch of him (but most of all from the reddened contortions of his plump face) was positively commanding us to enjoy every single second of this, our strict sixty-minute ration of military fun, or face the consequences! Never can a session of 'housie-housie' have been conducted with such unrelenting severity. You could say that we were mentally impelled into the game, near-hypnotised by the sheer glare from his eyes, as he manhandled those haphazard numbers out of the receptacle on his table and boomed them out to us.

The effect, nevertheless, proved quite out of proportion to the cause. That hour of entertainment – for such it was, Sergeant-Major or no Sergeant-Major – was a precious delight that I savour to this day. The emptiness at the finish of it, with the reappearance of the uncomforting cold as we slumped back to our barrack-rooms, was even worse than the anticlimaxes of those occasional Friday evenings of long ago when, after Mother had treated me to a show at the local cinema, we would be walking sadly along the cobbled streets back to drab normality.

From then on, we received this shot-in-the-arm of 'housie-housie' once per week; as regularly as clockwork (as the saying goes), but never more than the standard dose of an hour, timed precisely. Undoubtedly, it kept us sane, and comparison with our grinding, unchanging, work-scheduled existence continued to embellish it with a magnificence far removed from its actual rules and prizes – the latter being, indeed, so nominal that I cannot remember a thing about them. Were there any? Perhaps not: no-one could have protested, in any event.

The past had been just the same as now, contrast generating a magic all its own. No films could have been quite as wonderful as that; and these 'games' of the Sergeant-Major were, after all, only foretastes of the since jazzily-retitled 'bingo'. Against a happier background, they would have been mundane or even boring, however apoplectic his master-of-ceremonies activities. The national mania, post-War, for this trivial pastime – in whose cause, cinemas and dance halls and seaside stalls alike, in their thousands, have had to be commandeered to satisfy the universal craving – has long perplexed me. What sort of magic can possibly still cling to it? Now? In peacetime? Sadly, I have arrived at a suspicion. Its fanatical devotees may well have civilian lifestyles no more congenial or varied than ours were, enforcedly, in the drudgery of that Army Camp. It is a sobering thought.

At the time, at any rate, it was a veritable analgesic of a game against the discomfort of Army discipline. As if to ensure that it gave us only short-lasting relief, an automatic right to visit Richmond (or to go out of the Camp gates in any direction, for that matter) was denied us during the whole of the time we were training there. Weeks passed, in fact, before we were allowed our first visit; and, by that time, the vague feeling amongst us of being criminals confined in a close replica of Dartmoor had strengthened into a sense of near reality. That first venture into the town was, therefore, quite an event. As it turned out, quite an event, too, even before we set out. The matter of getting properly dressed up for it, I mean.

Now, you may well be wondering what was special about that. Cap, battledress, 'gaiters', boots; what else? We wore them all the time, didn't we? What was different now, simply strolling down to Richmond? Well, these weren't at all what we wore day by day in the Camp. The cap and the gaiters and the boots – yes; but for the rest of it we had to make do with much-loathed, dirty-grey-green 'denims'. More like 'boiler-suit' overalls, and miles away from the respectability of uniforms, these rough caricatures of battledress were patently unfit for any measure of public display. 'Denim' became a word synonymous with something to be rid of as soon as possible. (As with 'housie-housie', the notion that it would eventually become one of the most desired constituents of national fashion was unthinkable.) For the first time, then, we had to sort out the genuine articles, the battledresses roughly slung out to us on our original visit to the Quartermaster's stores.

It was remarkable how the Army dogma of 'spit and polish' managed, at the same time, to be so universally doubted and detested and yet individually respected and thought important. The daily grind of shining up everything metallic within reach, for no better reason than the patronising, critical gaze on the parade ground of the commissioned officer of the day, was so mindless as to defy any justification. Very nearly as lunatic as the rigid detail of the barrack-room 'kit inspections' to which we were frequently condemned. In these (something akin to the Drill Sergeant's obsessions about straight lines and right angles) there was a mania – where any article could be folded or tucked in, such as blankets or socks – for rectangular shapes, and most of all for 'square corners'; ideally, it seemed, to make them look like various sizes of parcel, all ready to be secured with string and sealing wax and taken down to the nearest Post Office. The impossibility of a respectable result to any of this caused – no doubt, intentionally – a frustration which was promptly increased by the inch-by-inch proper location on our bunk-bed of the rest of our kit, evidently in accordance with some inflexible map which had been handed down, unchallenged, through past ages. Apart from anything else, it gave limitless opportunities for inspecting officers to pick faults, and to ram home those same overall deficiencies in us. There was, however, no good reason within imagination for these repetitive purgatories.

On the other hand, there could be no better reason for any amount of salivary polishing and general immaculacy than an opportunity to mingle with what was left of the civilian community. The very thought of strutting down Richmond's main street, veneered in a smart khaki uniform – trousers creased, boots polished to perfection, cap-badge and buttons in sparkling competition – was enough to restore most of the pride that the Sergeant-Major and the Sergeant and the Corporal had done such a thorough, corporate job of removing. The key, of course, would be the uniform; the colour of khaki and the cut of our battledress masking the conviction of the Camp authorities that the lot of us were completely worthless. We would be accepted with admiring glances. Defenders of the country, no less – virile, tough, brave. In those days, after all, to be in any kind of Service uniform was to be firmly within

Of Straw And Stripes

the safety and surety of the sacred herd, flaunting the fact of 'doing one's bit for the Motherland'. It was the civilians, now, who might be feeling worthless, just by comparison with our splendour.

Unfortunately, the Military's determination to protect us from all of Life's dangers – with the peculiar exception, of course, of the War itself – got in the way of things. When we weren't having our legitimate sexual lusts deadened (for the legend of bromide was never officially denied), we were seemingly to be separated permanently from the perils of the common louse. To this effect, we were horrified to find our brand-new tunics ingrained with a white powder which had effectively mutated the healthiness of khaki into an agued condition of speckled grey. This, combined with an unbelievable degree of ill-fitting of the garments, the neckroom on my jacket having ample capacity for a couple of clenched fists as well as my head, threatened to highlight us, not as conquering heroes, but as very realistic inmates of a very realistic Dartmoor, if not indeed of Alcatraz.

In point of fact, I never in all of my Army life came in contact with lice of any variety, live or dead. Since hygiene, even real cleanliness, was absent during long periods of it, I have to thank my lucky stars. Certainly, it can have been nothing more than good fortune, in view of the quite vicious 'grooming' we gave those ailing uniforms. For what seemed hours of our spare time, we scrubbed away at them with the hardest-bristled handbrushes that we had managed to pilfer. Not a grain of that 'anti-louse powder' could possibly have survived the onslaught; and the Sergeant, as well as his clone of a Corporal, would have marvelled at the vim we secretly put into this particular species of 'spit-and-polish' (or should I really be saying 'scrub-and-blow'?) – urged on by the sight of the khaki's proper complexion gradually resurfacing out of the grey. No question about it; by the time of our first Richmond visit, we had regained much of our sense of respectability.

Sadly, Richmond itself was a supreme anticlimax. To have judged it a nonentity would probably have been over-praise. After the War, I recalled almost nothing about it, but that isn't the point: I had forgotten it even by the time we returned to barracks that same day. With one solitary exception, that is. For some reason, I was entranced by the little jeweller's shop right in the town centre. Maybe, because it reassured me that civilian life, somewhere or other, was still healthy and well – with its now unbelievable continuing requirements for gold

Of Straw And Stripes

bangles and diamond rings and pearl necklaces, just the same as a few weeks ago (or was it years?), when I was still my proper self. And also, I suppose, because of the quaint mechanism, right in the front of the window, which dared to call itself a clock.

Certainly, there was a recognisable clock-face to it, but the 'works' revolved around the performance (nakedly exposed for all to analyse) of a small, earnest, shiny brass ball. This persisted in trying to escape down a meandering, hopefully-sloped metal groove, only to find that the latter, with the tantalising reverse tilt of a see-saw, had suddenly turned the bottom into the top, as it were, thus precipitating a further despairing descent in the opposite direction. After a few minutes of these rather hypnotic repetitions (something akin to a trapped wasp negotiating a non-existent exit in a closed window), I began to feel truly sorry for the little fellow, so unfailingly was it deluded – and so frustratingly, with its obvious desperation to avoid both the limelight of the window and our persistent gaze. Nevertheless, a surprising by-product of its never-ending torture was the quite immaculate time-keeping of the whole contraption.

At any rate, there were more admiring glances cast in the direction of that window than at the whole lot of us put together; which, I may say, was a matter of very great numbers of soldiers indeed. That, of course, was the trouble. Any idea that our uniformed 'khaki veneers' would shimmer with attractiveness in the fresh air outside the Camp was soon rubbished by the competing overall veneer of khaki which effectively suffocated the whole town; thousands of us Servicemen blotting out everything from the landscape but ourselves. No wonder there was so little to remember! The few civilians around must surely have been swamped into visual non-existence, for I seemed to have seen none at all. It was almost a relief to get back to the barrack-room.

Not long afterwards, we had sudden and surprising word of a further diversion from our normal labours. Entirely unique during our time at the Camp, this consisted of a precipitous lunge – or, perhaps, slide? – into the realm of 'sport'. It is, of course, possible that the powers-that-were sensed a measure of failure; that the building up of morale (which must surely have headed their code manual's list of 'aims and procedures') was not working with us. Such perception wouldn't have needed even a touch of subtlety – just a quick glance at our faces, especially after the Richmond fiasco – but I suspect that thought wasn't involved in the slightest. The need to stage a mass cross-country race, with training squads competing against each other for positions of merit, was probably set out in rigid terms in the manual itself; and the Army has always worshipped blind obedience, even of printed instructions. The very date of the race may well have been inked in right at the start, and this religion of obedience evidently included not changing anything at all for any reason whatsoever. Otherwise, the weather would certainly have postponed it. While the falls of snow had by now tailed off, there was still sufficient underfoot to make any real talent for running an irrelevant nonsense. As it was, there simply came the inevitable democratic fetish of 'asking for volunteers' (which meant everyone without a brilliant excuse), and then, before we could change our mind, we were off – several hundreds of us; fairly early, on a morning still bitingly cold and white as far as the eye could see.

That day was a considerable adventure. As was each of the following two or three, though of a different kind altogether, and giving me no choice, either. If you are crying out that I had no wider a choice about the race itself, I must be honest. I confess that I was the most willing volunteer in the world. There was an exciting promise in the air, after all; a tempting challenge – at least 'evens', surely, to any respectable bookmaker. The Camp's assault course may have proved just as impossible as all those gymnastics, way back in the grammar school of my youth, but a cross-country race – why not? I had strong enough leg muscles, sound lungs, and a suspicion that I possessed a sufficiency of guts to complement them. I started off, therefore, confident for once about everything.

And, indeed, it turned out to be in that very order that I was tested; my legs, my lungs, and my guts. How surprising, mind you, was the amount of gymnastics I found mixed in with everything else; veritable snow-fountains of slidings and slitherings, which constantly interrupted my pounding strides into the front pack of runners. But the bravado of matching the best of them was inspiring an unusually certain sense of balance, to go with all the effort and determination which was boiling out of me. Reckless to the point of conceit, I simply 'went for it' as they say – at full stretch, and with no thought of keeping even a spark of energy in reserve for later on. It was glorious while it lasted.

Perhaps the most remarkable thing about the glory was that it lasted as long as it did; fully five or ten minutes – well into the surrounding countryside – before I felt myself flagging. And, even then, it was nothing to do with my legs, you must know. Looking down, I could see my feet, in their sopping Army boots, still squelching away as resolutely as ever through the snow. But my chest now demanded more fuel than I could gulp into it; and the aching protest of my lungs was spurned by a sudden and callous renewal of snowflakes, in their thousands, flurrying and scurrying around us from the sky. Presumably, this crisis must be what they called 'waiting for your second wind'. Feeling like this, however, could I possibly survive the wait? Buffeted by strengthening gusts, and tormented by snow (you could say) top, bottom and sides, those mythical odds now sounded increasingly generous – if only in terms of merely finishing the race.

As if by a miracle, my lungs did eventually find themselves 'topped up' for getting back into proper drive, but by that time the rest of me was disorientated, my balancing act now seeming a constant necessity, whatever the depth of the snow. Something certainly kept me going through what had become a swirling white haze, but I know not what. Before, there had been two inspirations; the raucous, sometimes blasphemous, encouragement from small groups of soldiers huddled at strategic points of the course (belabouring us with the honour of our respective squads), and, of course, the sheer exhilaration of being up with the leaders. Now, I hardly had the capacity to hear anything, and, dispiritingly, I could sense so many of the others passing me as to ram home a message of my frailties not being shared at all by *them*. To add to my misery, amidst these sprayed explosions of snow and ice and splashes from half-melted pools, the sogginess of my boots was now creeping up into my legs and my body and, it appeared, my whole soul. I was near to a saturated variety of numbness.

Astonishingly, however, I did complete the race – down amongst the last quarter of the runners, certainly, yet nowhere near the real stragglers, of which there were quite a few. But only just do I remember staggering over the finishing line. Less vaguely, there was the virtual heaven of the barrack-room coming into view, and then the deliriously comfortable luxury of that straw, as I collapsed on to my palliasse and panted myself into rest. At some time, I know, I must have climbed down to take off soaked denims and waterlogged boots and roughly dry myself; but then I went into a sleep as long and as deep as a coma, only to wake the next morning perspiring with all the sweat of a raging fever. Much the same, presumably, as that poor fellow who had collapsed on the square, I was whisked off unceremoniously to the Camp's sick-bay, where I spent days returning to an *unsticky* state of 'normality'; ready again for the barrack-room, and the Cookhouse, and the parade ground, and all the regulatory dogmas. Surprisingly, I was to find most things rather more tolerable, after the half-world of those misted days in the sick quarters. For a time, they replaced my comparisons with civilian life.

Chapter 5

There was no reason, you might say, to remember Richmond at all after the War, but the new age of the motor car was to make it just around the corner to Tyneside. After a few years, I found myself visiting it – or passing through it – quite frequently, and in its naked state, unclothed now by khaki, it is a likeable enough place. Yet at first it presented me with a disturbing mystery. Where on earth had reposed that Camp of ours? I could find no trace of it in the immediate outskirts of the town. Not a wisp of anything in the least military. Not a suggestion, indeed, of as much as a solitary soldier ever having existed in the neighbourhood. Not even the remaining concrete of a deserted barrack square.

It was a historical vacuum which bothered me. Certainly, the ramshackle Nissen huts forming a sizeable portion of the Camp had never seemed lasting structures; looking nothing more than the ugly interlopers of waste metal they really were – just dallying there, we hoped, on their way to the scrapyard (and the sooner the better). But that great, long, brick-built building which had, at one juncture, become our permanent dormitory, what of it? Nothing temporary, there. Of all considerations, built to last, I'd swear. If it were possible for a colossus like that simply to have disappeared into thin air, the claustrophobic torment which I remembered of its inner darkness could only, too, have been from my imagination! Yet never could there have been a dream quite so factual, so sharp, so absolutely realistic as that experience.

It wasn't one which I could have avoided, either. Nature saw to that. To put it basically, I needed to go to the lavatory, and my bunk was away up there at the very top of the room, the furthest of all from the exit. Now, that shouldn't really have meant more than a minute or so of separation from the warmth of my bed. The building was two times or more the length of our accustomed Nissen hut, and there were scores of bunks crammed into it. But these were, if anything, outnumbered by its windows, and 'navigation', in any event, was nothing more than a straight line to the door. This, however, ignored a prime fact of life in those days. All windows – in pain of court martial – had to be 'blacked out' after dusk, and no-one in peacetime can have any idea of how thoroughly effective was that procedure. Up to then, indeed, I doubt if I had realised it myself. So, swinging my legs over the side of the top bunk, it was in nonchalant fashion that I dropped to the floor to start what I imagined to be a routine trek. The room, by now, had certainly turned colder – it was hours after 'lights out' – but, never mind, I would soon be back in those heavenly grey blankets, relapsing once more, until reveille, into forgetfulness about absolutely everything.

Hitherto, I suppose, I had borrowed my concept of the worst possible War scenario from the cinema, and in particular from *All Quiet on the Western Front*; the landscape always liberally pitted with shell craters, and the shell-bursts themselves almost overhead (but with never a direct hit on me – since, presumably, I would have known nothing of it, in the event). At any rate, that was vicious enough stuff to merit anyone's terror. Set alongside, on the other hand, this situation was farcical. I was merely walking towards the toilet, down a very long room whose lights weren't switched on. Having said that, before even a couple of paces, I found myself panicking. All of a sudden, I had become totally and terrifyingly blind!

Groping and shuffling along this new mystery of never-ending bunk-shapes, ghostly in their invisibility, confusion oozed out of me in the stickiness of sweat. Not a gleam of light anywhere – nor any sound. Surely, by now, someone should have been snoring his very guts out? Or, at any rate, breathing heavily enough to reassure me that I wasn't, in fact, in some black parlour of the dead? At that moment, I would willingly have taken refuge in any of the shell-craters of my imagination.

Whilst I am unconvinced, now, that I travelled in any known approximation to the concept of a straight line, I did, at any rate, have the instinct to keep moving to some degree – inch by inch, foot by foot; and thus did I at last find the door, and the corridor, and – Heaven be praised! – the incredible miracle of its light-switch. Electric light, in an instant, changed the nightmare into self-ridicule. I was a little too old, I reasoned, for a repetitive dread of those unseen 'bogeymen' of my childhood's dark alley-ways! Switching off again as I started my return journey, I therefore re-entered the barrack-room convinced that I was fully re-insulated with normality. This, as it turned out, was only wishful thinking.

Before, I had commenced with the blackness, and the corridor's magic switch had always been hopefully in mind; whereas, now, I was plunged again into darkest oblivion from the other extreme of blazing light. Previously, the feel of a doorframe had been unmistakable for signifying success; but, presently, I was to perform a 'blind-man's-buff' search for a bunk-bed only distinguishable by the feel of its being unoccupied! After negotiating the first few of them, that meant fingering the blankets on each top berth for signs, perhaps, of a foot or a leg as warning for me to pass on and feel for the next bed. And all of this to be performed so subtly – so utterly delicately – as not to rouse any sleeping soul who might be attached to the limb I'd discovered! After five minutes or so of these furtive caressings of wood and wool and concealed flesh, you will not be surprised at my increasing desperation, with perspiration amounting, it seemed, more to pints than drops. Had I perhaps, this time, strayed into the wrong room altogether? Was I, in fact, properly moving up the middle of it? Compared to this, a London 'pea-souper' (with *everyone* in it lost and confused) had to be rated infants' play. Here, it was only I who was in any way astray. The rest of them (at any rate, if they woke) would know they were in just the right place, and at just the right time.

Reassuringly (confirming that I wasn't, after all, emotionally retarded), 'bogeymen' of any description didn't come into this predicament. Without doubt, I had left all of them behind me. At one time, there would have been crowds of them hiding around in a place like this, but my present panic came not from the darkness itself, but from the horrible sensation of being suffocated by the squeezing, all-sided pressure it brought. I was losing all sense of three-dimensional direction (or any other kind, come to that). And the frustration of it was the simplicity of suitable solutions – a torch, maybe, a box of matches, or, more logically, the foresight to have counted the bunks on my first, outward, journey. Any of these would have done the trick. Of course, even now, I could simply stand still and bawl out, 'For God's sake, where am I? Tell me where to go!' Assuming, however, that life was somewhere around – and these finds of legs and feet were proving rather too warm for the fare of any morgue – this would merely inspire blasphemous suggestions from all and sundry (after the usual preliminary of friendly obscenities) for me to turn on the light and find out. (But, in that event, where was the nearest infernal switch? Probably, much more unreachable than my bunk.)

Fortunately, against such possible further embarrassment, the dread of making a fool of myself in public was evidently more overwhelming than the rest of my fears put together, for I had no thought but to continue with this rather hopeless pathfinding operation of mine. Somehow or other, however, I did eventually get to a bed which felt colder than the others, with blanket-shapes more than usually dishevelled, and (crucially) no sense of anything remotely human about them. This particular palliasse, too, not only felt familiar, but imagination could stretch to the soft crackle of its straw even sounding the part! Levering myself up and sampling it proved the point. At last, I was back! Relief merged into the ecstasy of drowsiness, as the darkness around me softened to become as friendly and comfortable and warming as the blankets themselves. And, even now, the whole episode was starting to fade harmlessly away into sleep. Thereafter, in memory, one half of me would let it masquerade as a comic music-hall turn, good only for a laugh; one, certainly, that I could never confess to a single soul as having been the cause of panic. Yet the other half has continued to know it in its true colours. Vividly unfunny, it remains, in the background of my mind, a token of the potential horror of total blindness. Never, before this, had I realised how precious is the ability to see.

Passing again through post-War Richmond, I found myself pondering afresh my nagging fairy-tale of that disappearing barrack-room. Had there, I mused, ever really been tangible bricks and mortar to any of it? By this time, I had doubts. Not a scrap of it, after all, was now sharply focused for me, with the exception of that single frightening experience – which, you might say, had in any event been a matter of the most complete invisibility from start to finish! Certainly, by contrast, my mind-picture of our first Nissen hut quarters couldn't have been sharper were I stepping through its doors for the first time. Nothing remotely imaginary about it; nothing at all. Was I, then, wasting my time puzzling over the mere temporary disturbance of a common-or-garden nightmare?

Once and for all, I dismissed the idea as balderdash. What sort of dream could have dragged on into those subsequent self-rationings of evening liquid refreshment (against the need for any further indulgence in nocturnal pathfinding)? And, at that very same moment, there flashed to me the solution of the whole mystery. The barrack-room, and the bunks, and the corridor's lightswitch, hadn't in the slightest degree

Of Straw And Stripes

sprung from my imagination; yet it was also true that they had never existed in the first place! Nowhere in Richmond, that is. There had evidently been a gaping hole in my memory of those training days; right in the middle of them, in fact, when, without warning, our whole squad had been moved to the nearby town of Catterick, with its well-established cluster of permanent military buildings.

Belatedly (by a question of years) remembering the name of a place doesn't automatically resuscitate it. Catterick remains as anonymous for me today as it must have been then. I have never revisited it, and am unlikely ever to do so. Obviously, it must have had a drill square and a cookhouse and a canteen, just like Richmond. The impossibilities of its own particular brand of assault course had no doubt waited for us, just as innocently, around some corner of it. But the prototypes in my memory of these Army essentials are Richmond's alone; and the Catterick barrack-room – most probably standing there as stoutly as ever it did – still has its blackout curtains permanently drawn for me.

At first thought, in fact, the new Camp must have seemed so similar, in most respects, as to make the considerable time and effort in shifting us hard to justify. And then we saw Catterick's fully-fledged rifle ranges. That was it! Somebody – or, maybe, just another paragraph in that manual? – had decreed that we were overdue for 'finishing off' in our firearms education. To be sure, we had never seen anything resembling a firing range at Richmond, though whether we were yet ready to be let loose upon one remained debatable. After all, the continuing screams of the Sergeant (echoed as ever by the Corporal) still implied an obsession with dread rather than the possibility of any commendation. They hinted at untold danger, were we to operate the triggers half as clumsily as we drilled with the rifles themselves.

Few of us would have disagreed. Disillusionment with those accursed Lee Enfields had set in long ago. Savouring more of the First War than this one, it was hard to imagine them delaying the armoured columns of a German *blitzkrieg* – or even possessing the capacity to fire live ammunition of any description. In the overall saga of Life and Death, their sole purpose seemed embedded in the meaningless obligations to 'slope' them, or 'present' them, to 'order' or 'port' or what-you-will them of like artificialities. In no way could I envisage them doing much in the way of winning the War.

Fortunately for our general spirits, however, we had also been introduced to a shiningly sleek, veritable aristocrat of an automatic

Of Straw And Stripes

weapon – the Bren gun. Anyone (even we) could spot its pedigree at a glance. Certainly, Herr Hitler must have appreciated its lethal nature long ago, having made Czechoslovakia a top priority on his invasions list seemingly on nothing more than the country's invention and exclusive manufacture of it.

Now, the strange thing about these creatures' personality was their utter friendliness; from the safe end of the barrel, of course – our privileged position, so far. For a start, we didn't have to carry them around with us all over the place; not, at any rate, sloped on our shoulders or anything further of that nonsense. We felt quite relaxed with them. Indeed, they themselves always looked relaxed, as they reclined easily on the ground, each casually propped up on its elbows of a tiny front-fixed tripod. And that, in fact, was where we invariably practised with them – lying on the ground beside them. For the Army, whilst not to date letting us operate them, had still contrived to invent a drill of sorts, to keep us occupied; condemning them continually to be taken to pieces and then, just as promptly, put together again. Remarkably – since I am surely the most unmechanically minded of men – I could still undertake to carry out the task as easily and meticulously today. That part of our memory training must have been exemplary.

Perhaps the secret was the vague aura of femininity which the weapons conveyed. Not, that is, in their basic looks or character – which gun, after all, could possibly seem gentle in a womanly kind of way (particularly from the *un*safe end)? – but in their female associations; and evident attraction, too, for the fair sex. That weatherbeaten duo of Sergeant-and-Corporal, obviously all-knowing in worldly matters, was only too pleased to educate us at every opportunity. 'The ladies' delight!' it kept yelling, as (yet again) we would be dissecting the unfortunate Brens. 'Don't forget – the ladies' delight!'

In actual fact, the dismembering bit of the affair was comparative child's play; everything falling apart so unresistingly that one rather dreaded the same thing happening by accident in battle, leaving to hand only an unresponsive trigger. No doubt as potential damage limitation, therefore, great emphasis was placed upon reassembling the whole thing as quickly as possible. Surely enough, provided that the crucial element of its 'body locking pin' could be located, the one half of the gun slid smoothly back into the other; always remembering (and which of us had any difficulty?) that the first four inches of the pin 'didn't count' – as spoke the Sergeant, leering wisely at us – so far as a firm join was concerned.

By this time, however, all forms of firearms drill were showing up as hypocrisies. If, as we were entitled to suppose, the ghastly object of warfare – at any rate, the main ingredient for the finishing of it – was to kill as many as possible (preferably of the enemy), these non-availing struggles with the fine print from the drill manuals could be no more than pretence; continuing to play at being soldiers, as it were. What chance had all that 'spikiness', all those straight lines and right angles, against the might of the German Army? As yet, we hadn't even seen a bullet, let alone loaded one or fired one.

That rifle range, therefore, came to be what really counted with us. What would the imprecisions of our 'square-bashing' matter compared to hitting the target with live ammunition? We might yet confound that Sergeant.

Who can be sure, now, of the possibilities then? Quite reasonable marksmanship, perhaps, if only a small fraction of the time we had spent (and were still spending) on the sacred, bullet-less drill rituals had been allocated for firing practice. But the Army was always at its most proficient when shielding confidence from us. We were allowed two or three brief tastes of the range's facilities, and that was that; sufficient to convince us of the odds against the likelihood of ever shooting straight, but not at all of our capability to overcome them.

Even so, it took next to no time for us to be confirmed as disciples of the Bren gun. So far as it was concerned, outward appearance had told the entire truth. When fired, the ammunition sped from it with oily smoothness, its mechanism positively obscene in the way it was evidently caressing the bullets away on their potentially bloody tasks.

Sadly, however, in converse that rifle of mine proved no *better* than before, though my belief in the seriousness of its demerits – its overweightedness, and clumsiness, and general aura of primitive invention – may have sprung more from the awkwardness of inexperience in my shooting: any make of rifle would have performed just as badly for me, I suspect. There was the creaking of my leg joints (young as I was) and the straining of my arm muscles to distract me, as I lay flat on the ground, my legs forced uncomfortably astride (for stabilising the gun, they insisted – though with seemingly the opposite effect!), and my elbows forming an uncertain tripod which verged on the

Of Straw And Stripes

precarious, compared with the steel of the Bren's built-in variety. And then, after an age of delay in petrified tension at this 'ready position', the signal to press the trigger would inevitably result in that same, savage rearing up of the barrel as the bullet was released – a recurring calamity which made aiming a forgotten art, compared with the need to keep some sort of control over the weapon itself.

All in all, nevertheless, we can't have been such a complete disgrace, since we mostly got our shots somewhere or other on the target, even if not often in the more respectable places. And, in any event (if only we could have known), irony had been hovering over the whole of our firearms training. On active service, over in Europe, we fired not a single round from a Lee Enfield, and hardly saw a Bren, let alone handled one; our staple weapon being the light-as-a-feather Sten gun, easily carried by shoulder strap and completely unobtrusive. There was never any question of having to take it apart and then stick it together again: we had better things to do with our time.

However short and frustrating these visits to the firing range, there was a sense of finality to them. Surely, by now, we had felt the full force of everything which the Army could hurl at us? Foot-drill, arms-drill, 'assault-coursing', unarmed combat, route marching, and now (incredibly) the firing off of a few practice bullets. What further training could that manual possibly prescribe? Presumably, for infantry recruits, the extra target practice which we had been denied; perhaps, too, a taste of manoeuvres under live fire. But, for support troops like us, the latter could only have been a wastage of the training time that was available. Strange was it, therefore, to learn the nature of the 'lesson' which still remained in the pipe-line – nothing less than the final torment of 'throwing the live grenade'!

I have always wondered what this exercise was designed to achieve. The closest likeness must have been the 'live fire' experience which we were being excused. That would have inured us, I suppose, to the 'feel' of possibly being blown to bits at any moment by the enemy. The gnawing sensation here, on the other hand, could only be of imminently blowing *oneself* to bits!

I doubt, mind you, whether it must have seemed quite such a torment to the others. With me, you see, it was double-pronged. There was the frightening aspect of the grenade itself – nothing more in appearance than an innocent, grey-coloured Easter egg, but which, minus its retaining pin, was apparently for exploding into the terror of thousands of flying missiles. And then there was the equally unbelievable fact that I had never been proficient in the art of *throwing* things (cricket balls, or the like). To me, this failing boded tragedy where it was a grenade, of all things, which had to be got rid of; a scenario, in any event, savouring of potential (and probably posthumous) awards of the Victoria Cross, for valiant onslaughts on unassailable machine gun nests. Bravery unlikely in support troops, you could say, and most certainly in me.

Since these were my innermost thoughts, there could never be the faintest whisper of them to anyone whomsoever. That goes without saying. Or does it? Certainly, even in peacetime, there must always have been certain qualities, driven as undesirables beyond the pale by unspoken consensus; to be kept severely hidden. At present, for example, there is sentimentality and naïveté; the instinct to burst occasionally into honest tears (either from joy or from sorrow) and the sensitivity to be shocked. Not one of these outsiders is normally allowed to penetrate our assorted veneers against public disapproval. The penalty, after all, can be a reputation for foolishness or stupidity (or both); worse still, for being easily hurt or wounded.

But War generates its own values, savagely stricter, yet accepted by all. While romance and idealism positively flourish, there is an offshoot to them – the adulation of unflinching virility in the cause of patriotism; so overwhelming, indeed, as to intertwine the ultimate sins of fear and cowardice and make them indistinguishable from one another. Each becomes as unmentionable as the least curable of virulent diseases. And, much like the disease, no-one will admit to having it.

Age brings with it the luxury of comparative unconcern for the opinions of others, but in younger years they mostly rule absolutely and autocratically. I was the same as everyone else – I would not, and did not, admit anything. Looking a fool would have been serious enough, but to be *despised* was something much deeper down; probably necessitating (in my mind) the personal arrangement of a firing squad for the purification of my soul! How many hundreds of thousands of virile-looking young servicemen may have gone to their sudden War-death carrying the same, supposedly unique, secret with them into eternity? It is a morbid thought. All I know is that, as I approached that dreaded slit-trench, with the Sergeant nonchalantly cocooned in it beside his box of Easter eggs, I was desperately wishing I could look half as matter-of-fact as he. In reality, I remained convinced of the accidental horror which, in the course of the next few minutes, would finally solve for me the riddle of the After-life.

The built-in tension of the prospect hardly needed reinforcing, from my point of view; but the obvious necessity for 'waiting our turn' – in a safe cubbyhole, some distance away – gradually fermented a near frenzy of apprehension, as the vital moment neared. (In terms of real warfare, an unrealistic surfeit of thinking time.)

But there I was, eventually, crouching in the trench, my allocated 'egg' in the grasp of my hand, and the Sergeant in course of bullying me into pulling out the pin. There followed a few fraught seconds of stark realisation: only my grip could now be restraining the thing's vicious instincts. Was this, then, when I was fated to drop it, clumsily and fatally, on the ground? By this time, the Sergeant was booming a varied assortment of wisdom into my earhole. 'Get on with it, man! What the hell's the matter with you? Throw the bugger! Jilldie!' All of which added up to as big a mistake as he'd probably made for some considerable time, seeing that I promptly tried to put his advice into practice – not by gently lobbing the grenade out, but, with all my strength, *hurling* it far away into the safety of distance. In actual fact it merely skidded a few yards through the grass beyond the trench, before coming ominously to rest.

When, having heard the shatteringly close explosion, I realised that I was still in *this* world – such sharp hearing not seeming appropriate to the next – I noticed that Sergeant of ours wearing a brand new, awe-inspiring halo. He hadn't turned a hair, after all, apart from reinforcing the usual bellow of 'Get your bloody heads down!' with his forcible ramming of mine to below surface level. After which, it had merely been a matter of: 'Next one! Get a move on, there!'

I developed a peculiar notion. Perhaps this near catastrophe hadn't been so unusual as all that? What if, really, this was some sort of specialised training for the Sergeant himself – inurement, maybe, to future perils in assaulting those nests of machine guns? (Cumulatively, almost as hazardous, it seemed!) I will never know whether he survived the War. Left to me, I would have given him a medal in advance.

Looking back, the exploding of those grenades in solemn succession stands as a somewhat macabre fireworks display, in celebration of the end of our training. The three months which we had spent at the Camps had been more like three whole years out of each of our lives. But we had safely survived; and, before we knew it, we were packing up our essentials for the elixir of a couple of weeks home leave.

Chapter 6

I cannot believe that the London and North Eastern Railway Company Limited ever thought of the station at South Shields as one of the jewels in its crown, so to speak. While no worse than most, it had always been stark – desolate and cold, in spirit as much as substance; its sole warmth the steam which hissed aggressively from the engines as they came or went, either grinding percussively to a halt, or struggling, when leaving, in the apoplexy of getting their wheels to grip. Even this was only the heat of imagination, the reality of an engine's blazing coal furnace being usually masked from view by the driver and his fireman, standing on the footplate. As I alighted, on my way home, I should therefore have known what to expect, but there was now an additional sadness about the whole place, to dampen the pleasure I should have had at returning.

Outside, waiting for a tramcar, my disappointment persisted. What was wrong? Was it perhaps the *size* of things? To be sure, the buildings, the streets, the railway station, all the permanent character strengths of the town I had known from birth – they had seemingly shrunk alarmingly. Dirtier, too, and dingier; altogether less significant than I remembered them. Or was I now finding the comparatively deserted – and weirdly quiet! – nature of civilian life simply too strange to credit?

Just as there had been too much thinking space for me before dicing with that grenade, so was it now in the creaking old vehicle – surely meriting a shout or two of 'Jilldie!' – which alternately rocked and jolted me to the town's outskirts and my brother's bungalow. Never in my life had I felt more solitary. Or, come to that, more uncertain. What would I find waiting for me when I arrived?

Of course, the absence of anyone at the station to welcome me had been neither strange nor unexpected: in wartime, people have better things to do with their time. In any event, both my brother and sister (the latter, I knew, now back from evacuation to help with the care of Mother) would be out at work. But that left possibly only my parents in the bungalow, and with Mother hardly able to recognise a ring on the doorbell, let alone walk along the passage, it would be Father to let me in, or no-one. For all I knew (since I hadn't a key of my own), I might find myself serving a short sentence of tramping around the exercise yard of the back garden. In hindsight, I acknowledge the foreboding which must have dwelt within me, as, still hoping for miracles, I negotiated the path up to the front door and tried my luck on the bell-push.

The worry and apprehension on my Father's face when, at last, it poked out at me through the opening door, must just about have matched the look on mine. Either from forgetfulness or, perhaps, my brother never having told him in the first place, my emergence out of the coldness of the garden seemed to take him aback; but he was pleased enough to see me, smiling as wholeheartedly as his coughs and wheezes would allow at such short notice. For myself, I was so relieved that I very nearly embraced him on the spot.

And that, for me, was a truly extraordinary state of affairs. To start with, my family's repertoire of talents had never comfortably stretched to showiness – especially of emotions, which, by and large, were understood rather than demonstrated. Indeed, flippancies such as embracing and hugging, as well as all known varieties of spoken endearment, had been almost unknown to us. That said, however, I had never before *felt* affection for him. As a kind of distant figurehead, the upholder of discipline, if nothing else, Father had never fallen within the proper bounds of a human being. Compared with Mother's all-pervading influence, over so many years – as she 'skimped and scraped' to feed and clothe us and make us 'respectable' – he had seemed irrelevant, except in so far as I had always been afraid of him.

Yet, as he shuffled in front of me along the modern, green-panelled passageway, past the doors to the immaculate sitting room on the right and the spotless main bedroom on the left, I marvelled that he could ever have intimidated a single soul; a very old man now (far older than his years), with features both pallid and wrinkled, shoulders severely stooped, and the desperate gaspings of chronic asthma barely earning breath enough to keep him moving. How monstrous the ravages of old age!

That is not to say that I could ever remember him very much younger-looking. Factually, he hadn't been young when I was born. Middle-aged, you could say (even late-middle-aged, I suppose, for those days).

And, from the start – his affliction having come upon him years before I appeared – perpetually cursed and imprisoned by that relentless asthmatic catarrh, which had grown to be an unfailing barometer of the prevailing weather outside our windows, or even approaching them from the near distance. The slightest wisps of fog, for example, would find him already on his hunkers in front of the living room's bright coal fire, retching cataclysmically to get the clogging of bronchial phlegm spat out into the sterilisation of the flames – a convenient form of hygiene now no longer to hand, unfortunately, with nothing more basic than a gleaming electric fire in this present sanctum of modernity. Sadly, at those times, I was probably as close to the heart of him as ever I would get; but there was always a barrier beyond the mere physical distance. With such unpleasant displays liable to recur unheralded, it is perhaps no wonder that he had engendered more of a revulsion against the nature of his disability than the sympathy he really deserved.

A step or two more, and we had reached the third door, the one at the end of the passage; and through it, looking rather better than I had expected to find her, was Mother. Perched on her accustomed place, the edge of the fireside chair overlooking the electric heater's artificial coal effect – a poor substitute indeed for that cheery old black-leaded grate! – she presented herself as a trim and compact little lady, looking almost as good as new, with the blue-blacks of her hair hardly affected by the few half-hidden greys, her brown eyes as lustrously large as ever they had been, and a friendly appearance doing its best to deny the nearing of old age. There was, however, that one telling change from the past; the strange, unconcerned placidity which had replaced her perennial trademark of constant bustling activity and worry. And, just as she hadn't known who it was going away into the Services, she had no particular recognition of me now, coming back for a home break.

This was the supreme tragedy of our family. Whereas the health of my Father had been slowly worsening over many years, the unexpected and alarming collapse of Mother, from the vibrancy of hard work into the lethargy of premature senility, had taken less than two. Looking at her now, after three months of jostling with all the health and vigour which the Army took for granted, was to realise fully the 'death within life' – non-speaking, non-feeling, non-caring – to which she had been cruelly reduced.

It was hardly the most welcoming of starts to a homecoming; and ironic, too, since the Mother I had previously known, forgetting her inhibitions for once, would surely have greeted me with open arms, and tears of rejoicing that no harm had come to one of her 'bairns' (as she would have continued to think of me). She had loved all us 'bairns', all our lives, even though, with her temper crotchety from overwork, some of us, for moments, may have doubted it. As of now, however, I had to make do with just the outward semblance of her, eked out by Father's well-meaning but empty small talk, and, at tea-time, the return from work of my brother and sister – who, in turn, were largely absorbed in the priorities of Mother's needs and the tidying up of the house.

That first day set the low watermark against which the tide rose not an inch during the rest of my fortnight. I had to get used to doing nothing and not needing to feel guilty; but that, in itself, wasn't either difficult or unpleasant, with memories of the Training Camp's forced labours. While I was indoors at home, however, embroiled by the utter hopelessness of my parents' situation, I was useless, and that was a different matter. If I knew it, so must these siblings of mine, probably hard-pressed to conceal their irritation. I was simply 'in the way' of the smooth running of affairs: to have stayed put at Catterick would have been best for everyone. The conclusion was especially galling when I thought of the rest of the squad, undoubtedly wallowing in untold arrears of family affection – and not just a question of parents, either: often there would be wife and children, and the warm reassurance of the connubial bed thrown in for luck! You will see that I was just as healthily self-centred as any other young man.

Indeed, as my leave crept uneventfully onwards, I found myself thinking more and more about myself, my own misery, my own predicament in this no-man's-land of civilian stagnation. Soon, there was no room in my head for anything else. Surely, it argued, I needed to be 'recharging my batteries' if I were to survive the full impact of Army life when I went back as a so-called fully-trained 'fighting man' (sic)! Yet those 'batteries' (wherever they were implanted in me) were still draining current, not receiving it, and, at this rate, I would be in a rare old state of depression at the end of my leave. It was my turn, now, to feel secretly irritated – with my brother and sister, and even with Father himself. If their life-styles were humdrum and monotonous, there was at any rate a settled permanence to them – with nothing of the unpredictabilities of Life and Death which were embedded in *my* immediate future. Before I knew it, I was wishing myself back at the barracks, without further ado.

Of Straw And Stripes

* * *

On the morning of my last day, I rose early, as usual. 'Reveille' at the bungalow was little later than Catterick's, and Mother, who was gently stirring into wakefulness, needed to be tended before all else. Father, beside her, seemed not yet ready to leave a pleasant and unfinished dream. It was the longest sleep that he would ever sleep. When we drew back the blankets, he was stone dead . . .

Chapter 7

It was my first experience of a funeral, as it had been my first glimpse ever of death itself. Of the two, unexpectedly, only the funeral was repellent. What remained of my father still smacked remarkably of the living; rather healthier-looking, in fact – less lined and wrinkled and worried – than I had known him for some time. His face, no longer contorted with the constant struggle for breath, had assumed the waxed veneer of ethereality; or, in this world, of a Tussaud's effigy (as if, suddenly, he had been elevated to all the greatness and fame required for that museum's public display of queuing reverence).

As it was, the half-dusk, half-dawn of the bedroom's closed curtains saw him laid out in an incongruous condition of hushed and breathtaking dignity which seemed magnified, rather than reduced, by the fewness of those who came to look their last upon him. I was one of the even fewer who lingered sentimentally over the process, perhaps secretly in penitence to him for my recent egotism. Gazing down, awestruck, upon the mystical stillness of death, I was mourning him as a stranger who was nevertheless the origin of me. Only if I had been on this earth much earlier would I have stood a chance of properly understanding him. That incredible ancient photograph, mind you, had never ceased telling me its fairy-tale vision of such a handsome, tall, upright young man, standing proudly beside the gorgeously beautiful and youthful version of Mother; their first three children, neatly posed into the picture, scarcely recognisable from the grown-ups I had always known. For some reason, I began to feel vaguely ashamed of myself.

But the whole of the funeral ritual which followed carried its own shame. Shallow, hypocritical and bleak (in every sense), it removed all traces of the spiritual aura which had surrounded Father as he 'lay in state', you might say, in his last home; the only thing subsequently around of any real depth being the frightening gravediggers' pit into which he was finally lowered – protecting him, at any rate, from the harsh farewell of a particularly biting airstream.

The coffin's submergence beneath all that sea of soil is almost my only memory of the proceedings, up to our returning home for the 'tea-and-sandwiches' refreshments which were seemingly, by tradition, an indispensable tailpiece to such an occasion – presumably to remind us all that, being still of this world, we had a bounden duty to enjoy ourselves. My mental blanks of the journey to the cemetery, and of what went on within the religious sanctity of its chapel, lead me to conclusions which are poles apart. I can assume that our travel was smoothly uneventful, but never that the pulpit's offering can have been inspired, or even properly comforting – more likely as coldly routine and remote as in most of the funerals I have since had to attend, particularly where the dead individual hasn't been a member of a clergyman's regular flock. And Father, though a man of morals, probably hadn't seen the inside of a church since I was baptised.

When it was all over, I was beginning to realise that the most memorable part of a funeral is not, as I would have expected, the prayers for the soul of the departed or the burial of his body. Rather is it the 'get-together' of the relatives and hangers-on, after the grizzly part of the affair has conveniently and hygienically vanished; the laden trays of cakes and sandwiches, in combination with uncountable teas and coffees, letting loose – as if it were a pack of snapping, confined hounds – a sheer torrent of frantic, accumulated gossip.

Having said that, I was pleased enough to see the several who had turned up; my Auntie Annie, genially bespectacled and beaming camaraderie to one and all as she proceeded to talk the hind legs off a donkey, as they say; inoffensive Uncle August, her husband, smilingly complementing her by not saying a word; Auntie Mary, slower and rather hesitant of speech, as kindly as ever and leaning forward from time to time with wisdoms about the family's past (each ever so well-considered before she spoke); and a cluster of thoroughly grown-up cousins, most of whom were brimming over with all kinds of enlivening trivialities. In addition, of course, there was the twosome of Hilda and Jim themselves, floating anxiously around in general control of essentials – in particular, the teapots; while my other brothers Tom (the artistic one, down from Scotland) and the more scholarly Andrew (back for the occasion from his evacuation in the Lake District), as well as my sisters-in-law, were doing as much to assist in the organisation as their only recent arrivals would permit.

This was the stuff of which jolly family reunions are made, and a funeral is no hindrance whatsoever. Cram together a few far-flung relatives who haven't met in force for years (some perhaps not at all), and the sheer novelty is guaranteed to melt seriousness into a whimsical catching up with history, in which family anecdotes become vaguely amusing on their way to guffaws of laughter. While yet to grasp that it was a common danger of the species, I could sense the party spirit round our particular tea-table warming into near oblivion what had brought us together in the first place. Not only was Father no longer on anyone's lips, but my poor Mother, tucked away on her chair beyond the fringe of the babble of talk and looking puzzled and disturbed, had evidently been put to one side and written off as a nonentity.

Looking across into her unblinking brown eyes was to plumb the depths of human sorrow. What was to become of her? More to the point, how much of her remained for becoming anything at all? It was difficult not to see her still as she would healthily have been – at the very centre of affairs, running here and hastening there to pick up every scrap of responsibility, and with all things (including, you may be sure, each of the teapots) totally dependent upon her. In my capacity as the youngest by far of her brood, she had doted upon me, and I upon her; the more so since, never minding the ample size of the family, I had grown up more or less as an only child, encased by kinsfolk sufficiently mature to have been plausible uncles and aunt, had I not known them to be brothers and sister.

It seemed that, either way, I couldn't win. Father haunted me because I hadn't ever known him, but this current edition of Mother was equally as disturbing; in reverse, as it were. The closeness to me, her supreme importance over so many years – how *well* I had known her! And now she was no more meaningful than a kind of fairy-tale of the past. This time, I felt wretched for no *longer* knowing.

On balance, it was doubtless a mercy that none of the hubbub from the tea-table can have made sense to her, nor, for that matter, the sight of so many comparative strangers sitting round it for some unknown reason. Certainly, for some time past our household, during its increasing poverty and domestic difficulties, had known no visitors at all; and, whilst evidently perplexed by the prolonged disappearance of her partner, Mother had no comprehension of his death.

In this way, the story of my parents' marriage had no proper ending. I was left with only the imagination of how it might suitably have finished, given a background of reasonable health. Callous, maybe, even to think, but a good, honest paroxysm of grief from a more cognisant version of Mother would have set the world to rights for me at that moment.

This, of course, was to make a somewhat precarious assumption; that the close and untroubled partnership of the two of them over the past year or so hadn't, in itself, been merely the *product* of their ill-health. It had certainly been the reason for their roles within the family, and towards each other, being turned inside out; Mother, no longer the resilient organiser of slender resources, now becoming dependent on everyone else, with Father (the traditional 'provider') soon unable to provide anything other than his presence beside her – but with all the time in the world, nevertheless, to go through the motions of protecting her.

Arguably, such an absence of financial worries throughout their marriage might have meant never a word of anger between them (albeit with boredom a likely consequence). In any event, however, they – and, not surprisingly, the rest of us – were highly-strung creatures, with the knack of erupting stormily every now and again, if only by instinct. Ironically, the most 'peaceful' of my brothers, Tom, left the household when I was but seven years old, for work as a commercial artist up in Scotland; leaving behind Jim and Andrew, each of whom frequently didn't see eye to eye with Father, and Hilda, who was just as often in disagreement with Mother. I was never more than vaguely aware of the reasons behind the flare-ups, though it is now obvious that shortage of money was the main cause.

All I know is that the whole house seemed dangerous tinder at these times; the more so, I see now, with the need for money highlighted by that strange and increasing family instinct of ours. This consisted of an alarming (some would say heinous) tendency for stepping out of line from our 'proper place' in society; running amok from the herd, you might almost describe it. I suppose it was Father who had set the pattern in the first place, way before I was thought of, when, instead of sensibly and safely vegetating as a routine workman, he had established himself as a 'master painter and decorator', complete with a couple of employees, an assortment of ladders, and the most unsure and spasmodic level of remuneration imaginable. As if this were not sufficient in the way of adventure, he had insisted on purchasing our home 'on mortgage' (a rarely heard concept in those days of almost universal renting).

It wasn't, after all, that either of my parents had more than basic education, though their standard ration of six years had achieved literacy comparable with much of today's stretched variety of eleven. Jim and Tom, too, had got by quite well with their equally few crumbs of learning; needing to slave additionally at evening classes, but getting respectable jobs, all the same, at the end of them – out of the ordinary ones, indeed, compared with shipyard work, or coalmining, or serving customers in a shop (the destiny of most of the other eleven-year-olds on leaving school). Being accepted as an apprentice draughtsman at an electrical engineering works set Jim immediately apart from his friends, whilst Tom's eventual ability to switch from trained instrument-maker to well-paid commercial artist was something to shout to the housetops. However, when the turn of first Andrew and then Hilda came round, *their* potential began to revolve around scholastic achievement, and that contrasted even more sharply with neighbourhood tradition.

It was at this juncture that all concerned really began to feel the pinch, further education seemingly being so obsessed with the future as to ignore the necessity for surviving the present. Hilda won entrance into a respectable teachers' training college – and subsequent election as its 'head girl' – without the money to buy clothes to supplement her day-to-day outfit (hardly a boost to confidence), while Andrew's plight was no better. Despite winning a scholarship which paid all his fees at the local University, it provided nothing to bolster his weekly pittance of pocket money – a solitary halfcrown. From now on, it was a question of living (or trying to) beyond their means, the same strictures applying, for that matter, to the whole of the household.

With Tom's departure, you must see, there was only one regular earner among the six of us, and that was Jim. Father's cashbook receipts alternately stuttered promisingly and dried up altogether; often with the seasons, for outside painting jobs were apt to be hampered or ruined by the harshnesses of winter, to say nothing of the occasional spring. Since holidays were unknown, there was no obvious sedative against the build-up of tension, and the strong arguments which occasionally resulted could develop into frenetic rows – such as the occasion when Father, presumably at the end of his tether for the moment, flung a shovelful of coals across the living room at the truculently grown-up edition of Andrew; his aim, however (I'm sure intentionally), falling far short. No doubt, Mother often received an unfair benefit of the doubt in my secret judgements of these affairs: in my eyes, she was usually as completely blameless as Father was completely in the wrong. Personal acquaintanceship with fatherhood now makes me suspect a more reasonably balanced blame, though I cannot deny the violent nature of his bad temper when he was goaded into it.

Not that – now I think of it – he ever actually raised his hand in anger against any of us. He had no need. His was a simmering personality which mostly only threatened to spill over into drastic action. Since it rarely materialised for proper measurement, this unknown quantity became all the more dreaded. In point of fact, the most ferocious thing he ever did in my presence was directed, not to any human being, but to the crockery set out on the table for our midday meal. Storming out of the house in the course of a particularly warlike confrontation with Mother, who had probably been badgering him again about his failure to get clients' bills paid on time, he swept cups, saucers and plates alike on to the floor, shattering them to pieces and us into near terror with his shouted intention of getting drunk at the nearest public house. I recall him bawling out 'Whisky!' as the speediest means of achieving his promise.

I could only judge the abominable nature of the threat by its evident effect on Mother, for I knew as little of drunkenness as of alcohol itself. Within my life-span, there hadn't been a drop of strong drink around, with ginger wine, so far as my childish knowledge went, the only special beverage ever invented for occasions like New Year's Eve. And yet – rather mysteriously – Father was apparently an entrenched member of the Gospel Temperance Union, with the unspoken assumption which came with it of the unchecked vice fermenting beyond its pale. Perhaps (I can now suspect), he may have had first hand experience of these depravities, to be so afraid of them. As on most other aspects of the family scene before I arrived, I was an ignoramus; but, in any event, who was I to have been bothering myself about such ancient history? Nevertheless, Mother's fright sank into my very bones, and I remember vividly the taut and mounting anxiety, as we waited for the return of what I imagined would be a vicious, drink-sodden condition of my Father – maybe wreaking a havoc on everyone in his path as cold-blooded as his savagery of the crockery. Armageddon for the entire household, as it were.

Strangely, I felt both deflated and disappointed by the eventual result of his brief spell of debauchery. I didn't even witness it. After the dread creaking of the front door as it opened, there were just a few unsteady footsteps coming along the passage, before I heard them turn stumblingly up the stairs in the direction of the bedroom. And then – nothing but the snuffles and snores of a pole-axed variety of sodden sleep. The next day, life rose again into normality, with never a further word spoken of the original argument, Father back in comparative favour, and forgetfulness everywhere thriving.

This was the usual pattern with us, though not of drinking habits – complete teetotalism never otherwise being questioned, apart, that is, from Andrew's later liking for the odd 'half' (but imbibed elsewhere) with his University friends. We were, as a whole, a decidedly stormy lot, but the storms were infrequent and mostly over and done with in a single flash of lightning.

But several bolts of what must have been the forked variety, in the form of a bitter dispute involving Jim, did eventually hit us, splitting the family apart in the process; a disaster which was lasting and largely irreparable. It probably had to happen some time; Jim, with his regular if low-paid job cultivating an increasing sense of independence, Father doubtless in the midst of one of his cashbook's blank spells, and the two of them with identical, flammable tempers. Mother, as well, must been at the back of it all, more irritable than usual from the impossibility of her economics ('Where's this month's mortgage to come from?' I can still hear her lamenting), with Jim, who adored her without question, always dogmatically on her side in any exchange of hard words.

Whatever the cause, the confrontation was evidently cataclysmic; so serious as to make father and son entirely incompatible from then on. Whether, at that point, Jim was verbally *told* to leave the house and get lodgings elsewhere, I have never been sure; but, in follow-up to the incident, the arrangement for a 'solicitor's letter' to be sent to him (with the situation set out in the severity of black and white), was surely the greatest blunder of judgement which Father can ever have made. It certainly achieved Jim's prompt departure, together with all of his belongings, but it also drove a wedge between my parents, whereby Mother spoke not a single word to her husband during the course of the next two years!

This was my initiation into the subtle technique needed for 'living in two camps'. Later, within the house itself, I was to be the common denominator of the living room's workaday culture of my parents, and the more intellectual conversations of Andrew and his University friends in the next-door sitting room. Whereas that was mere artificiality, the quarantining of supposedly different 'classes', the present alienation went deep down into classless basics – even the geography of it; Jim always meeting Mother outdoors, and sometimes treating her to the entertainment of a bus trip into the country, for the temporary cheering of her existence. Since I was still a child, I was always taken with them, thus emphasising, when we returned home, the difference of the two sides of the argument. It left me with all the sadness of an unnatural state of affairs which I suspected was to last for evermore.

Everything was reinforcing my belief in the past. The best, I was more than ever convinced, had always happened somewhere behind my back. My parents had been young and vibrant – even sleeping in the same bed. There had been communal family parties at Christmas time, with a plentiful supply of joviality and of relatives whom I had since hardly seen; to say nothing of the hard-practised 'magic' of Jim and Tom which often led the entertainment; a choice of witnessing an impossible escape from the innards of a padlocked mailbag, or one of them being sawn in half, inside a wooden box dangerously resembling a coffin.

Jim, additionally, had been the enthusiastic core of a local concert-party, as comedian and ventriloquist, while Tom had dabbled in the first glimmers of photography – with Father himself experimenting in 'cat's whisker' wireless reception. But with the exception of the 'cat's whisker', which was, indeed, still sharply defined for me, the rest were no more than chapters of folklore. Others had witnessed them: I was only the listener.

And now, as I continued to gaze at Mother, sitting over there in a world only she knew, I wept inwardly, not only for her but for the 'running-down' process of the whole family, the only part of its story, I realised, to which I could really testify. While Mother's 'Coventry sanction' had tailed off eventually into splutters of terse, essential conversation, the merging of these, ever so gradually, into a reasonable flow of normality with her husband had coincided with – just as gradual – the onset of her own chronic illness. Who, then, can tell whether their final reconciliation was complete or only roughly patched up for the sake of convenience? I like to believe in the possible – that at any rate a little of the early prosperity of their marriage vows, the loving respect for each other which still shimmers out of that ancient photograph, had resumed its proper place before ill health's final blurring of the realities.

Of Straw And Stripes

When the bubbling animation which marked the celebration of the funeral – for that was what it was; like the rest of its genre, a total irony – had dispersed, the four of us were left, in the blanket silence of the bungalow, to relapse into more serious reflection on the changes in our life-patterns. Mostly, perhaps, in those of Hilda and Jim; since mine was already swallowed up in the uncertainties of the Army, and Mother, in any event, couldn't really have been reflecting at all, just vaguely sensing a difference, with no answer to what and why.

In fact, of all the people who had been buzzing around, it was my sister alone who must have grieved wholeheartedly for Father, for she had never had a serious dispute with him, and he had been behind her throughout, insisting on the extension of her education and even the peculiarity of pursuing a career of her own. (This, in the days when, more often than not, the odd girl out in a household was earmarked to 'stay behind' as its sacrificial and permanent caretaker; insurance, as it were, for the eventual arrival of its old age.) Hilda, as honest and well-meaning a girl as ever there was, had emotions which were deep-seated and linked with the strongest sense of family loyalty. This, as long as I knew her, contrived to keep her persistently in touch with all her kinsfolk, near and far, readily accessible or not. Father's death, as well as obliterating the only true supporter she had ever had in a near all-male community, must have seemed to her the first tremor of an earthquake which could split her family from top to bottom. In the midst of a flood of tears, she could look just like my Mother of old in her times of exceptional trouble; a summary of all the sadness and bitterness and misery of the entire world. Though she was presently restrained and quiet, she may well have felt that way now.

Jim was of different mettle, though he may have started off much the same, since even now he remained as deeply emotional as his sister. But having been placed outside the educational greenhouse for hardening off at the tender age of eleven, he had learned that practically nothing in such circumstances is earned without a fight or a struggle. As a result, he had, I suppose, grown excessively hardy to the point of dogmatism. His allegiances were not, like Hilda's, spread far and wide: within the family, indeed, you could say that they were confined to Mother and myself, extreme youth evidently providing immunity from all ongoing disputes and quarrels – though not from my hearing or sensing them.

And yet, with a strange twist of Fate, it was he whom the outbreak of War chose to suck relentlessly back into the family's very heart. All of a sudden, he found himself the odd man out for supervising its process of gradual disintegration. He had absolutely no defence against the unwelcome appointment. Tom was up in Scotland for good, and with Hilda and Andrew whirled away to the Lake District, that left no protection for the old house from the auctioneer's hammer, following the inevitable collapse of 'the mortgage' (Mother's permanent nightmare finally turned fact!).

Father being well into his own disintegration, Jim's reappearance within the walls of the dying house – a development which hitherto would have been as explosive as incredible – became nothing more than a readily accepted mercy visit; but it left the matter of the original quarrel in nothing better than a state of permanent abeyance. No-one apologised; no-one seemingly regretted anything at all. On the surface, indeed, it was forgotten; but the reversal of my parents' roles, which was already under way, proved trifling compared with the necessity for revised status between Jim and Father.

Unlike the ultimate feelings of my parents, one to the other, I have never doubted the extent of Jim's lingering animosity towards his senior namesake. It was obvious only in a negative way; the absence of a willing concern for non-crucial needs – the reluctance to indulge what he judged merely the whims of his parent. Concerning which, I may say, he was firmly dogmatic; surprisingly so at times, when it came to medical matters outside of his certain knowledge. Father, for example, had long been taking a certain patent medicine for the relief of his asthma. He was convinced that it was of benefit to him (which was probably the most important thing), whereas Jim considered it useless quackery and a waste of money. While he never specifically forbade it, the begrudging attitude must have nagged Father with an ever-increasing anxiety, during this new and complete dependency upon his son.

In fairness, this wasn't quite the unsavoury victimisation – the unreasonable picking of an unreasonable dispute with a weak old man – which it may appear. To my brother, belief meant total belief, even if it approached bigotry, which he would never have believed of himself for a moment. The rooted, often peculiar, convictions which he held on a whole range of topics included a near religious fanaticism for fine-tuning the health of mind and body alike. Moreover, he brainwashed himself with his recipes just as much as his listeners, engaging in a course of 'Pelmanism', for the nurturing of his memory and general brain-power, just as enthusiastically as he would sometimes suffer the starvation of a few days 'all fruit diet'. The latter (he constantly sermonised) was the real secret of happy life; killing off all of the body's accumulated impurities, and largely, at the same time, the necessity for any continuance of the medical profession as a whole. His extreme seriousness about so many things was in stark contrast to his past triumphs as a comedian in the concert-party, and, even now, to the 'jolly face' which he still managed to present to close friends, liberally spraying them with conversational jokes from his wide repertoire.

Nevertheless, whether or not he properly acknowledged it, Father had finished up subservient to Jim in everything; an unenviable situation, with not a penny left, from a whole lifetime of hard work, for bolstering what must have been his fading sense of independent worth. He merits my full sympathy, but sadly only now, reflectively, when it is too late to be of use.

My brother, on the other hand, with all the good health in the world, and, by now, very respectable earnings to go with it, was in even worse a predicament, and had been from the moment he took on his elderly tenants. From then on, whichever direction the story-line might have taken, there could never have been a bearable solution for him. The moot point throughout was simply which eventuality would prove the worse. Would Mother be the first to leave this earth – or was it destined to be Father? I'm not suggesting that he was sufficiently morbid to have sat down and, head on hand, brooded solidly over it. But he must have recognised the disaster which constantly kept close company with him.

After all, what even now was left of the life-style he must have been planning for himself when he bought this state-of-the-art bungalow, hopefully to blot out what he thought the denigration of his years as a lodger in 'digs'? The whole situation, in itself, had been a wrecking operation when it first arose. Still in his mid-thirties, he would never yet have surrendered belief in meeting the right marriage partner, his long-term philosophy. Of course, putting the cart before the horse like this – or should it be the 'house before the altar'? – may now seem absurd, but he was a man who really did believe that he could plan everything; that steely determination, combined, as here, with unswerving savings from only moderate resources, could achieve limitless goals. As always, there had been no-one to help him but himself: most would never have thought of the idea, let alone succeeded in actually buying the house.

If there is such a thing as Fate, it only emerged, in this situation, by virtue of the unsuspected fragility of Father's heart mechanism; selecting him authoritatively for the first scene of the Final Act and leaving Mother in uncertain rehearsal for the second. On the face of it, this should have been the kinder alternative for Jim; who, whilst willingly sacrificing himself for the rescue of his beloved Mother, would bitterly have resented the residual horror of being left in isolation with his Father – into an extension of old age which might even infringe upon his own.

No sooner had one variety of Doom been side-stepped, however, than another appeared in confrontation. While the continuing care (however indefinite) of his widowed Mother would have been a more than acceptable chore, this had turned to sheer impossibility. Father would have been able to fend for himself, to some extent, but Mother, needing constant attention, couldn't be left for a moment in an empty house. Though Jim and Hilda didn't involve me directly in what must have been suffocating worries about her, I sensed, as I prepared to return to Catterick, that her sole future feasibility could only be as a long-term resident in the local hospital. It was a shattering thought to take back with me.

* * *

The coarse din and vigour of Army life seemed peculiarly attractive, as I resettled into the end-of-training transition period at the barracks. Mercifully, domestic concerns were part of a world which was so infinitely remote from this one, in which too much of immediacy was brewing up to allow an iota of pensive sadness or nostalgia. We were, in fact, on the point of being split up into our permanent assignments, spread around mixed regions of the United Kingdom. Most untypically, we found ourselves asked which of half a dozen different areas each of us would prefer. It seemed of such little importance, in view of my eventual destination abroad, that I merely indicated, at random, 'near London' or 'somewhere on the South Coast'; instinctively, I suppose, to get forgetfully as far away as possible from Tyneside.

Certainly, even now, during the couple of weeks which passed before our 'postings' came through, recent purgatory did, indeed, begin to soften. Obsessional curiosity about the directions in which our assorted lucks were about to drive us was seeping into everyone; and when, out

Of Straw And Stripes

of the blue, I was summoned to attend the Camp's Adjutant in his office, I at first imagined that it must be my particular piece of 'news'. Entering the room, I came dutifully and passionately to attention, and saluted him with all the concentrated 'spikiness' which my memory of 'Longest way up and shortest way down!' could muster; only to realise that this couldn't be anything at all to do with the contents of that Army manual. For a start, instead of 'Stand at ease!', I was being motioned to a seat in the nearby armchair; more alarmingly still, I was spoken to both casually and with the most unmilitary kindness. And, when it finally came, the news was far from what I had expected. This time, it was my Mother who was dead.

Chapter 8

This second funeral lingers in the memory as a dull echo of the first. I arrived again at the bungalow as if in a dream; very promptly, it seemed, and with little sense of having been carried there in any steam-train or tramcar whatsoever. Inside the now familiar coffin in the bedroom, I might not have been surprised to see the resurrected shape of Father (buried surely only in my imagination?), but no, it was, indeed, a fresh coffin and a fresh corpse – an immaculate, china-doll replica of my Mother, ever so calm and youthfully serene, as it lay motionless before me.

I had no room for any emotion other than thankfulness that it was at last over for her. This present vision was only material confirmation of a death which had really taken place long before; and, as I shuffled awkwardly out of the bedroom, I was making that my excuse for not having bid her any sort of farewell two weeks ago – though I felt a twinge of conscience not even to have kissed her goodbye. (Too late, I mentally whispered affection in the direction of her spirit-world. Would that, during her lifetime, she had been quite so happy as she looked now!)

With no stomach for the unavoidable repeat of that hollow 'last rites' ritual – concluded for Father only a few moments ago, I'd have sworn – I was glad when the proceedings got under way. There would have been nothing to prevent their completely cloning what had gone before, if the 'audience' hadn't now included a member or two of Mother's own clan; notably her sister Lily (whose coarse, loud-mouthed contributions to the conversation quite contradicted her history of coming from the same stock) and her brother, my well-liked, smiling Uncle Jim, who was a trawler skipper by occupation, and even quieter by contrast than August was to Annie. But there was a universal peculiarity at large amongst us at the time; and this, I think, now stands out (by omission) from all of the chatter at this particular tea-table. It was simply our complete lack of *curiosity*. Why and how had Mother died? No-one seemed at all concerned.

One thing is certain: she died in the hospital to which she had been admitted little more than a week before. That is what (now, when there is no disturbance to reasoned thought) continues to provoke unsolvable mystery; yet at the time, I think, it had the effect of concealing it.

That she had come to her end in a cocoon of medical people, all supposedly skilled for her condition, may have anaesthetised us from recollecting that she was not yet properly an 'old lady'. Full five years younger than her late spouse, who (despite the ravages of ill health on his appearance) had himself only struggled to his late sixties, there had never been an inkling of weakness in the condition of her heart. Nevertheless, it had certainly failed, one way or another. Had it, I wonder, been stunned to a halt from fright, suddenly finding around her no-one she knew? Or, maybe, with her partnership with Father as solid in reality as in my dreams, had her heart simply *broken* from the unbearable truth of it – from the sheer loss of him?

Travelling back to Catterick yet again, on what was becoming a veritable carousel of a round-trip journey, I was possessed by a feeling of hollow, aching emptiness. It was only afterwards that I had the luxury of puzzling out what it was that had gone out of me; and only then that I could realise the strangeness of it. The truth of the matter was that my Mother, in death, had ceased to haunt me; which was, you could say, the wrong way round, since she had relentlessly bewitched ghostly and sorrowful recrimination into me throughout her remaining time in the land of the living.

It needed no such nicety of analysis, however, to be shaken by the sledgehammer impact of the past fortnight's happenings. That small portion of 'civvy-street' which I had so far cosseted in my mind's eye, as reassurance of the eventual sanity of the human race, had been near-obliterated; leaving this particular journey back to Yorkshire with all the feel of a 'Single ticket only, please!' variety. It was indeed a cold thought, but, with virtually nothing behind me now to justify a return fare, I was for the first time going home to the Army.

Chapter 9

The five years which I spent in the Forces divided themselves naturally into three distinct phases, each with a substance and spirit quite different from the others. The first was the training stint and the last the active service; but the better part of two years which came in between is more difficult to label. I can best think of it now as yet another period on remand, waiting to learn my eventual fate in terms of my part in the actual fighting of the War.

My arrival once more at Catterick, where I must have entered the record books for near-linked spells of compassionate leave, was this time for little more than collecting my posting notice. Borehamwood, in Hertfordshire, meant nothing to me, but my atlas showed it to be almost the same place as Elstree, where the films were made; titillating me at once with the thought of more civilised scenery than these far-flung, half forgotten wastes of Yorkshire. London's bright lights, too – though doubtless dimmed by the regulations, or even stifled entirely – were near enough on the map to cheer me from the mere idea, soon, of their near presence.

Certainly, Borehamwood itself was to prove agreeable enough so far as it went. Which, mind you, seemed not such a very long way at first sight; but it had a compact, cosy aura to it, a reassuring contrast to the rugged nature of the training camps.

And I had absolutely no reservations about 'The Grange'. This was the elegant, generously detached house, nestling snugly in its own protective greenery, which must surely have been the contented home of privileged families over countless years, but which now, called up like the rest of us, was masquerading as a Regional Headquarters Battalion Office of the RAOC – and, for good measure, as my assignment for the foreseeable future. It provided a delicious reminder of the better things in civilian life; even if, as lip service to current realities, a couple of Nissen huts sprawled repulsively nearby as makeshift sleeping quarters for its Wartime interlopers.

Of Straw And Stripes

Nor was it just the old building which I found so congenial. Inside, its daily routine was of a different world – the whole pattern of it, the whole atmosphere. Busily and exclusively an administrative office job, there was no time (or need) for the niceties of saluting, and heel-clicking, and spikinesses of drill which I had come to assume were the prerequisites of all Army activities. Here, indeed, was an aspect of the military machine that I had never suspected, with all those shell craters of my imagination crowding out the organisational side of things.

In point of fact, the very informality of the place created a strange anomaly. On the one hand, there was a welcome and permanent relief from the staccato commands which had hitherto echoed around me, it seemed, from every direction of the compass. On the other, however, I found myself immersed in the continuous preparation and issue of 'orders' of a different kind (less abrasive, no doubt, though equally effective), by way of the written word. By nature, they had to be thoroughly unstylish, impassive affairs, with titles sufficiently unimaginative as to match their contents. There were orders, for example, which were labelled 'Part One', and some which would only answer (but just as tersely) to 'Part Two'. Others needed even more distinctive categorisation, appearing in print – yes, you may have suspected it! – as 'Part Three'.

None of these editions, then, would have attracted a modern publisher with any proper sense of profit and loss or, more particularly, with an eye only for 'best sellers'. But this was wartime, and literary skills were trivialities. Content, not style, counted most, and, here, that was almost always important enough to douse potential boredom. How many times, in fact, may it have meant even the balance of life or death to the reader!

Since much – in fact, usually everything – hung on the luck of the draw where 'postings' were concerned, I soon got to absorbing the sense of innate power which pervaded the unit. This was reassuring, yet dangerous in the false belief which it encouraged of our being in some way infallibly inoculated against any close-quarter confrontation with the War itself. For the moment, at any rate, we were always in the fortunate position of *making* the draw, which in turn meant that we were never in it. Of course, people like me were only the minions who operated the machinery, telling the various RAOC establishments which of their soldiers were needed, and where. The decisions themselves rested with a tall, slim, cultured gentleman with the rank of SQMS,

Of Straw And Stripes

who displayed much the same sleeve insignias as yesterday's ruddy-faced Camp Sergeant-Major. Looking and sounding meek and mild by comparison, at the end of the day he wielded power which was considerably longer lasting – and without the need for such apoplexy of effort.

There was always that element of unpredictability about the moves of personnel which his superiors (up in the clouds) needed him to arrange. It was as if they required him to sit permanently at his desk with a half-loaded pistol in his hand, so that we should always be kept guessing as to the timing of the next explosion in his game of Russian roulette. Some of his directions, on face value at any rate, were 'blanks', simply transfers of men from one home establishment to the other, but quite frequently there would emerge a troop movement to some bleak (or, mostly, broiling) quarter of the globe; the Far East maybe – a regular hot-bed of fighting like Burma, whence everyone recognised the niggardly chances of coming back alive. And that, we knew, must often have been as good as his bullet through the heart of each of those involved.

His must have had a slight flavour of the job of a staff officer; that lofty profession which, I have since learned, inhabits and sustains all the High Commands of all warfare, constantly directing military formations (in their anonymous form of small flags pinned to maps) to positions of maximum destruction of the enemy. Callousness, to some degree, has obviously always been an essential for this kind of efficiency; and, since our SQMS clearly wanted to prove himself worthy of higher things (possibly as high as those same rarefied clouds?), he had not only steeped himself in it from the beginning, but had seen to the numbing of the minds of all his staff, too. So it was that a name in typescript became for us just that and nothing more. If we weren't operating that Gestetner copying machine, others would be. Nothing, after all – except an awful lot of killing – was going to stop the whole system of the War. And we merely turned our minds to other things.

As it happened, this wasn't in the least difficult. You wouldn't have expected it to be, would you? Not with all those girls around – working with us; mixing with us! There must have been a full dozen of them, at any time, employed at The Grange alone; like us, all of them in khaki, but suddenly making it an altogether more attractive colour than ever before. They were, of course, members of the ATS, which, after all these years, may need elaborating as the 'Auxiliary Territorial Service'

77

– in other words, women soldiers; just as, in those days, there were women Air Force personnel (WAAFs), and women Naval staff (WRENs), to say nothing of those labouring away – rather less dashingly, outside the actual Forces – in the Women's Land Army. These particular girls at The Grange were trained specialist clerks, roles much less unexpected than the rougher, manual jobs like anti-aircraft gunners and driver-mechanics which many women were tackling elsewhere (and often enjoying to the full). But what did their precise jobs matter? Just being amongst them was a delight!

These, of course, were the days when qualifications for the accolade of 'girl' were rather more liberally sprayed around than now. In practice, any eligible female the right side of thirty – and the wrong one, too, on occasion – would shudder at no longer finding herself thought of and talked of as the genuine fledgling article. Allusion to her in terms of 'woman' tolled the bell, as it were, for the worst fate of all; being 'left on the shelf' in the stagnation of permanent spinsterhood. Hollywood itself had no doubt about it: 'girldom' was the essential ingredient for attracting men. Not that the leading actresses of its silver screen were anywhere near teenage. Thoroughly moulded into womanly maturity (and probably because of it), most of them radiated sex appeal from their every pore, as well as the promise of similar powers of seduction for years to come. And all of *them* were 'girls', weren't they? The male leads, at any rate, were quite sure of it, and who were we to argue with the experts?

But this is not to suggest that there was anything to argue about where the present assorted samples were concerned. Not one of *them* needed to worry for a second: no dictionary in the land could have found fault. Young ladies, at the very most – and not so much of the 'ladylike' bit of it, either. The combined miseries of wartime could never have stifled youthful spirits like these. They simply effervesced amongst us, concocting a continual brew of good humour, cheerful laughter and all-important forgetfulness. Which is to say nothing of the sheer attractiveness of the lot of them.

The features and personality of several linger in my memory as brightly as ever, the very names tripping off the tongue as I write. Lily Bragger, Dorothy Ward, Netta McVie, Josie Brooks, Connie (whose surname has absconded), and of course the vivacious Eddie Lees, with whom I became thoroughly infatuated. How unbelievable is the passage of time! They remain for me so perennially youthful, so secure in their *eternal* girldom.

It occurs to me that it is only now in my Army story that I am mentioning individuals by name. The fact that I have never been strong at remembering names as such has had nothing to do with it. There was simply no-one at the Training Camps (save the Sergeant-Major and the Sergeant and that ambitious, cloned Corporal) who had seemed to *matter*. No more than a corporate mob of drudges, we had generally been too tired at the end of each day for much more than humorous obscenities, embroidered with the monotonies of bad language, to be echoing somewhat anonymously round the barrack-room. Of course, there had been Reg Mitchell, whom I *do* remember. Riven into khaki from his peacetime profession of bank cashier, his suitability for private (the Army's lowest form of life) had been most doubtful. Grey-haired and bespectacled, suave and cultured, he sticks in my mind for none of these things; rather for possessing the secret of the origins of our young, patronising, 'toffee-nosed' Commanding Officer, Captain Corbett (whose name I find also resuscitated!). Not so long before, this living god's powers had seemingly been limited to those of a mere office boy at the bank. His miraculous transformation of personality was, I later found, typical of commissioned officers 'rising from the ranks'; most of them managing within weeks – in addition to the patronage – an incredible change of accent!

The Grange, on the other hand, was a revelation. There, almost everyone was rememberable. And not just the ATS, mind you. *They* would have seemed special at any time. In the youthfully imperative state of my sex glands, absolutely everything in skirts had come to seem memorable to some degree. After all – unbelievably, by modern concepts – this was my first measurable contact with the opposite gender, even for the innocence of 'chatting it up', as they say. Being shy hadn't helped, but the dogma of strictly segregated schools, reinforced by the confining walls of my own household, had ensured that not a single gilt-edged chance of meeting girls could ever come my way; and I had gone on to work in a very small office which simply hadn't any on its staff. Most distastrously of all, whilst not lacking the impulse, I had had in my repertoire neither the guts nor the adventure to 'go exploring'. The existence of attractive girls had, therefore, tantalised me little more directly than from the pages of a book or the screen of a cinema.

Set against the sudden emergence of so much feminine charm and

Of Straw And Stripes

high spirits, it has, indeed, to be unexpected that I can still recapture even a few of my fellow conscripts of that period in anything like their present sharp focus. I have never found members of my own sex particularly intriguing; and, of the four who immediately spring to mind, two seem hardly deserving of this permanent niche in my memory – they each sported a couple of stripes, but, in civilian life, neither might have warranted a second thought. Corporal Hubert Smith had, at any rate, the combination of rare and commonplace in his name, but, beyond that, he was just another from the 'Reg Mitchell' stable – quietly unassuming and refinedly polite, as he floated round the office, never issuing an order or raising his voice or getting engaged in confrontations: he simply oiled the mechanics of the whole establishment with his own unobtrusive efficiency. In that respect, I suppose, he (like the SQMS) *was* remarkable, in his unmilitary approach to getting things achieved. Reg Kemish, on the other hand – a short, stocky, slightly balding man – bustled flutteringly all over the place, his pleasantly earnest, bespectacled demeanour concealing a well-rooted dry sense of humour. He, too, was obviously well educated, and his enthusiasm for classical music ensured that he became a good friend of mine; or as good an acquaintance, you might more properly say, as I was ever likely to meet in these circumstances. (I was still too much of a 'loner' to develop a 'best friend', the basic instinct of most men from their earliest schooldays.) Thinking back, he was fussy and somewhat effeminate. Nowadays, I might have wondered as to his possible homosexuality, but the word and the notion didn't then exist for me. He was simply a refreshingly nice individual: I appreciated him as a reminder of the intellectual values to which one day I might return.

Now, I may be able to recall the characteristics of these good souls, but that doesn't turn them into genuine 'characters', the sort that can illumine the pages of a novel or add quaintness and zest to an anecdote. These are rare birds; but a few of them, here and there, did flit in and out of my long pilgrimage to the shrine of demobilisation. Savouring them again in general, I find Dick Watson and Mick Gilgallon still holding their own against all comers. They hadn't a solitary stripe between them, but what did that matter? Advancement (I have since gleaned) so often sits solemnly on the other end of the see-saw to personality: there is not much amusement to be found amongst drive and determination.

Dick was the one with the versatility. I never doubted that, though at

Of Straw And Stripes

no time did he supply visible proof, going about his Army chores as routinely as anyone else. But I have always thought of him as a potential *actor*, rather than any variety of a military man (which he most certainly wasn't). Full six-foot-plus of lanky, loping, cheerfully benevolent humanity, he could – minus the khaki disguise – have stepped straight into a Hollywood movie as a veteran, tobacco-chewing cowhand of the Wild West, or, just as convincingly, as the laid-back farmhand of a remote English village, chewing the alternative cud of a strand of straw, and drawling rustic anecdotes to his cronies in the languid sunshine of the fields. Or, with the added sanctity of a 'dog-collar', would he not have made a believable, reassuringly-calm Church of England vicar? Who knows? If he survived the War, some perceptive repertory company may have discovered him for a succession of parts requiring a natural, beaming wisdom of worldly affairs. Stranger things have happened – particularly in the Hollywood of those days. But I am not so convinced that he would ever have passed an audition for the role of a soldier. That was doubtless what made him the leavening, soothing ingredient of our motley society.

While you might say that Dick gently persuaded his carefree cheerfulness into the rest of us, sometimes with no sense of his even being in the neighbourhood, Mick Gilgallon was for spreading his particular brand of smiling bonhomie in more determined fashion. A small man, with close-clipped dark hair that was as straight as the rest of his rather stiff posture – can ever a man have been blessed with a more 'bent-back' spine? – he was seldom to be seen in serious mood: in olden days, he would have been smiling just as broadly on a compulsory walk to execution on the block. And I am reasonably sure that he would have gazed full-eyed and fearlessly at the waiting headsman. There was certainly never a suggestion of a 'shifty look' about Mick.

That, after all, was what made him so remarkable on first acquaintance – his eyes, as round as his face and ever so honestly penetrating, with their irrepressible twinkles of lurking humour. There was no avoiding them: he seemed to know the very depths of one's soul in an instant, and to have the ready experience available to advise on its tribulations. They were, in fact, the most monopolising male eyes I had seen for a long time. But, as I eventually discovered, also the strangest! For, despite the testimony of his 'AB 64 (Part 1)' – the soldier's bible of personal details – that he had been placed in the very top category of medical fitness, there was only one of them, of recent years, which could have had anything like a proper 'look' about it, or (rather more to the point) through it. The other was only for show, a thoroughly inanimate glass ornament! I can only think that, when he joined up, there had been the utmost desperation for new recruits; though how that particular optic could have passed any test sanctioned by science must remain a miracle. Eventually, on the advice of all of us, he applied for a second medical examination, and was promptly discharged as unfit for further service. But it was several months before he got round to taking this obvious course of action, and in the meantime, like Dick, he pleasantly flavoured the assorted mix of us.

Both men were in their mid-thirties, though Dick (as versatile in his seeming years as in the rest of his potential) could have passed for any number up to fifty. With Mick, you got what you saw, with no variables. In view of the vibrant personality of the man, it is ironic that now (somewhat cruelly), I recognise his features in two alternative artificialities; the wooden head of a ventriloquist's dummy, and, even more so, that of a fairground's 'laughing sailor', imprisoned in his glass case and ready to cackle loudly for minutes at the drop of a penny.

It has been, at any rate, fair judgement to remember him in close company with entertainment, for, with his daily attendance as well as the girls', time of a sudden stopped dragging its feet, and even got to swirling by in ever more pleasant fashion. I could almost come to forget that, outside The Grange, the War was continuing its plodding, unfathomable course seemingly to the end of eternity. Strangely, ever since joining up, I had been out of contact with all of its customary civilian-life manifestations; the air raid sirens, and the anti-aircraft guns, and the searchlights, and the bombs. It was as if the safest place to be, in this country, was *inside* the Armed Forces! Short-term safety, maybe, but a further, pleasantly puzzling – unbelievably lengthy – breathing space before whatever was going to happen finally came along.

Instinct having prompted me against examining the mouth of this particular gift-horse, I unexpectedly discovered a sense of adventure to go with my good sense; and, before long, I was applying for weekend leave of absence to explore the awesome unknown of the City of London.

It was to be the first of very many visits, almost all of them in no-one's company but my own; the only sure guarantee, I was convinced, of unhindered, spontaneous sorties of discovery in the spirit of the moment. But that first expedition was the one which really counted, the one which finally banished all self-doubts of my navigational aptitude in a foreign jungle of this density. I had in my pocket the strategic reserves of a solitary half-crown, and in my mind the barest scrap of information – the easy accessibility of the Tube station at nearby Edgeware – as I left for a voyage of discovery every bit as unpredictable as Columbus's to the Americas; and, in my terms, probably even more daring.

A more rational frame of mind would have seen to it that a map kept company in my pocket with that lonely half-crown; perhaps (for the realisation of its hints), a small field compass as well – the more so since my sense of instinctive direction was, and still is, as minimal as the traditional absent-minded university professor's. Nevertheless, it turned out that I needed neither of these lifeguards. I survived very well, thank you; without, however, this reflecting anything at all upon me of heroic glory or suchlike. I simply found myself self-sufficient. Any variety of imbecile, I decided, could have used that London Underground system with impunity. It was simple and foolproof, even for me.

I knew it early on; almost when I first stepped on to the first stair of the first escalator of my life, and, glowing with the most surprising self-confidence, started the descent into my first reconnoitring of the bowels of the earth. How could anything possibly go wrong? Only, I concluded, for the colour-blind. For the rest of us – to go by the large route-map displayed in the station – red was still red, blue as blue as ever, and black was there also to be picked out from the rest, signifying a certain 'Northern Line' which promised to hurry me along, the most directly of all, to the very heart of the City. The names of its stations, as they now displayed themselves, successively on offer through the train's window, all reeked of magic; most of them seemingly ideal for the start of a titillating safari, though 'Leicester Square' – hadn't I heard that somewhere else, in a song about a different war? – smacked of special romance. At any rate, even that fabled professor could have developed a sense of direction within this system. The alternative, adjoining platforms at every stop would each of them be ramming their pointing arrows and heavily-printed destinations into any normal eyesight like mine. And (the most comforting thought of all) those twinned platforms were permanent institutions; lurking there, all along the line, for retracing mistakes of the moment. When, at last, I stepped

Of Straw And Stripes

off that further escalator, and up the concrete steps to the fresh-aired actuality of Leicester Square, I was as relaxed as I had been for a long time, and thoroughly ready to enjoy myself.

Was it simply the froth of my enthusiasm for the miracles of its cellar which had effervesced into that first sight of the City itself? Or was everything around me really so bewitchingly beautiful as it seemed at that moment? To be sure, when I revisit these days, most of the glamour has gone: there is worn shabbiness everywhere, drugged destitution only half hidden, over-dense crowds stifling comfort, general overheating of the whole scene. But the London which loomed around me at the top of those steps knew nothing of this. Presenting herself to me in overwhelming dignity, every cubic inch of her vast buildings seemed to radiate history; none of the modern multi-storied interlopers (near suffocating of venerable neighbours) being as yet in place, or even in concept. Bustling civilians, to my surprise, I saw in their thousands – how could so many be exempt from National Service? – yet I sensed no piece of surplus humanity amongst them which might need hiding away in shame. (Presumably, the Forces were hiding all of *them*.) As I wandered bemusedly into the heady atmosphere of Leicester Square, there was clearly a veritable Arabian nights of legendary things and places for me to find and savour in my travels.

Chapter 10

That first sauntered inspection of London's West End must indeed have been a delight of all the delights! So much so that – though I recognise the imagination of it – part of me still insists that I digested the memorabilia of the whole City at the one go; from Madame Tussaud's to Marble Arch, National Gallery to Soho, Houses of Parliament to absolutely what you will. Chelsea's football stadium, of course, and Lord's cricket ground, too; which is not to overlook the theatres (a new world in themselves), or – Heaven be praised! – the swirling intoxication of the music concerts.

There were, in fact, to be untold 'Edgeware to Leicester Square' journeys before I reached anything like this stage of my London experience. But all of the explorations remain, to this day, so enjoyable as to seem mere instants in my life; finishing educations, certainly, which I wouldn't have missed for worlds. Had it not been for the uncertainty of the length of my tutorial, and the sense of what might follow it, they would have constituted unsullied tastes of Utopia.

Strangely, however, of all the fabled 'sights' which London displayed for me, the most unforgettable – if for nothing else than it was soon to be a phenomenon only of folklore – turned out quite as sightless as that glass eye of Mick Gilgallon's! Come to think, there was nothing at all of real substance to any of it; more of an *experience*, really, than visual treasure trove. Perhaps I should simply judge it to have been the most gigantic of magicians' disappearing tricks – perpetrated right in front of me, in the falling dusk of an autumn evening, in a matter of seconds!

At times like this, it is important to be able to remember the factual, visible world immediately before its descent into unintelligible chaos. Otherwise, a lapse from overall sanity may subsequently be suspected. But I do know that I was walking (quite uneventfully) along the pavement of a London side-street, mingling with many others of the same aimless mind. I am sure of that, at any rate. There was nothing particularly special about the street – or about the weather, for that matter. The darkening sky was still adequate for lighting my surroundings. Very shortly, I would be seeking out the Tube for Edgeware again. It had been another exhilarating sample of the great City's offerings. There was no warning whatsoever of the further 'offering' which suddenly engulfed me.

I had had no sense that I was even approaching anything notable, and I certainly didn't walk into it, in the nature of turning a corner and seeing, say, Nelson's Column for the first time. Yet neither had it exactly crept up on me. More truthfully, you could speak of its galloping headlong into me at full speed, making close-pressured acquaintance front, back, sides and top – the densest cloud of creamy-grey, sulphur-fumed gas. For a split second I had the sacrilegious idea that the weather was simply 'turning foggy'. But – foggy indeed! The dictionary needed a new entry! To call it ordinary, mediocre 'fog' grossly insults the impenetrable London 'pea-souper' which now petrified me in its stifling embrace.

Now, while I was taken aback by the abruptness of this communal blackout of the elements, it wasn't seemingly alarming in itself. After all, my fellow pedestrians couldn't possibly be as disorientated as I. To many, this would be only a routine hiccup of the weather. Indeed, all around me, weren't they excellent buffer defences? (Difficult, at any rate, to collide into anything harder than human flesh!) I could certainly distinguish, near and far, their assorted shouts and cat-calls, some good-humoured, others more foul-tempered – from the failure of even died-in-the-wool Londoners always to find their way. But I also heard, here and there, the hooting of car horns, one or two sounding (suspiciously, indeed) rather too much of 'here' than 'there'. And when a hard, solid shape – strongly suggestive of the side of a taxicab – brushed past me, I realised in shock that I had succeeded in wandering to the middle of the road!

This was the time, if ever, for quick solutions. Quick direction-finding, most of all, since my present path evidently diced not just with danger but with suicide itself. Unsure as to whether I was walking obliquely across the road or parallel with the curb, I put my despairing bet on the latter. Turning sharp left, and shuffling forward as fast as I dared, I passionately willed my next point of contact – something, anything – to be friendlier than the death-trap of another vehicle. By now, the clogging haze was dissolving outlines barely a foot from my eyes. Further than that, literally everything had already disintegrated

Of Straw And Stripes

into mystery.

How long was it before I stumbled over what surely had to be the curb of that Heaven-blessed pavement? Probably only seconds; yet seconds which had endured more like minutes, and the longest minutes of my life, at that. But now, I found nothing more lethal than a pedestrian for bumping into, followed by the unmistakably rough-feeling bricks of an ever-so-solid building. Not long afterwards, making sure this time that I kept securely within the herd, I discovered the life-saving oasis of steps leading downwards to yet another Underground station, and to the unrealistic luxury of the whole episode suddenly turning enjoyable in recollection.

For this purpose, in a peculiar kind of way, it is perhaps fortunate that the priorities of post-War legislation have been obsessed with Hygiene, however sadly to the detriment of Art. London's aesthetic charm may have suffered somewhat in the process, but the arrival of a compulsory 'no smoke zone' for the area cured for ever the time-honoured plague of this exaggerated 'smog'. As a result, I can now savour the experience of that evening as a nostalgia – of the old London of legend, in which thick damp fog was always around, wasn't it? Never mind Dickens, where would the creepiness of the Jack the Ripper murders have been without it? Or the city's background for Holmes and Watson? (Even the Baskerville business. The animal may have been bred elsewhere, but not the denseness of the fog – surely cloned, in inspiration, on London's.)

Against reason, indeed (and my own close-quarter schooling in their immobilising discomforts, even dangers), I find myself secretly bemoaning the extinction of those gloomy pea-soupers. Yet, in moments of sanity, I have to be thankful that they are now but shadow-mists of the past, since, in their hey-day, they can only have been eccentricities which were sustained by the past itself. Had the nineteen-forties' nature of society survived to this day, such tantrums of the London weather might still, of course, be tolerable. There were far fewer vehicles on the roads, after all, and the non-aggressive common sense which generally prevailed translated into supremely lower speeds when the need arose. At the worst of that fog, nothing can have been moving at more than four or five miles an hour, making imagined danger minimal in practice, and probably only for novices like me for whom, with experience, 'pavement drill' would have conquered all future crises. Yet my mind shudders at the thought of the present M25 motor-way, for example, operating in similar conditions! Modern fogs, with their visibility of at any rate twenty yards or so, have already caused horrible carnage on occasion, with half-blinkered drivers thoughtlessly chancing fifty miles an hour or more. What would they be prepared to risk with only a foot of visibility in front of them?

Still, the visits of this trouble-maker of a fog cannot have been so very frequent, since I never ran into it again (or it into me) during any of my subsequent visits to the City. If the episode hadn't been quite so startling in its unexpectedness, I might have forgotten it altogether, in competition with the myriad of (unobscured) sights which continued to entertain me. And there were the sounds, too.

While I had previously heard about most of the things I saw, I had, of course, *properly* heard Big Ben. How many times indeed, back home, with his meticulous timekeeping booming round the sitting room from the depths of our Murphy wireless set! I knew the exact sound of him; his very last harmonic, the last echo of his last chime. I was sure of it. Until, that is, the evening when I was settling down, as I imagined, to a particularly luxurious sleep between the spotless-white bedsheets of my bed in the Church Army's hostel for servicemen, just across the way from the Houses of Parliament. But it was a night which degenerated into what you might call continuously prolonged consciousness. If ever I should have had premonition of the lack of 'high definition' in the radio transmissions of those days, it was now! So *this* was Big Ben! Rendered realistically, he would surely have blown the loudspeaker of the Murphy to smithereens! As to the notion that there could ever be a terminating point to the echo of any of his chimes, I wouldn't that night have credited the possibility. Not with his resonances ricocheting ceaselessly, it seemed, round every cavity of my brain. Only dawn brought sizable relief. I never set foot again in that hostel.

All of this fitted in with the general pattern. Nothing was proving less than expected. The streets were busier, the shops fuller, the buildings grander, and, now, the proclamations of Big Ben much, much louder. Their North-Eastern counterparts were puny by comparison. But, while the big clock was what you might call one of London's natural progeny, it was the sounds of her foster-children which made the biggest impact of all on me; probably because, back home, there had been nothing like them ever born. The extensive scenario of music concerts, available for choice in so many scattered locations around

Of Straw And Stripes

me, I found breath-taking.

Did I consume all of those as well (in addition to the 'sights'), in the course of just a few excursions? Far from it, but they have become inextricably entangled; jostling so tightly and competitively through my past that I would be hard pressed to place them in any sort of order of hearing. They crowd in on me as I write. The stout, middle-aged figure of Myra Hess, for example, seated commandingly at her piano in the unlikely setting of a National Gallery lunchtime recital; managing, somehow, to soften the severity of the whole place with her glittering Mozart (the sonata with the Turkish finale). How different from the pianism of the more youthful Cyril Smith, whose short, black, Brylcreemed hair gave him more the look of a film star than a classical musician – and his pyrotechnics, in my first hearing of the Rachmaninov concertos, a wondrous aura of the near supernatural. On a contrasting front, there was my reassuring ease of entry into the Wigmore Hall's intellectualism, in a sudden, precipitous, daring sally into previously off-putting chamber music. Not quite so overwhelming, nevertheless, as my introduction to Tchaikovsky! – the first of those several Sunday concerts under the baton of Anatole Fistoulari; a vigorous, wavy-haired, dapper individual who seemingly disdained the help of orchestral scores, conducting everything and everyone from effortless and flamboyant memory. Yet even this magnificence cannot downgrade the evening spent in the stalls of the Sadlers Wells Theatre: I could but marvel at its colourful offering of Smetana's *Bartered Bride*, with the historical bonus of President Benes (exiled from his Czechoslovakia) looking on from the Royal Box.

Having developed an addiction, over those first few months, for fairly frequent concert-going, my first sampling of the Promenade variety of the species was not, in itself, to break particularly new ground; although the venue of the Albert Hall did succeed in producing another of my gasps of astonishment – this time, at the sheer size of the auditorium. Perhaps this was why I decided to plunge in and test the deep end, as it were. Meaning, of course, the only unusual thing about the proceedings; that crowded 'standing room only' zone, quite against the logic of the place's huge capacity, but thriving on the evident tradition that Music's genuine stalwarts were always to be found there – braving the elements, you could say, so as to show their true artistic mettle. Recalling the stamina-sapping potential of the drill square, I vaguely wondered whether my current leg capacity would, or could, 'stand up to standing' for the full two hours, without anaesthetizing all musical enjoyment by the effort. Certainly, I soon found that those around me seemingly took stoutness of thigh muscles for granted. Theirs, I sensed, were rather steelier than mine, maybe because so many previous performances (or, rather, listenings) may have completely destroyed the inclination ever again to rest them – even on some magical chair or sofa, if it were now suddenly to materialise alongside them.

But, manfully, I 'stood it out' (literally) and achieved both the distinguishing and relish of those parts of the programme which reached me, however improbably, via the narrow channels between packed heads – stalwarts, indisputably, all of them, each thoroughly petrified, within their respective 'mettle', by the music. Not a solitary conspicuous fidget amongst them; probably not even the thought. Would that I could have said the same for me! Not that the overall concept was unworkable. A realistically populated 'promenade' – with the option of strolling even a foot or so in any direction – could have made matters enjoyable enough, but this would have meant 'exiling' a full half of the stalwarts around me to places of less obvious mettle. As it was, I found the whole experience so foreign of any kind of movement as to constitute a balancing act – first on one leg, then the other; for, unlike the rest, I had evidently no ability to put either of them on 'automatic hold'. And to shuffle anywhere without pushing, noticeably, through the queue, was an absurd notion.

It was to be another six or seven months before I discovered, at a more routine concert and, even then, almost by accident – from a spontaneous decision to 'be different' and, this time, climb the stairs to the Hall's balcony – that this other, much more spaciously genuine 'promenade' had been up there all the time for me, circling the entire inside wall of the building and simply crying out to be investigated. The generosity of its empty floor spaces suggested, indeed, a similar ignorance in many others.

Whether or not it was a place for the purists, music (I soon found) could flourish largely untroubled up here. Admittedly, high though it was above the orchestra – to look dizzily down upon the scene below was as if from a hovering helicopter! – it wasn't at all a 'half-way house to Heaven'. More factually, the direction was merely towards the ceiling; but possibly the most infamous ceiling in the land, presiding over so distorting and persistent a reverberation as to have become part of British musical folklore. (A nuisance, nevertheless, since cold-

Of Straw And Stripes

bloodedly obliterated, by the ghostly, scientific umbrella-shapes which now 'squat' permanently and permittedly up in the building's stratosphere.)

In truth, however, my ears had been adjusted too long to the warped atmospherics of those days' wireless transmissions to pick out this iota of digression from pure sound. In practice, I found nothing wrong with these higher-stationed acoustics. And, in any event, there were bonuses. For a start, the instinct for dozing off, under the combined influence of a tedious item and a comfortable plush seat, was entirely removed. I could either stand propped up by the rear wall, or sit briefly on the ground with the same support; while there was always the alternative of merely 'promenading' – gently, and in the whim of the moment, without having to push a single soul out of the way. Moreover, since sight of the actual performers was only obtainable by leaning over the balustrade (with the deterring reality of the distance down) there could be few of the usual visual distractions from the music itself. I gave that balcony my practical approval by revisiting it more than once; each time, ironically enough, against more normal competition from the ground floor, with its reversion to all-seating arrangements for the return of ordinary concerts.

But even a semi-illiterate like myself, musically speaking, could sense these not to be on the same level as the 'Proms', however roughly equivalent the programmes. As far as I knew, no other long-standing series of concerts could claim to be the ornament of a single man's vision; the pioneering of a veritable colossus in London's music scene, past and present. Sir Henry Wood *was* the Proms, after all; always had been. Now, it seemed, prepared to gift some of the conducting to others – as well as, to the London Philharmonic, a foot-in-the-door of the BBC Symphony Orchestra's previous monopoly – legend continued to magnify the lustre of past years, when he had run the whole show by himself, effortlessly and with just the one orchestra.

The venerable copy of the prospectus for that 'Forty-eighth Season, 1942' lies happily in front of me as I write, now surely belying its marked price of 'twopence – by post, threepence' by having turned into a historical curiosity. But for it, I might well have forgotten the early starting time of the concerts; especially those in the latter half of the series – no later than six of an evening, with the finish scheduled for half-past-eight prompt (thus avoiding as much of the 'black-out' as possible). Or that, presumably for getting the old boy home before

Of Straw And Stripes

dark, someone must have persuaded Sir Henry into the first half only of most performances as his share of the responsibility; one of the associate conductors then catering for the remainder. Those who had known him at his full, younger resilience would no doubt have held this to be self-evidence of his waning years.

From the strangulated viewpoint of my first ever Prom, I had, of course, hardly been able to consider his features, let alone his general state of preservation. In their job of chasing after the orchestra's response to his waving baton, my ears had quite monopolised the rest of me. I was, nevertheless, sufficiently intrigued to attend a further two of the series; and the fact that I could hear *and* see in each of them betrays my resignation, at the time, to having neither stomach nor legs for further involvement in true-mettle promenading. My short experience in that direction had surely been amply graphic – almost challenging that 'pea-souper' of a fog – to need nothing by way of repetitive emphasis. I paid a little more, and enjoyed in full the sacrilege of sitting.

Perhaps I am tacitly stealing the whole credit for my good sense. Maybe it was Reg Kemish, after all, who whispered the advice. Exceptionally, he tagged along with me to the Albert Hall on both occasions; the first of them resulting from his seductive conversational hint that he was on speaking terms with a member or two of the BBC Symphony Orchestra. This was too good an opportunity to miss; and, sure enough – during the mid-way interval of the concert – I stole along with him to a room behind the scenes which simply buzzed with the chatter of practising musicians, amongst whom two or three (surprisingly young) women violinists readily exchanged familiarities with Reg, and even flattered me with a few words. For all I knew, they may have come merely from the back row of the 'seconds', but the sheer glamour of the whole situation was sufficient, in any event, to flush my cheeks with exhilaration. More seriously, not far off, I could see the very leader of the Orchestra, the illustrious Paul Beard, in full flow of relaxed banter with his colleagues; a deep contrast to the juncture – only a minute or so away – when he would be left in isolation before returning, last of all of them, to the public glare of the concert's second half. Though he had not as much as brushed me in passing, I almost felt that I had got to personal terms with him, as, with newly sprung steps, I resumed my more subordinate role out in the audience. The rest of the performance throbbed for me with almost ethereal glory.

It left me smacking my lips for more. But when, some weeks later,

Of Straw And Stripes

I felt a jogging of my arm to the effect that the last of the concerts was almost upon us, and that I must on no account miss it, there was inference for me of nothing but the uncertainty of the times. Overlook this opportunity, I accepted, and there wouldn't be another Prom anywhere to be heard until next year – when God alone could know of our likely whereabouts! Looking down at the programme itself, as we took our seats in the crowded and exceptionally vibrant auditorium, there was nothing particularly special about it except the multiplicity of conductors; Sir Henry, in charge at the start, being scheduled for replacement first by Sir Adrian Boult and then Basil Cameron, before having his rightful mastery restored for the whole of the second half.

Difficult though it is to pin-point the alchemy of that concert – an exhilaration still, amongst my memories of the long ago – I have always recognised the power of understatement which lay concealed in its entirety. I suppose that, from the beginning, I should have suspected the almost self-conscious, over-well behaved nature of the creature. All around had seemingly come simply to enjoy the music. There was to be no trace of a celebratory end to the series; nothing of that nature. And, indeed, there was a plentiful variety of goodies on offer; no fewer than seven items in the first half alone. None of which, I admit, would still have been registering with me, save for my ancient relic of a programme, which recalls Beethoven, Coleridge Taylor, Delius, Liszt, Rutland Boughton and Tchaikovsky, to say nothing of the first performance of a symphonic poem entitled 'Knight in Armour' by a certain Ruth Gipps (an individual who must, I imagine, have faded instantly into oblivion alongside the final chords of her composition).

The applause, mind you, I *do* remember. Everything, that night, received it in good measure; presumably even the Gipps effort, to which, no doubt, we gave our benefit of the doubt for 'future promise'. Within the atmosphere of that particular concert, we were catholic in our enthusiasm: enjoy one, enjoy them all. Yet, for all that, there was nothing so special about it as to have bred this increasing sense of expectancy amongst the audience around me. Not even the impressive reappearance of the Old Man himself, after the interval, with – let me see, now – 'Purcell's Suite for organ and orchestra', really justified that.

Neither did the very last item of the whole series possess the necessary ingredient. Not to start with, at any rate; though I had to concede its slight difference to the rest – a 'Fantasia on British Seasongs', seemingly arranged, as well as conducted, by Sir Henry. (Since when, I wondered, had his musical scope stretched this far?) I had never previously heard of it, let alone heard it; but, delightfully, I found all of its tunes as second nature to me as the nursery rhymes of my childhood. Not that I had, in fact, really heard them before; certainly not displayed so seductively as this, with the sentiment of them squeezed out to the last drop by differing instrumentalists who were popping up out of the orchestra, here and there, to make their point. The tunes were turning into melodies, mostly slow, sometimes sorrowful, always emotive. I was entranced first by a trombone solo, and then by the principal cellist, who made his particular contribution seem as heart-tuggingly important as any respectable slow movement from a first-ranking concerto. After this, however, just as one was wondering where the first violin had got to, there he was all of a sudden, jigging away – ever so lightly and softly and delicately – with the first few bars of the 'Sailors' Hornpipe'. How and when the rest of the orchestra came into the picture was hard to define, but before we knew they were all hard at it – unobtrusive, but managing, nevertheless, to work up a fair frolic of a rhythm to the piece. There must, I thought, be some particularly subtle combination of percussion to give this mounting momentum to the dance. But what, exactly? It took the first few moments of the gradual crescendo in the music to solve the puzzle. Feet! That was it: feet – nothing else! All around, initially, there had been the very lightest of tapping from them; perfectly in time, mind you, and in utter sympathy with the conductor, but soon increasing to an overwhelming *stamping*. The only alternative, they seemed to signal, to dancing on the seats themselves! Never again in my life have I heard such shattering, yet controlled, frenzy in the course of a performance. The whole Hall shook with the insistent emphasis of those feet of ours. Until – as soon as ever that hornpipe finished – there was the complete reversion to a concert's normal discipline. Not a further whisper from the lot of us. An immediate re-adoption of our proper role as mass listeners.

It was very probably this strictly maintained self-control which eventually exploded into such extravagance of noisy applause at the finish; a sort of accumulated 'thank you' for all the musical fare which had been on offer, not, of course, just that evening, but in the course of all the other evenings of the splendid weeks now past. I suppose, strictly speaking, that proceedings should have been halted there and then, with workmen hurriedly summoned for the erection of a proscenium arch complete with drapery. Certainly, never minding the imaginary

Of Straw And Stripes

nature of the curtain, there was no shortage of calls to the front of it. All three conductors claimed their share, and found us anything but niggardly: we were in the mood to enthuse over everything. As an audience, we finished the whole thing off with a performance to rival even the orchestra's.

This universal furore could easily have ended up losing its meaning; somewhat like the official British honours system, spraying out accolades with uninformed generosity, merited or not. Fortunately, the closing, persistent recalls to the podium of Sir Henry – remarkably short statured and inoffensive-looking, I thought, for a colossus (the first of the species I had ever encountered) – quickly restored a proper sense of critical proportion. *This* was what it was all about! *He* was what it was all about: the founder of the feast, no less!

No-one could suspect this volume of acclaim of being in the slightest uninformed. At least six or seven times was he called back to acknowledge it; a stocky, solid man, whose innocently rounded features managed to convey both geniality and determination; yet, apart from the serious nature of his beard, with little of the high distinction which he had achieved over the years. But the audience around me, knowing it full well, was seemingly loath to let *him* forget by ever letting him go. So enthusiastic were we that I can graphically remember his final appearance before us, clothed in full top-layered outdoor regalia; black overcoat, white scarf, walking cane in one hand and top hat in the other. With this demonstration of unchangeable resolve, it only needed the 'full-stop' of another, this time sweepingly exaggerated, bow before – motioning Paul Beard to follow – he was at last allowed to walk briskly off the platform and away.

In total, that evening was very special indeed. You may, of course, be tempted to ask why I am making such a big thing of it (as they currently say). When all is said and done, the ritual of the 'Last Night of the Proms' is common enough nowadays. The (by now) routine miracle of television beams it annually all over the place. We most of us know the 'Sea-songs fantasia' by heart, whilst aggressive clapping to the rhythm of its hornpipe has long become an ingrained tradition, and the closing verbal benediction to its massed disciples notable only for which conductor, this time round, is having to mouth it. So what, you query, was so different about the 1942 variety? I am sorry, but, if you are in this mind, I have to suspect both your judgement and sense of good taste.

Of Straw And Stripes

Comparison can only be of chalk with cheese. That one had been a relatively austere affair, centred strictly around the music and thriving on contrast – combined with wise self-rationing of our 'foot-timpani' to the late appearance of that solitary dance. Never the whisper of a risk, even then, of disturbing the authority of Sir Henry's beat (though who, of course, would have dared?) or, more to be expected, of drowning the sound of his orchestra. The present television mutations, on the other hand, nourish an ever-increasing, overheated atmosphere of carnival-like abandon, such as almost to push serious music out of any justified presence. The massed Promenaders – with their funny hats, and little Union Jacks, and toy pistols and trumpets, and coloured streamers, and (here and there) even painted faces – suggest more of a reincarnation of the Chelsea Arts Ball (which ushered well-heeled Londoners of the past into the New Year) than the adult enjoyment of a music festival.

That 1942 hornpipe had arrived as a complete surprise. The only unexpectedness embedded in this present, gaudy panoply of juvenility, however, is the silence which it still volunteers during most of the music. But the occasional pistol shot or trumpet call which bursts free during a gap between items – unexpectedly, like an animal suddenly taking the bit – reminds us of the pulsating fervour that's around for getting to the *clappable* part of the programme; or, equally delectable, to anything which lends itself to the fashion of communal, rhythmic, arm-linked *swaying*. Each of these modern catastrophes of audience participation makes for a confusion of opinions on the proper speed for the piece; to say nothing of the devastation of a beat transmitted by hand-clapping – not a patch on those previous subtleties of our feet! – in obliterating both the conductor's poise and the last vestige of audible orchestral sound.

Yet there is another side to it. In the strange, contradictory riposte which the majority of the audience (those mettle-less non-Promenaders, sitting in their comfortable seats) makes to this popular trend of indiscipline, comes an amazingly coordinated burst of glorious choral singing. Two bursts, in truth – 'Rule Britannia' and 'Jerusalem', each so strictly controlled from the podium as to return much of the confidence of colour to the conductor's cheeks. Neither of these items, or the stereotyped speech which now unavoidably follows to spoil them, existed in the 1942 proceedings. As it is, Sir Henry's bust needs an annual, placatory laurel wreath around its neck for it to bear to look down in bemusement on the inebriated atmosphere of the place. Certain is it that *he* had the right idea – a top coat at the finish, in place of even a single word. Perhaps a future leader of the orchestra might always keep a loaded coathanger within arm's reach, for the similarly streamlined escape of his conductor of the day?

Be this as it may, I wasn't then so burdened with hindsights. As Reg and I made our way out of the Hall and back into the unfriendly blackout, I was merely sure that I had been part of a very celebrated occasion indeed.

Chapter 11

From this distance of time, my London trips can easily become magnified into weekly salvations from a dull monotony back at Borehamwood. But it was not so. Army life there was no worse than a normal office job; routine maybe, tedious even on occasion, but, with the constantly cheerful back-chat from those ATS girls (as well as from folk like Mick and Dick and Reg), how could it fail to be reasonably enjoyable? Certainly, I never dreaded the arrival of a Monday morning, as do so many shop-floor civilians – and even more of those 'higher up the line' – throughout their working lives. Of more direct (if unlikely) concern was each arrival of my turn for a home leave pass. Ordinarily signifying a happy seven-day holiday with one's family, it was a different creature for me. Regenerating the nostalgia of my rootlessness and loss of future purpose, I was to be crucified again and again on the no-man's land of my past.

The exclusive topicality of life at the Unit, with no time for the fairytale of the past or the unreality of the future, had been the safest of buffers against sentimentality. But going home again, even for just a week, posed unescapable questions. Where exactly was it? Where, amidst all that distant normality, did I live? Was I, anywhere, still a fully paid-up member of it? On the occasion of the first of my leaves, I simply went by instinct and made for Jim's bungalow. It was where both of my parents had last lived, after all. As 'homes' went, my own last stopping-off place. A place with, at any rate, a spare bed.

Not, mind you, that I set off gloomily. Just a slight suspicion, at the back of my mind. The family, in its undemonstrative way, had always been very fond of me: I knew that. Constantly gnawed by poverty, wasted by the feud between Jim and his father – in direct contradiction of this, there had been an underlying, cohesive pride to it which had started me off with a sense of direction; given me standards of desirable achievement. I found it hard to accept that this background to life had wholly disappeared. Some remaining, near-magnetic force still seemed to be pulling me back to the North-East.

This time, there wasn't a welcome for me anywhere at all. Jim's house had become as anonymous as the railway terminus. Even more so, you could say, since there was still the usual miscellany (albeit of strangers) frequenting the station, as opposed to the bungalow, which was quite as empty as Mother Hubbard's cupboard when I arrived – just a vacant shell of a place.

Not entirely bare, of course. Tentatively opening the front door with the key I had (relievedly) found still in my trouser-pocket, there was the same lining of near-new carpets and furniture and fittings that I remembered. But nothing of nourishment for the soul; nothing to compare with the dusty shabbiness of the old rooms in the terrace house of my childhood. They had added up to our home: this was merely an immaculately smart house. And lifeless. The void left behind by my poor parents was everywhere. Only now was I accepting the amount which they had contributed, even in their final decrepitude, to a lingering aura of family traditions – obstinate linkages with the past. Whilst, on the evidence of my present gaze, this modern assortment of spotless bricks-and-mortar had long since reverted to the safety of its original, characterless, builders-yard virginity. How I would have rejoiced to be able to hear those friendly gasps and wheezes of Father, ushering me as before along this green-walled passage! Even though, at the end of it, there could now be nothing better than another vacant space (amongst so many!), in place of Mother sitting patiently in her chair.

It cannot have been so very long, but when Jim eventually returned from work, I had been lost forever, it seemed, in contemplation far removed from the brusque, bawdy Army existence of past months. Not even a single pin was around for dropping into the silence, making it easy to have imagined a sudden petrification of all living things in the neighbourhood – something in the nature of a modern 'Sleeping Beauty' scenario. But my brother, bouncing in as lifelike as ever, re-entered my life as I had always known him; still distanced from me by his persistent veneer of contrived joviality. Recent sadnesses might well have been only imagination. There was never a mention of them.

Perhaps this simply measured the depth of his feelings; for I never doubted his devotion to Mother, and the concluding chapters of her life had most probably left him in turbulent desolation – despairing of a meaning to it all. Avoiding the subject would have gone hand-in-glove with the impossibility of sharing his grief with anyone else, the prevalent harshnesses of existence having long ago taught him to marshal his own defences. In any event, he was the eldest of the family, wasn't he? The one for the others to look to for advice and comfort; never the reverse. If only, now, he could have brought himself to do 'the ordinary thing', shedding, even for a moment or two, that constant, protective layer to his innermost thoughts! Not that complete normality was ever a prominent feature of my family. Talent we had in abundance, but poverty, unfortunately, more than matching it. And this combination had always been the breeding ground for secretiveness. Keeping things from the others had so often been high on our agendas; not, you must understand, slyly or deceptively, but most often with unselfish purpose – to avoid spreading additional and useless worries. Unsurmountable predicaments make hypocrites out of soothing words. To this day, I continue to find most adversities actually *worsened* by discussion; never improved. Each is like a spasm of toothache: sympathy cannot help, only a visit to the dentist.

All things considered, we were very much two of a kind during that week, each of us as artificial as they come. Somehow, it was impossible for me to ask about Mother's demise, and, clearly, Jim's concept of 'head-of-the-family' didn't stretch to informing the youngest of it of anything so crucially important. Conversing, therefore, in nothing more significant than friendly trivialities, we must have exhausted all we had to say in the course of a half-hour, after which I felt increasingly the sense of emptiness crowding in on me. By now, of course, Jim was well settled into the full-time life-style of a confirmed bachelor, living entirely on his own; a state of affairs which was to remain unchanged for the rest of his life, though probably never accepted by him in its full inevitability. Hilda, now returned permanently from evacuation duties, was lodging elsewhere in the town, whilst Andrew and his wife, similarly returned, were in rented accommodation nearby. Consequently, a great deal of my leave was spent elsewhere than the bungalow, in renewing acquaintance (of more relaxed nature) with them, too.

On certain days, these enthusiastic excursions made Jim's home, I suppose, little more than a 'bed-and-breakfast' staging post for me. A little guilt crept in at times, even though I was showing no more discourtesy than that of many adolescents, at some stage, to their parents' house in which they may have been reared since birth. But

Of Straw And Stripes

Jim wasn't a parent at all, and with no similar built-in liability for being taken for granted. He said nothing (typically), but reacted in writing, not long after I returned to barracks at Borehamwood.

His letter arrived as a surprising landmark in my life. It was the one and only he ever sent me during all my long years in the Forces. Friendly, and outwardly concerned only with my wellbeing, it served to sever, at a stroke, any remaining connection I might have had with the bungalow. The sentences and phrases, carefully and gently calculated, nevertheless blared out Jim's seemingly unshakeable 'conclusion'; that, for future leaves, I should stay with 'others of the family'.

The message, however meant, reeked of ignorance of its likely effect. If anything, Jim was revealing how blinkered he had become by his own situation. No matter how self-convinced to the contrary, this was seemingly the tidying-up process to a new life-pattern, a honing of the neatness of his self-contained bachelorship. And, too, it evidenced the continuing rift between him and the rest of the family. Breeding insidiously throughout his system, like some untreated infection, ever since the quarrel with Father (which had, after all, turned him into a kind of domestic outlaw, banished from the normality of the family scene), this had evidently worsened into a festering sore from the juncture when he was left with sole responsibility for his sick parents. Penalised, as he would have seen it, for the sin of not being happily married.

Or was it all mixed in with that early kick-start he had had to adult life? Education – or his believed lack of it – was an unacknowledged 'chip' which, never leaving his shoulder, had doomed the rest of him to an instinct of inferiority, kept at bay only by his aggressively jovial dogmatism. In the process, I think he had arrived at a positive jealousy of Andrew, not only now a married man, but who also had had all the benefits of a grammar school and a university behind him from the beginning. Or their supposed benefits. The important thing was that Jim hadn't *participated* in them: crucially, he *imagined* he had missed so much.

To have to ponder over that phrase 'others of the family' was, come to think, a somewhat incongruous exercise, set against the insulating background of throbbing military activity which had already repossessed my mind from any remaining thoughts about the sadness up north. Forcing myself back into it, I could only reason towards an answer, by way of inference, in the direction of Andrew and his wife, with whom

Of Straw And Stripes

I must have spent a disproportionate amount of my leave. Tom and his family I ruled out: they were surely too far away, up there in Scotland. And there were no other candidates. No other possible bed-space that I could think up.

Ironically, of all of them, it fell to my sister (in lodgings) to be the only one with no possibility of a future billet for me; Hilda, who, from the goodness of her heart, would normally have rushed unasked to help out. If anyone merited the title of my wartime fairy godmother, it was she; my sole consistent correspondent, for a start – the only one with the staying power to keep me continuously in sane contact with the outside world. I don't blame the others as such; but, during their later spasmodic lapses into anonymity, they were surely wearing blinkers as thick as Jim's. Letters from home, always lifeblood for soldiers, were most especially so in those days, for the host of uprooted civilians like me. It was in sardonic contrast, therefore, that I suddenly found *myself* the letter-writer, for keeping (desperately) still in touch.

Perhaps unfortunately, my response to Jim is still with me, in all its detail. Sadly, at his death some years ago, I was to find it cosseted as securely as ever amongst his meticulously filed papers. Drafted in pencil, painstakingly and in a most immature and unstylish stage of my handwriting, it testifies to the near Uriah Heep unctuousness with which I went about preserving links with him. The protestations of how much I had enjoyed my recent stay, my acceptance of the ways in which I might have stretched his hospitality, my fervent hopes of meeting up with him on future leaves – all this now savours of over-acting to such a degree as to approach 'ham' status. As I rarely heard from him again throughout the War years, it cannot have been so very convincing.

For all I know, of course, Jim may have remained in prolonged expectation of further statistics from *me*. When would I be in the area again? When (precisely) would I descend upon the bungalow? But formalities of this order rarely work. In actual fact, I was never to contact him; the longer the passage of time, the less even the possibility of my doing so.

In reassuring contrast, my brief correspondence with Andrew couldn't have been more relaxed. Unlike Jim (who inherited much of Father's aura of distant, indefinable menace), he had never overawed me or frightened me. I had admired him, yes; taken my artistic cue from him; 'hero-worshipped' him, even, in my childhood days. Yet, despite his adult wisdoms, he had remained understandable as a brother;

easily approachable, and with his often novel and intellectual ideas always opened for debate. I had never found a trace of dogmatism in him, except for an unshakable prejudice against dogmatism itself. Whether this civilised façade would have survived being put out to work at the age of eleven is, of course, problematical. It was one of the undoubted legacies of the grammar school and the university; and, in fairness to my eldest brother, it was Jim who had had to take over the parental 'bread-and-butter' economics of getting me started off in a job, and letting me into the secrets of organising my resources. As always, I was split down the middle in my allegiances, and it explains my initial near-panic when the parting of the ways from one of them arrived on my doorstep. Leaving Jim behind me, however – casting off the pilot, as it were – was to prove my most positive step thus far towards eventual, unshackled happiness. From what, I was not certain, but I had a sense, increasingly, of freeing myself.

This was encouraged by the prompt offer which arrived from Andrew of a haven up at his place, whenever I needed one. Sounding spontaneously warm and genuine, it merited a sigh of relief, somewhat in the nature of having been allowed in again from the cold. I had one port of call, at any rate.

Certainly, there couldn't have been a shortage of indisputably proper homes for most of the others. The Service authorities themselves hadn't a doubt of it. Against a spreading unbelief in their promised 'Second Front' into German-held France, home leave remained the main prop to morale; and my venerable 'AB 64 (Part One)' testifies to regular Tyneside leave passes every three months or so. Gradually, these short spells with Andrew and his wife Dorothy were to soften my continuing sense of disruption, as the successive welcomes for me, both from them and from my sister, cajoled me into a vague belief of having a home base after all. Nothing, of course, that would last into peacetime; but who was to care, anyhow, so far ahead?

And, in wartime, there is no better antidote to the relentless undercurrent of death than the insistence with which the green shoots of new life optimise the future. Being so exaggeratedly the fledgling of my family, I was already, as in everything else, the 'in-between' – this time, of the generations. An uncle to Marie and Tom's son when I was a mere boy of eleven, my sister-in-law had since additionally supplied me with a niece, to 'make the pair'. Thriving, both of them, way up there in Scotland, I had glimpsed them only occasionally. It was

Of Straw And Stripes

Andrew's wife Dorothy, however, who now assumed the attitude of defiant pregnancy; and, surely enough, there was soon another continuing hope for the world by way of a small boy called Brian, together with – happiest tonic of all! – the effervescent novelty and wonder and ambitions of new parents.

If I envied them a little, it was not abrasively. And not at all because of the relative pleasantness of their daily life-pattern to mine in the Forces. That never entered into it. Indeed, it continually enlivened me to think of those left behind with the luck of their normal civilian comforts. I liked the light to shine brightly, you see, at the end of my tunnel. But – could I still be under Jim's shadow? – I knew that this married kind of luck would never meet up with me, wartime or peacetime or any other time you could think of. It was one of the absolute certainties of my youth; a very obvious fact of life, I thought. Evolvement of such last word in 'properness' of a home base needed the asset, to match, of a proper – or was the word 'steady'? – girlfriend; and I hadn't any sort of approximation to one of those. Never an unsteady one, for that matter, and no-one realistically in prospect, my debilitating dread of making a fool of myself (amidst such a welter of worldly-wise onlookers) leaving petite Eddie Lees still no more than highly desirable fantasy. And myself still encumbered with that most shameful secret of all for any young man – my undoubted continuing virginity.

In those days, it was yet another of the disadvantages of being young. The pecking order of society was today's stood completely upon its head. 'Experience' constituted the prevailing gold standard; youth merely a temporary blight for surviving, as patiently as possible, until that elusive maturity (which went with the interesting jobs) hopefully arrived. There was a universal requirement for 'waiting one's turn', for serving tortoise-speeded apprenticeships, and, of course, for being suitably deferential to those into whose shoes we hoped to step.

That was the way of it in peacetime, at any rate. The War had altered the criteria, admittedly, for those of us in the Forces. In the commissioned officer classes – subject to the ability at will to diffuse an aura of aristocracy – youthful appearance seemed no particular disadvantage; whilst, for the main mass of us ordinary individuals, an aggressively brusque, pushing personality became the key to getting ahead, however young. No-one asked for previous references, or, for that matter, proof of experiencing anything whatsoever. But a good, rumbustious grounding in sexual conquests was always a necessity for general acceptance.

Actually, this was a variety of 'experience' which would have nullified itself as a basis for comparing promotion contenders, since just about every soldier appeared to have had a positive glut of it. Never could I have imagined the full glory of their sex-lives. On the face of it, I wouldn't be able to find a companion virgin amongst the whole lot of them. Every one an expert practitioner, mind you, and with such sex-appeal that, from those returned from home leave, there was often a welcome for the relief from seemingly insatiable demands upon their passions, which were then lavishly described for all to savour.

But I am misled. My ears were so constantly monopolised by this eroticism that I, too, now exaggerate; almost forgetting that there were many who talked only sparingly, and some hardly at all. The latter were mostly the older ones of us; sober, respectable, married individuals. As well grounded in amorousness as any, you could say, and with no need to boast about it. They were also uninhibited, and several found no difficulty in striking up enduring friendships with nearby ATS members.

Their prosaic choice of partner, however – more often than not a quiet, plain-faced, stolidly serious young woman with not a scrap of feminine charm to her – only confirmed, to my mind, the dull staidness of their own personalities. Yet there was a certain pleasantness to the sight of a couple like this, strolling gently along arm in arm amidst the dusk of an evening, all the while conversing innocently and amenably with one another. Not everything had to be of the blood-and-thunder earthy coarseness which brainwashed me every moment of the day. Pleasant – yes; but not so interesting as all that. Never a trace of the steam of a torrid romance. What did they call it? Platonic? I gave them not a second thought. Nothing at all for me to envy.

In fact, after a first, whimsical surprise at the unexpected durability of these little liaisons, they ceased to be of day-to-day interest to any of us; a dispassionateness which even extended into the eventual (almost unnoticed) splitting-up of three or four of them. Unavoidably more arresting, however, was the news which subsequently filtered through from ATS Headquarters, explaining the magically sudden disappearance, in each instance, of the feminine element to the pairing. The message was repetitious: they were all, quite irrevocably, pregnant! So much for Plato, I thought.

Chapter 12

Arthur Pratt! Now, that's a name for you! A character in itself, quite apart from its owner; who, nevertheless, more than matched up. An intriguing fellow, just as quaint in his very different way as either of the Watson-Gilgallon duo. Without question, therefore, I would be slighting Borehamwood if I failed to write him, too, into some sort of posterity, before passing to the wider-world expansion of my story.

His absence thus far from these pages simply derives from his later appearance on the scene than the others who caught my eye. On my scene, that is; for the responsibilities of his two stripes lay elsewhere to our office and its routines. More amongst the drivers and the driver-mechanics and the storemen, stationed nearby, who were our *raison d'être*, after all – the fodder, you might say, to feed our continuing appetite for posting them all over the place. I never learned the extent of his duties, nor was I really interested. But that he pursued them in dynamic fashion, with a lively mixture of flair and resolution, you can be sure. He was that type of a young man. Above all, he was an enthusiast; and there are few enough of those, at the best of times, for the savouring of their intoxicating joys.

I couldn't help noticing him occasionally exploding into us, for some sorts of essential paper-work from the top table; authorizations or the like, I imagine. A slimly built, tallish individual, with his goodly supply of thick top-hair well brushed back from an ample forehead, he seemed indeed a prime example of perpetual motion; with correspondingly speedy verbosity, but in such a strange, grotesquely exaggerated accent – which only later could I credit as being quite normal around Birmingham – as to make it difficult to grasp all that he was saying. He had a lean, expressionless face – but no, that's not quite right. It simply displayed much the same expression all the time. Perpetual surprise. That was it. With just a suggestion of his being in the course of asking a question for which he would never receive the reply, and sometimes (without altering any other feature) the permission for his mouth to crease into cheerful evidence of the otherwise 'dead-pan' sense of humour twinkling in his eyes.

His excursions into comedy were apt to be precipitous, and the nature of them just as unexpected. Such as (during an early conversation) his brusquely common-or-garden invitation – bawled into my very earhole, it seemed – of 'Want to hear a joke?' Bored revulsion boiled up in me. Had I really to suffer yet another sexual extravaganza, and, again, simulate the obligatory coarse appreciation of it? (The latter, of course, for defence against any continuing suspicion of my shockability; always a danger from my cursed birthright of boyishly innocent features.) Arthur's preliminary of asking whether I knew the French for 'war' and for 'railway station' didn't help, either. Was this supposed to be an even more titillating, *French* version, perhaps, of smutty eroticism? I sighed resignedly, before finding myself treated, instead, to the following.

There had evidently been, at some time, a high dignitary of a small French town – the elected mayor, no less – who had received an invitation to an important function in his honour in the adjoining town. Encasing himself, therefore, in his full regalia (chain of office, robes – the lot), he travelled by train, with his complete entourage of deferential officials, to the next stop up the line and the colourful reception committee which would be there to greet him. Unfortunately, the train driver was inexperienced, and overshot the platform by quite a few metres before the brakes took full effect. Anxious to get on with the ceremony, the mayor hurriedly opened the carriage door, stepped vigorously out – and fell flat on his face on waste ground by the side of the track. Rebalancing himself with difficulty, the shell-bursts inside his head a celebratory fireworks display in themselves, a bemused, wondrous smile illumined his face as he looked to the sky. '*C'est magnifique,*' he said, '*mais ce n'est pas la gare!*'

Now, you must not suppose that I'm expecting you to roll around your armchair in helpless mirth over this little anecdote. Indeed, on the couple of occasions when I have retold it to an acquaintance, there has been not the vestige of a smile, let alone a sign of laughter. Nor did I myself react at all for a few seconds. I was, after all, temporarily dumbfounded by hearing such a completely 'clean' story: in the Army, nothing could have been more original. Arthur must almost have been reduced to offering an explanation – the surest of gallows for humour – when sudden comprehension made it the most hilarious affair I had heard for years, engulfing me in absolutely unstoppable merriment for several minutes. It still earns a broad smile, just to think of it. Perhaps it was the mixture; the overflowing (if confused) emotions of the mayor, stirred in with the entire unconcern of Arthur's features as he rattled – I very nearly said 'prattled' – the whole thing off, in his incredible combination of Birmingham English and Birmingham French. Ironically, whatever its secret, I took him much more seriously from then onwards simply because of his ridiculous funniness. He was evidently something of an original in his own right.

And so it proved; though not on the basis of any other of his jokes, none of which were equally memorable, and few with similar ingenuity for omitting sexual padding. There was, at first, little on the surface to distinguish him from the rest of the mob. In present day terms, you might pigeon-hole him as noisily 'downmarket'. Never short of a girl-friend; happily integrated into the subservience of Army life; readily accepted by most. And – to me, hardly endearing – a popular music addict, to 'jazz fiend' heights of fervour. A single-minded mania which, as far as I could see, excluded anything else of more serious substance.

Against all the odds, however, conversations with him were never one-sided. He could be a surprisingly good listener; and, of course, I was arguably just as manic as he, but in the opposite direction of classical music – for which, conspicuously, I must often have drooled my saliva. Jazz was but the entertainment of the moment, 'real' music a varied, often ethereal world all of its own (by which the rest of life could only be compared). The two of them as different as *Comic Cuts* and Shakespeare. That was my youthful, unshakable dogma. Only later did it soften realistically into its present, relatively mute, tolerance.

Perhaps the strangest aspect of our developing contacts was that I should ever have ventured, in the first place, a whisper of anything so dangerous as artistic enthusiasm; for, ever since schooldays, the inadvisability of bringing this out of hiding had been deeply ingrained into me. In the 'Juniors' (amongst the rough and tumble of the neighbourhood), its existence would have gone hand in glove with a reputation for being a 'proper cissie!', and at Grammar School there had been much of the same – still that repulsive whiff of unfashionable seriousness which would forever block free and easy access to the contented security of the herd. Adulthood had taught a continuing but different reason for reticence; the stonily infertile soil in other people's gardens for the seeds of music. How obstinately prevalent their blinkered requirement to 'understand' it (as if they were tackling some geometry theorem or algebraic equation)! Music needed listeners, not talkers or scientists. Other people's ears must simply be taking in different sounds to mine: that was it. One way or the other, however, keeping my treasure to myself remained as judicious as ever it had been.

However improbably, therefore, Arthur and I must have shared the same aesthetic wavelength from the beginning; receptive to much more than just the dazed dignity of that ridiculous Frenchman on the railway track. Yet there had seemed little of mutual interest in our musical tastes. Not even (for mental exercise) anything in this jazz of his that I needed to 'understand'. It was pleasant, often lively, stuff, but nothing more than reasonable entertainment – a few minutes here and there. Too related to those hideous 'eight-in-the-bar' piano-bashings which I had to endure each day, seemingly from every tone deaf clodhopper who entered the NAAFI canteen, for it willingly to be endured for longer periods. Worse still, to be discussed even for shorter ones.

It all finally merged into the classic example (in all respects) of a mountain and a Mohammed. In the course of the comparatively few occasions when we ran into each other for conversation, I began to realise that I was already trading with the converted. Soon, from 'going over the top' where jazz was concerned, he it was who now extolled – with that everlasting look of surprise – an ecstasy of newly-discovered classical treasures.

I imagine – in fact, it must have been – that Arthur had artistic reference points back home; possibly friends who were musicians. Certainly, though I was evidently the catalyst for this change of direction in his enthusiasm, I cannot recall ever propagating specifics to him; generalising, more usually, on the broad, shimmering musical landscapes which I had so far viewed and sampled. As yet, in any event, my range of vision was strictly limited, with most chamber music, for example, still hidden behind initial suspicion. When, therefore, a month or so on, he got to eulogising over delicacies like the Beethoven Rasoumovsky string quartets (even to the extent of humming their themes with the repetitive adulation commonly reserved for catchy dance-band tunes), I marvelled at the wholesale extent of his transformed outlook.

He would have been the first to admit, mind you, that these vocal emphases of his new musical crusade weren't miraculously remembered, all of a sudden, out of thin air. They were the direct result of the little affair (or was it barefaced fraud?) of the gramophone records. But, of course, that in itself was his doing, his bright concoction, from start to finish, wasn't it? I had better explain.

This had been the way of it. The writer of Army directives, seemingly plagued by a rush of blood to the head, had momentarily overlooked the most sacrosanct of military principles; the quarantining of all commissioned ranks from the rest of humanity – a precaution carrying with it not only the implied superiority of their intelligence, but indeed of their whole culture (a matter of educated gentlemen, as it were, pitted against labourers). Those with a mind, and the rest of us with nothing more than a body, for the purpose of saluting and obeying. Somewhat outside these limitations, however, Arthur had a positive genius for nosing out, from the top table, any surreptitious item with even a glimmer of potential personal advantage.

It was just as well. Had it not been for my eardrums and his gabbled euphoria, I would never have suspected the availability, from Army sources of all places, of this godsend of classical music records – seemingly to choice and free, too! At the same time, since I never saw the 'small print' of that memorandum (nor any of the rest of it, for that matter), I was able legitimately to believe in Arthur's more democratic, and self-centred, concept of 'availability'. This, in place of the strong probability of it all being for educational purposes only, and, even then, strictly within the Unit itself. The thought must have been very much the offspring of the wish; and he was so very convincing, after all.

In support of his eloquence, there was the authoritative reassurance of his stripes, but, even so, a lingering sense of guilt was part reason – after poring over the HMV and Columbia catalogues of the day (the only ones in existence) – that my share of the conspiracy amounted to no more than six selections. To be honest, however, it was more probably the prospect of having to manhandle them home which first seeded this upsurge in my morality. Noticeably, Arthur himself can have had no such inhibitions (physical or spiritual alike), since he wholeheartedly ordered at least two dozen of the blessed things. Or so it seemed, to go by sheer weight – and who better to know than I? For, in the event, his powers of persuasion proved easily extendable to the engagement of me, one weekend, as 'fellow-porter', all the way up to his Birmingham home for a generous sampling of most of his acquisitions.

Of Straw And Stripes

With the passage of the years, those gramophone records loom large in significance. They educate me afresh; astoundingly so. How incredible the transformations in Life's artificialities, the gadgets, the inventions, notwithstanding the flesh and blood of it remaining much the same throughout, disguised but poorly by the constant succession of fresh faces and dress-fashions and manners. All of the recorded music on those cumbersome, heavy, fragile, black-shellac monsters – three or four minutes only a side, and needing constant changes of steel 'needles' to reproduce their coarse, crackling approximations – could now be embraced by five or six compact discs; light, largely undamageable, and as truthful as a live performance. The whole lot of them, you might say, made to measure for the recesses of an Army battledress blouse, with need for not an iota of additional porterage.

But where, then, would have been the adventure of it? For that matter, where are now the limitless artistic wastelands for virgin exploration? What to compare with the enhanced adrenalin of imagination – the holy grail of an eventual live performance, with its proper, gloriously undistorted and non-fragmented sound-picture? Or – earlier, perhaps – when the scientists might have found the right weedkiller for the veil of atmospherics choking so much precision out of the wireless? The future held a lot of promise. In the meantime, there was the compensating art of getting the most from the existing product. Whilst, nowadays, one merely has to press a button to obtain near perfect renditions, almost as much then depended upon the proficiency of the operator as upon the gramophone itself.

Especially do I remember the essential, light-fingered subtlety of it. For simulating near-continuity to the several chunks of a longer work, there was the instinct for sensing the impending end of each side; the gentle removing of the gramophone's arm to its 'rest' position; and then – the crucial incision of the surgeon's knife, so to speak – that adroit reverse-juggling of the disc, before caressing it back to the continuing revolutions of the turntable, for reacquainting needle with grooves. Even this was as nothing to the extra speed required to replace one disc with the next in sequence, with as little a gap as not to ruin the illusion altogether.

Such expertise, nevertheless, was nigh impossible until the acquisition, at Andrew's establishment, of a second-hand 'electric pick-up', since the winding up of his existing portable machine – with the precise pitch of the reproduction sadly linked to the state of the

Of Straw And Stripes

clockwork mechanism – was too much to combine with all the rest. Even so, it gave the operator still greater a part of the actual performance; with the occasional necessity for stuffing a pair of rolled up socks into the creature's speaker, to control its volume of sound. And in any event, nothing could mask the quality of the music making itself. No amount of clicks, or swishes, or crackles could spoil it, not even the occasional stutterings of 'groove-jumping', or the mushily clotted approximations of the loudest 'tuttis'. These were performances, indeed, for real pride of participation, if only in playing the instrument of a gramophone's needle!

Well, Arthur's machine, as I recall, was rather more refined than Andrew's portable; the electricity of its innards being, however, offset by a complete disregard of the need for aesthetic manipulation of needle, disc, or anything else. With *his* playing method, gaps and suchlike were, if anything, exaggerated. Take it (the music) or leave it, warts and all: that must have been his philosophy. Needless to say, I took it gladly, simply letting my imagination work overtime. His unbounded enthusiasm, washing over me in waves, made up the balance, and left me all the more impatient to get my own assortment home for testing.

At the same time, this missionary fervour of his had its off moments. It could give rise to occasional and unexpected embarrassments; situations from which the opening up of the earth's bowels would have been welcomed as a suitable refuge. Take for example our brush, you might say, with Beethoven.

An upright piano of respectable appearance, resting demurely in the shadows of the Birmingham household as we listened to the records, had been quick to seduce me; first, into gnawing regret at all the other musical titbits which the War had outlawed, and then into the more factual temptation of going over and trying out my fingers on it – against their very likely infection with forgetful insensitivity. The instrument was of excellent tune and touch, suggesting regular usage. It simply radiated friendliness. Involuntarily, therefore – by way of a handshake – I found myself coaxing from it a fair amount of the Moonlight Sonata's first movement. Such joyous relief! These were fingers which matched my brain's memory of the music itself; solving again (in tandem with instinctive foot-pedalling) their previous secret of expressive, 'singing-toned' legato. The piano, the fingers, my right foot – all of them were combining nicely to produce as reasonably pleasant a sound as I could expect. Nothing much out of the ordinary, mind you, but with promise,

Of Straw And Stripes

in the misted possibilities of the future, that I might just about be able to get back to square one.

Our Corporal Pratt, to be sure, would have none of it. For his money, I was there already, as good as ever I must have been. Most impressed he was; properly 'knocked over', you would say – perhaps as much, however, by my having even a scrap of memorised repertoire, in the first place, as by this impromptu performance of it. All of which may have been understandable enough; hand-in-glove, probably, with his not being any sort of instrumentalist himself. To the unenlightened, the very ability to turn black paper-dots into living music must, after all, seem quite remarkable, let alone any carrying of the translation in one's mind for future use. In actual fact, of course, mind-power never enters the equation. Where pianism is the concern, only finger-muscles have much of a say in it, even a suspicion of considered thought dispersing the memory in a trice through the back door. It thrives only if the fingers and the keys are left to themselves.

Or so it was with me. Not so much, I have always thought, a separate or deliberate talent, as simply the natural (and surely inevitable) progression from the initial reconnoitring of sight-reading to its logical advantage at the other end of the spectrum; the freedom from always having to play by courtesy of the printed page – when, having been 'read' so many times to the confidence of unfailing accuracy, the staves are reduced to occasional reminders of marks of expression and the like. And, soon, to the realisation that they have now become completely unnecessary bystanders. In pursuance of this so-called 'learning', not a scrap of extra hard work or even conscious effort has ever been needed. It goes automatically with all the rest.

Having said that, how many (I wonder) from that throng of struggling apprentice pianists who saturated the sound-waves around me, as I grew up, had even a bar or so of any of their party pieces in a personal memory bank? To go by the persistence of their haphazard inaccuracies, most must never have got beyond that 'playing by sight' bit of it; the mind no doubt becoming uncertain of what it *should* be putting in store. (Probably the reason, too, for the creeping state of boredom which paralysed so many of them into never again touching a musical instrument as soon as they had a choice.)

So much more mystifyingly wondrous, at any rate, was that rare gift – especially when (as typical) demonstrated by an unlikely illiterate in the reading of paper-music – for playing a keyed instrument 'from

Of Straw And Stripes

ear'. In its own right, honest, unpretentious light entertainment of this sort would have sparkled against any backcloth, but to have it materialising out of the fog of thumped cacophony which was the normal output of the NAAFI piano seemed the provision of manna from Heaven. Such miracles! – the sumptuous harmonies which, all of a sudden, would be dressing popular tunes of the day in clothes of positive splendour. Not a wrong note, not a single alien chord! An exclusive craft, surely, to those born with the instinct; never, of course, to rival the more creative flair of a musician improvising at will on a given theme, but close enough for comparison, I think.

That, indeed, was a talent which I have long wished had been in *my* genes; and never more so than at the Battalion's Christmas dinner festivities, held imposingly enough at the vast Elstree film studios nearby. In defiance of the grim world scenario outside – and in common, I imagine, with what remained of civilian households throughout the country – a determined effort had been set up to pretend, whatever else of normal existence might be destroyed, that Christmas was cocooned automatically against all of that; left inviolate, as warm and cosy and friendly and idealistic as ever. By long tradition, we 'other ranks' (usually the lowest of the low) were due for treatment as gods for the duration of the feast; all officers, commissioned and non-commissioned alike, being unexpectedly transformed into subservient waiters upon our table, serving us, in addition to the seasonal fare, a fleeting sense of friendship from fellow human beings.

Just before the meal got under way, there developed, spontaneously and with readily volunteered items from amongst us (comic ditties, songs, jokes and the like), a quarter of an hour or so of what you might describe as self entertainment. All of this was proving enjoyable relaxation, until Arthur chose to lob one of his Molotov cocktails in my direction. Perhaps 'lob' isn't the right word: actually, it exploded into my realisation of things without the slightest of warnings. 'I'm now going to call upon Private Lawrenson,' he joyously boomed out to all around, 'to play a little for us from Beethoven's Moonlight Sonata!'

It was hardly the situation for playing anything whatsoever from the classics, let alone this, amongst the slowest-paced and most atmospheric of deeply emotional music. Added to which, I had no idea whether, apart from those relatively few bars of my Birmingham 'recital', I had reliable memory of it. Giving a realistic demonstration, therefore, of what must have appeared absolute gutlessness, I could only stammer

Of Straw And Stripes

out an emphatic disclaimer of knowing the piece sufficiently well. To cover my confusion, one of the commissioned ranks stepped in with a few minutes of light pianism, and our impromptu divertissement jogged along without further embarrassment. But it was a prime example of Arthur's never sensing the need for a suitable ambience for the savouring of serious art.

Perhaps unconsciously in deserved retribution for my weak-kneed performance (or lack of it), one of our 'waiters' subsequently developed a new variety in the methods of serving soup, delivering a noticeable spattering of it down one side of my battledress blouse. All in all, my appetite was left without its edge, not only for the soup which actually reached my bowl, but for all the rest of those particular festive proceedings.

This was the first of two demonstrations of my friend's complete ignorance of 'proper time and place'. Any imbecile, I later decided, would have recognised that vast corner of the film studios, packed with khaki effervescence, as the setting for earthier entertainment than meditative artistic culture. This had been *Comic Cuts* territory, never the footlights for Shakespearean drama. But those hostile vibes of the second example merited analysis of some subtlety: it was a full-blown symphony concert, after all, and in a tailor-made location.

Of course, Leicester itself now seems thoroughly out of place (both for this chapter and Borehamwood's map reference), quite apart from the actual venue of its De Montfort Hall. Why (I ask myself) were we there at all? Come to that, what could any of us have had to do with Cambridge, an even more unlikely destination? At this late stage, my memory has been tested in rediscovering the connection. But I recollect now that, of the two, we had been prescribed the University City (understandably) for a permitted 'educational break' – as that Army Manual no doubt listed it; nearby Leicester merely cropping up as the adjunct for an interested few out of the main group of us, after Arthur (who else?) had spotted the advertisement in the local paper.

I may have expected too much from the concert, but not unreasonably so, I think. It should have been a fitting epilogue to our conducted tour of the Cambridge establishments; such a sparklingly refreshing contrast to the boredom of military dogmas! One by one, the massive old colleges had peered beneficently down at us, each clothed with an unexpected, yet insistent, aura of scholastic unchangeability (War or no War); enclosed and encouraged as they were, on all sides, by that unbelievable, segregated, sanitised oxygen of peaceful contemplation.

If the overwhelming sense of time-travel, several generations backwards, had needed the slightest reinforcement, the identification of our guide as the venerable Doctor Trevelyan – a colossus amongst historians of the day – would surely have done the trick, as he trotted enthusiastically in front of us, his black gown frolicking merrily in the whims of the breeze. He looked quaint – with, I thought, no relevance whatsoever to the precarious realities of current events; whilst the cluster of us, in his wake, must have seemed even more incongruous for *his* world – the men amongst us clattering along in the heaviness of Army boots, and with our assorted ill-fittings of battledress propagating a collective absence of higher culture.

It was a comparison of such inequality as to be embarrassing. Yet the Professor, for his part, evinced neither conceit nor condescension, not even a suspicion of a patronising attitude, during the whole of our encounter; evidently recognising no worthwhile difference in our respective rations of intelligence. This was a compliment which, somehow, we were able to infer from the very beginning (when he had hardly spoken a word to us). It gave so much of a fillip to our corporate ego that, while still panting from our efforts to keep up with him, we found ourselves welcoming with confidence his eventual invitation to the place's 'inner kingdom' – those secluded interiors of the colleges, or at any rate a few of them.

Passing inside was to flick back through countless more pages of history. Nothing at all now remained of the present. Walls, floors, ceilings, furniture, the very air for breathing – all were exclusive in their honouring of years and happenings long gone. And, most particularly, of the galaxy of celebrated men who had seemingly lingered here at one time or another; many of renown during their own lifetime, all, with the benefit of the grave, now magnified into supreme legends of accomplishment. By this time, their names alone sufficed to heat the imagination, breeding the absurd notion that short-term tenancies of particular rooms must have bequeathed to them the lasting enhancement of a kind of spiritual glory.

It seemed to me that, in Trevelyan's case, this constituted a very positive and inflexible *belief*. As he exuberantly pointed out the hallowed resting places of these Cambridge heroes, it was as if they were all still very much alive; briefly away on visits, as it were, leaving him to make sure that no-one trespassed more than momentarily into their reserved

Of Straw And Stripes

lodgings. Fleetingly, I doubted the *existence* of current, flesh-and-blood usurper-tenants. The factual concurrence of the University's summer vacation – *did* such luxuries still exist? – might explain, at first sight (or the lack of it), the complete absence of undergraduates around us. Yet it added to the unbelievability of the whole scene. What possible justification could there still be for such a refinement as studentship? Assuming these particular 'holiday-makers' to be more than just a collection of medical rejects, most must have conjured deferment far in excess of those pathetic, soul-searched five weeks of mine. Justifying, one would think, a savager examination of 'War effort relevance' than my final, ephemeral little pianistic escapade can ever have merited.

In the absence, so far as I knew, of a chair in Advanced Explosive Technology or facilities for reading Theory of Blitzkrieg Warfare, it was hard to appreciate how anything or anyone within sight could be helping to win the War. I remember the blissful calm of the whole establishment, nevertheless, as the miracle of miracles of the War years; providing the possibility, amid all the ghastly destruction of the shells and the bombs, the air raids on civilians, and (though yet to be revealed) the mass racial cruelties and exterminations in Europe, for people still to dabble in Arts and Classics and the like – diplomas certifying faith in the future, you could say, as much as anything else. Had I but known, of course, there was, even now and out of everyone's sight, an additional unknown horror; the concentration of more practical academics, in their anonymous laboratories across the world, on solving the secrets of the atom – in particular, of how to split it.

Fortunately, the bliss of the air around us extended into this measure of ignorance. When the last of the colleges had been explored, the lustre of their pasts expanded to the point of the Professor's scholastic ecstasy, we trudged outside again in a state of rather sad bemusement; sad, because the quiet beauty of what we were leaving would probably never again touch us, amid the uglinesses of warfare. Or that is how I felt; I cannot speak for the others. Peculiarly, of the factual information which had been sprayed liberally over us, I remember nothing; not the names of those past gods, not their respective colleges, not even any of the historical anecdotes dished up as sauce and gravy to the rest. The very buildings themselves were to merge in my mind into distant, ill-defined cathedral shapes with none of the sharp edges of reality. (Long after the end of the War, with our younger daughter at Trinity Hall for the finishing of her education, a revisit found all of them complete strangers – seemingly as unacquainted with me as ever.)

The brevity of my rapport with them may partly have resulted from their initial reticence in the realm of visible evidence. Had any of these famous people *really* stayed there? We had the Professor's word for it, of course, but stories endure best from the pages of a book, and much had seemed mere word-of-mouth fairytale stuff at the time. I am, however, close to overlooking those most intriguing of all fossil-remains (as I now think of them); relics which we were able to examine at length and at close quarters – the indestructible 'graffiti' donated to posterity by many of the past Cambridge cognoscenti, as sworn affidavits of their sojourns.

No entry in the English dictionary highlights a more swiftly changing phenomenon of life than that for the word 'graffito'. Generally unknown and unused in those days, only latterly (and plurally) has it entered everyday language. More a question, indeed, of having forced its way in, from the sprawling proliferation of the thing into such present voracious parasiticism. This has been to vilify an otherwise worthy instinct – against the frightening oblivion of future death, for laying a scent of 'having passed this way' (or that) whilst still alive. Blame it, if you will, on the invention of felt pens, spray-paint canisters and the like: they have made it easy to besmirch a whole wall with indelible obscenities in less time than the former innocence of a single set of initials, carved painstakingly and hopefully into a wooden future.

The years seemed to have shrivelled to days since my sister Hilda had been showing off hers, neatly engraved into a secret corner of her favourite bench in the local park. Unostentatious, almost artistic in their way, they had constituted as permanent a record as she could possibly have envisaged of her time on earth – subject only to the long-term ravages of the English climate on the seat's timber. Sadly, most of the benches have long since weathered away into the scrapyard. The initials have gone with the rest, as irreplaceable as Hilda herself.

At the time, however, the somewhat more pampering indoor climate of the colleges promised near-immortality for every material object in sight; endowing them, certainly, with futures far beyond imagination, and maybe to the fringe of eternity itself. I believed it then, and I believe it now.

Within the University, after all, when can furniture or trappings of any substance ever have been discarded as outdated, too old for further use, overdue for modernisation? Seldom, I suspect. Even if I wouldn't now be able to find that particular college again, let alone locate the vast dining hall of the place, I still view its great table, out of the corner of my inner eye, with no difficulty at all. If nothing else, it was (and, undoubtedly, still is) substantial! How many massive oaks must have lost their lives to ensure its muscled longevity, against the hordes of undergraduates testing it over the centuries! With, quite apart from the relentless weight of the platters of food eaten from it, the whole storage tanks of beer drunk, certain persistent individuals, it seemed, using it for more than just their meals. If it were initials one was after, here were dozens of more intellectual ones than Hilda's, for resuscitating with our microscopes of eyes.

Even the nameless sets, however, had needed the Professor's pointing finger to discover their map references on the huge wooden surface, running almost the length of the room and long-since aged into wrinkled antiquity; with the handful of famous specimens proving as elusive again as spots of gold dust in a worked-out mine. Nevertheless, while these identifications had to be taken on trust just as much as the other stories, it is a fact that the simple incisions brought History briefly alive, as we pondered over them in wonder.

These few were to become legends in their particular fields. They had no need to advertise their existence, to boast of being at Cambridge. It was Cambridge which would soon be for boasting about them. But perhaps this stamps them, after all, as having been more normal pieces of humanity than I had suspected. (At that stage, evidently still unconvinced of their future greatness, and quite unknowing of the benefit to be had from timely interventions of the blessing of luck; a commodity – who knows? – which may have avoided some of the anonymous amongst the engravers altogether.)

Whatever else my mind eventually carried out of that oasis of learning, it was the calm relaxation of the place which lingered the most influentially, serving as a delectable diversion to its undercurrent of gloom and uncertainty about life after Borehamwood. And there was that nice thought of the concert still to come: how better to get back to ground level without too much of a bump?

Unfortunately, that was not at all how it developed. Even the label of 'neutral' for the experience would have constituted blatant flattery. As far as I was concerned, 'catastrophic' was much nearer the mark, feeling as I did that I had been returned to earth so forcibly and abruptly as to have broken both legs in the process. And all because of Arthur's continuing bad judgement. Whilst this time he had got the place right (and the contents of the programme, too – nothing wrong there), he had still ensured a faulty component to the final mix; that of the audience itself. Or, at any rate, the single member of it whom he was directly responsible for dragging along.

She didn't *look* like a philistine, mind you. My concept of the species was rather vague, but instinct painted it for me as having been predominantly male and fiercely muscled; hairy-faced and hairy-chested; scruffily aggressive, above all, towards anything faintly resembling civilisation. And Betty – Arthur's latest (and, this time, surprisingly 'steady') girlfriend from the ATS – was, of course, none of this. Her forte was nothing more pretentious than the allure of youthful femininity. Dark-haired, fresh-faced and pleasantly curved in all the right places, a slight tendency to plumpness did her no disservice at all. Indeed, the nearness of these assets might have been expected to distract me in any event, never minding Arthur's prior claims on the girl. Significantly, however, I have no recollection of the colour of her eyes. (I was still as besotted as ever by the perpetual twinkling laughter in the grey-blue of Eddie's, back at Borehamwood.) No – it could only have been by virtue of her fully-fledged philistinism that she made such an impression that evening. No possible doubt about it.

Of course, for all I know, she may only have acquired the trait when she passed through the doors of the De Montfort building. Certainly, she didn't like the look of its interior from the very beginning; even as she was walking to her seat, and long before a note of music was offered up to her for approval. Her own 'look' was ample evidence – a combination of distaste, non-understanding and premature boredom. Was it, in fact, her first experience of a concert hall? As the evening progressed, I became more and more convinced that it would be her last – despite Arthur's seeming ignorance of the sufferings next door to him, as she fidgeted constantly and impatiently, and with far more glances at her wristwatch than ever at the orchestra.

Sat there together, they presented a peculiarly ill-sorted pairing of souls. He, completely insensitive to her mental discomforts; she, equally numb to the emotional message of the music which he was sensing so deeply. As for me, it was an occasion when almost everything of beauty reaching my ears had ceased to mean a thing. I doubt whether my mind heard much of it, let alone found any remaining appetite for its digestion. Could it be that she was actually *groaning*? Or merely sighing? Perhaps neither – audibly, that is; yet her spiritual moans and groans were reaching me just as destructively. I was in the presence of an alien (in aesthetic terms) who blocked the enjoyment of all things artistic, for the time being.

That evening, Betty slotted a significant addition into my understanding of the human condition. She became for me the prototype for the whole tribe of cultural philistines continuously infiltrating the intelligent world. Out of that brief, two-hour session of unadulterated purgatory in the De Montfort Hall, came two gradual realisations. The first, beginning only with suspicion but since solidified many times over, was of the numbers who are constitutionally blighted, for all time, against the enjoyment of artistic glories. The worst of them suffer from the undisguisable calamity of colour-blindness, or tone-deafness, or (Heaven forbid!) some combination of the two. Mostly, however, they have otherwise healthy ears or eyes which seem not to have been sensitised enough, at creation, for the aesthetic subtleties dividing us from the animals. Mercifully, most are quite unaware of their disability. Something akin to being born without legs and never getting to know that all the others have two apiece.

The fact that, with the concert concluded and the auditorium itself well in our wake, Betty could emerge again so quickly into the sparkling vivacity and humorous repartee of her proper self, served as a suitable (if, at the time, contradictory) tailpiece to the main lesson of the evening. The Bettys of this world, she and her fellow 'artistic outsiders' of either gender, are at their best on their own pitch, substantially distanced from the foreignness of orchestras and conductors and the like. Only outside the Artistic Pale do they exhibit their true worth; often as the most interesting and intellectual of individuals, and providers, above all, of the perfect antidote for that disease of confined, tribal artificiality which can so easily choke Art into near heart failure.

This, however, is medication which needs, at the same time, a somewhat realistically restricted attitude towards friendships from different sides of the divide. The trick, I was later to find, lies in keeping to compartments. Most haphazard mixtures have proved ugly with me, highlighting not only the yawning and bigoted gaps in the non-believers' ideas of beauty, but the warping 'funnel-vision' as well of some died-in-the-wool artistic types. Increasingly, my ideal has become, at any one time, the mingling in one of the camps to the complete exclusion of the other – not only in actual company, but in areas of conversation. With luck, one may then enjoy the complete scope of the human scene, without, for example, the inner fury from the tittle-tattle which can suddenly sever a compact disc's symphonic slow movement – an unrecognised sacrilege, worsened yet again by the encouragement to 'carry on enjoying the rest of it'!

All such theorising was for later, of course. Looking backwards is the time for that; and I was still languishing in a seemingly perpetual condition of merely starting out in life. What should have been a soothing evening's entertainment had simply demonstrated the blunt end of the argument in advance. As for Arthur, it was clear that nothing whatsoever had disturbed his own entire enjoyment of the occasion.

Nevertheless, the day as a whole had, for me, fizzled out meaninglessly. And, as we travelled back to Borehamwood, I had the vaguely sad feeling at the pit of my stomach that my time there, too, must be getting very near the fizzling-out stage.

Chapter 13

Whereas, to this day, it is hard for me to think of the Yorkshire training stint in terms of months, rather than the years of my mind over which it undoubtedly stretched, the Borehamwood episode was pleasant enough, by contrast, to make the weeks and months of it skip away much more briskly. For that matter, the years themselves were almost in process of joining the helter skelter. 1942 had melted into 1943, and 1944 was almost in sight round the corner, when it all, eventually and inevitably, came to an end. With another Christmas but a few weeks away, the scenario changed at a stroke to the preliminaries for my proper participation in the harsher side of the War. Everything to date, I suspected, had been in the nature of charades. Evidently, at long last, it was the coldest of realism which lurked for me just around that corner; and, with Yorkshire now light-years into my past, I felt as untrained and unready for the coming fray as if I had never been up there in the first place – never even seen Richmond or Catterick; nor, for that matter, any Lee-Enfield or Bren or grenade that had ever been invented, or a square inch of any parade ground whatsoever or wheresoever.

Yet I cannot maintain that my enforced exodus arrived abruptly or unexpectedly. Over the previous few weeks, even the densest blanket of wishful thinking couldn't have concealed the signs, both outside and inside the Battalion Office. The whole country was increasingly seething with thoughts on two equally weighty conundrums, each centred upon an idea to which the lengths of continuing official silence threatened embalmment into a myth. This was the suggestion (hope or dread, dependent upon the viewpoint) of a 'Second Front' against Hitler and his Germans. Was it, we wondered, really practicable, with the European coastline encrusted, as it was, in armaments of the sort to send stomachs retching from the *thought* of them? And, if a storm in some brain or other were to rubber-stamp this degree of recklessness, would any partial success be worth the cost? (In this respect, a recent visit to the local hairdresser's had proved typically dispiriting. The chattering background of waiting customers – in unanimous opposition – were seemingly in disagreement only on the scale of the resulting bloodbath!)

It would have been comforting to imagine that the British and American High Commands were currently thinking along lines similarly dismissive to those of these amateur staff officers, unconcernedly awaiting their turn for a civilian haircut; though how and when the War would then ever have ended is more problematical. But the changing pattern of our work within the Battalion Office told otherwise.

Not that there was much alteration to the basic routine of it. The dictatorial posting of unfortunates here, there and everywhere continued just as before; but, swiftly emerging, came an overwhelming emphasis on 'here' to the virtual exclusion of 'there'. New units in England, needing the swiftest of reinforcements, were evidently springing up overnight, resulting in the strange demotion to second-rank urgency of replenishments for the Far-Eastern zone of operations (Burma and the like). There was a strong overall sense amongst us of these switching balances of importance, which implied an added seriousness for 'home' postings – most often, now, to addresses sounding suspiciously like transit camps. (Up to the present, it had been 'away' assignments which had carried the worst of the odds against long-term survival; the lengthy spells of 'phoney war' blessing this side of Europe never, for example, being anywhere known around the vast and bloody battlefields of South-East Asia.)

Intermingled with the issue of ever more personnel movement orders – noticeably draining our nearby reservoirs of human fodder – there was an unwelcome suspicion. Were our own destinies quite as secure as so many months of The Grange's stability had suggested? The unspoken message of the old building, that our inviolability as directors (as distinct from the directed) could somehow last out the War, was now frozen with the realism of current developments. There was the hitherto unthinkable question: might some of *us*, indeed, be next for the executioner's block?

When I claim to have sensed more than a trace of apprehension knocking around, I find myself (not for the first time) imputing to the others my own feelings and reactions; a judgment which may have been true enough, but without anyone I can recall supplying conversational support to it. This wasn't really so surprising, however, since no-one talked at all of such serious things. What now seems an

Of Straw And Stripes

odd characteristic was one which inhibited everyone, civilian and soldier alike, throughout the War years. Non-confession of fear, that is, or of any sort of reluctance for entering into the heat of battle. This would have been a self-indictment of intolerable sin, instantly translated as lack of patriotism (that fixation which is so often ridiculed in peacetime, but generally held in awed reverence during hostilities).

In any event, I hadn't to wait so very long for news of my future. The gradual, week-by-week crystallising of those first faint intimations of its fragility grew disturbingly into a day-by-day mounting of the suspense of near certainty; during which time, for the summary administering of my fate, a scaffold hastily hammered itself together in the recesses of my mind. In terms of what actually transpired, I had to climb its steps not once but twice. On the first occasion of my name being bandied about and then 'pencilled in' it was a matter of the dreaded Burma – complete with thoughts of blazing heat, steaming jungles and life-sapping forced marches, against a constantly threatening background of Japanese sadists sniping from the treetops.

It was bad enough – at the mere scratching of a pen nib, you could say – to have to make such a lightning-quick adjustment to the culture shock which now awaited me, half the world away from Borehamwood's more understandable civilisation. But, with my intellect persuaded into unaccustomed resilience, and only the keys of the office typewriter needed for the finality of the posting, the 'top table' found it in them, even now, to shatter me afresh; a revised and entirely different permutation of the whole transaction serving to deposit me once again at the foot of the steps. Quivering in bewilderment and confusion, it was as if I had suddenly been granted a temporary pardon; back to what remained of normality at The Grange. Yet still with the requirement to be retried for the same crime.

I was never so stupid, however, as to expect a respite of more than days: being the youngest candidate around, I must already have achieved – no trouble at all! – the top honours on any existing sacrificial list. And so it proved. Very shortly afterwards, a posting authorisation which had, in fact, survived the typing stage arrived in front of me, coldly and without ceremony. By comparison with the lurid Far-Eastern landscape still lingering in my imagination, it sounded routine; prosaic. I was to travel up to East Anglia, to join a unit called '107 Armoured Ordnance Sub-Park'. The location (seemingly every bit as humdrum) – Swaffham, in Norfolk.

Chapter 14

If that first adventure-journey of mine, way back up there in Durham and Yorkshire, had never really registered in the memory – only my arrival at the end of it exciting anything like a lasting imprint – this time it was just the opposite. No-one could impassively have endured the viciously crushing and stifling mood in which, at this time of day, I found London's Underground. It was nothing like so friendly as in my 'Edgeware to Leicester Square' weekend routines of only yesterday. On a Saturday, certainly, there had been crowds for wriggling through to the trains; but now, of course, in addition to this unyielding melee of city-goers (none of whom must ever have heard of a call-up notice, let alone received one), I was having to contend with my encasement in the heaviest of Army greatcoats – surmounted by a full display of 'webbing', including back-pack – and the need to supervise a cumbersome kitbag, precariously balanced on my right shoulder.

I don't know whether it was the greatcoat, or the people packed in around me, or, maybe, a mixture of both, but, long before I got as far as Kings Cross, I was sweating my guts out, as some say. It could also have been the sheer anxiety of keeping myself in a state of balance. In all senses, that is; for, even with the financial security of my travel warrant and the posting order's clear directions, I had only the vaguest of hopes of getting to the right place at the right time. While most moves from one unit to another involved at least three or four personnel, travelling together, this one had turned out so solitary an adventure as to be ironic. Though normally as natural a 'loner' as they come, I found myself longing for the reassurance of any sort of companionship! Squeezed and pushed and buffeted by this horde of frantic Londoners, I was, nevertheless, as totally isolated as if the carriage had been empty.

More than anything else, it was the resurgent, unbroken anonymity of all the people and places around me which I now found dispiriting to the point of near despair. I felt as if, torn savagely away from the bonhomie of all those good friends – now, belatedly, recognised as such! – back at The Grange, I had been thrown out coldbloodedly on to some kind of scrapheap. With the exception of Mick Gilgallon, latterly possessed of a broader grin than ever and with better reason, following his discharge to home and family, all of them would probably linger on at Borehamwood quite a while longer; yet I knew full well that, save possibly dear Eddie (with whom I had agreed to correspond), I would never see any one of them again. It was an awesome thought to take with me on the steam train up to East Anglia.

Having expected so little of it in the first place, Swaffham, an inoffensive little market town, came into view, and my life, not so much as a disappointment as a non-event. There seemed even less to it than Borehamwood, and (unlike the fringes of the Metropolis) nothing bigger and better, either, 'just up the road'. More to the point, the large print of my posting document finally guided me to a scenario redolent of Richmond and my training days. I was evidently to be enmeshed once again in the grey, drab monotony of Nissen huts and the like. There were, however, several Army lorries stationed like some petrified forest around the huts, suggesting (as, indeed, it came about) that, from now on, they would always be part and parcel of the activities of my new unit.

Bearing in mind my instinctive shudder at the prospect of returning to basics, it surprises me even now how smoothly and rapidly I managed to settle into this new variety of anonymity. My initial revulsion at the well-remembered, bare-boned nature of those monopolising huts, with all the crudity of their furnishings and facilities, softened into an acceptance of the comparative benignity of their ailments. This conversion was helped along by the improvement, over only a day or so, of many of the nondescripts inhabiting the Camp into separate individuals; though the ghosts of Dick, and Reg, and Arthur, and, above all, that angel of a girl Eddie, continued to haunt me more graphically than anyone closer at hand.

It would be nice, of course, to preen myself with the supposed surfeit of sturdy resilience I displayed in adjusting to the new regime. But that isn't realistic. Choice for servicemen is always fragmentary, particularly in wartime, and unpleasantness or even horror irrelevant so far as running away from it. Arrest as a deserter brings untold family shame (quite apart from the firing squad), and mere disobedience the introduction to one of the Army's 'glasshouses' – suitably much worse than anything which has been disobeyed. Dictionaries published during the War might well, in fact, have deleted the word itself, 'resilience' becoming an antique form of the more straightforward 'survival'. And, below the surface, no-one was confident of a long-term version of that. Especially at this juncture of the War, with all the signs around of the imminence of its final viciousness; the make-or-break offensive against the French coast and the toted odds of that barber's shop.

Yet, taking stock, I found my new circumstances more tantalising than foreboding. There was nothing of the expected adrenalin of excitement of forthcoming battles coursing through my veins, only puzzlement at the unchanging, uneventful limbo of the whole concern. It had even less of the feel of a front-line unit than The Grange! And, being so well distanced from the South Coast (the likely jumping-off area for the big onslaught), it could hardly be available for quick transportation to France. Unbelievably, I had travelled all this way up the country – from the mounting expectations of civilian-like Borehamwood to what was supposed to be an active service unit – only to find myself *really* back to basics, marking time yet again for that proper climax to the War. Life at Swaffham dragged on, in fact, for all of four months before anything significant developed, and by that time I had got to believing that it never would.

For that matter, what *were* we awaiting? I had never been crystal clear of it, but the concept was becoming hazier as the weeks went by, with the sight of all this motorised transport standing around – presumably ready for something or other in the near future. But what? My original background tapestry of shell-pitted fields and muddy trenches had, of course, long since been donated to history. Cinema newsreels and newspapers had seen to that, with their startling revelations of the German armoured *blitzkrieg*: profusions of tanks demolishing everything in front of them by awesome, sweeping 'pincer movements' and suchlike state-of-the-art carnage. I had some sense of the part infantry soldiers might still play in the overall battle-scene (flushing out the enemy in street battles?), and of artillery-men being able to add to the havoc of the tanks – the necessity, too, for big dumps of ammunition and stores (even if some way back from the front line). But what of ourselves? We might have 'Armoured' in the title, but none of it that I could see in our make-up, either for protecting us or for damaging anything German. And all of these Army lorries put together wouldn't carry enough stores, surely, for more than a couple of days of battle expenditures.

Of Straw And Stripes

Nevertheless, the contents of some of them were interesting enough to keep my curiosity whetted. The fleet of vehicles was larger than I had first supposed, and some of them were evidently intended as miniature (and mobile) warehouses, in contrast to others which, from time to time, were bringing in fresh stocks from some larger base in the region. Two or three of the fleet were quite monstrous affairs – ten-tonner Chevrolets, no less – and near one of these an accumulation of sizable items was stacked; complete engine assemblies, rear axles, replacement tyres and wheels, tank tracks and the like. These were the kind of thing I would have expected the Unit to be stocking; but, inside certain of the standard three-ton lorries, I was taken aback by the myriad of smaller items held, and the meticulous way in which they were stored and categorised. Spare parts of all kinds and complexity were there in thousands, as well as profusions of finer details – screws and bolts and washers of all sizes, and the subtlest shades of difference in delicate copper wire (in strange competition with all the varying stoutnesses of more substantial electric cable). A compact version, you could say, of the most well stocked of hardware and electrical and motor-spares shops put together. Military precision of a type I had not previously suspected.

While I could come to believe, with a little stretch of the imagination and a rather larger amount of good luck, that the contents of those trucks might get to France still reasonably organised, the 'Office' lorries were less of a realistic bet. Amongst other things, they housed a close-knit family of filing cabinets, each one holding trays of indexed record cards (one for each type of item stocked); and, alongside potential next-door neighbours of German mines and machine guns and artillery, it was hard not to see the cabinets shaken on to their sides and the cards strewn higgledy-piggledy all over the place.

My instinctive reaction was a mixture of disappointment and dismay. If what I was seeing was the skeleton of a blueprint for active service procedures, it must have come from boffins who had never been outside a military academy; without a sniff, you could say, of an actual battlefield. To me, those finicky record cards looked bogus. There was a pseudo-civilian fragrance about *them*; a scent, I may say, which strengthened as I gleaned the theory of what we were supposed to be up to. The supply lines: that was it, of course! Needless to say, I'd heard of them – cutting the enemy's was supposed to be 'half the battle', wasn't it? – but I hadn't so far thought myself quite so 'cuttable' as the

Of Straw And Stripes

Unit's scheduled slot in the European battle-scene, only a mile or two behind the front line, was likely to prove. All the more reason, then, for strengthening the shock absorbers and, thus, the cabinets, or (just as important) coating all the vehicles with armour-plating, to assure longer 'usable value' for both ourselves and the stores. These were no more than facetious thoughts, but, in hindsight, they could so easily have been to the point.

Against this feeling of being among the innocent, ready for slaughter, there were, however, the two small animal pictures, woollen-woven on to cloth, which had been issued to me shortly after my arrival. They were my regulatory 'corps signs' (one for the top of each battledress sleeve), advertising the larger Army conglomerate of which the Unit was part for combat purposes. They depicted an inoffensive mouse-creature, reared up on its hind legs for no particular reason that I could think of. My new powers-that-be not having thought to introduce me properly to the little fellow, its true significance took a while to sink in; and when, eventually, I learned of its being in fact a jerboa, this, too, meant nothing, until I was reminded of its common nickname – a 'desert rat'. When, all of a sudden, the recent nondescripts were elevated into truly illustrious company!

Humdrum, indeed! Even the mechanical drone of the Unit's title now developed an underlying lilt to it, especially when the instinct was indulged of dwelling upon the figure '7' in its numbering. For that, as I had now decoded, was its obvious proclamation of parentage; the fabled '7th Armoured Division' of the British Army. *The* 'Desert Rats', no less! It says much for their feats in the North African desert campaigns of the earlier part of the War, that, half a century on, assumption of any need to restate them remains patronising. Books, and films, and documentaries have, in turn, drooled quite sufficiently over the Battles of El Alamein and Tobruk, the first defeats of Rommel and his German 'Panzers'. Whether the 'Seventh' was General Montgomery's finest jewel, or Monty the Seventh's, is a fine distinction, but, between them, they had generated the only light so far seen through the monotonous murk of German domination. Bright enough, certainly, to have spotlighted the matchless quality of the Division amongst British armoured columns. In consequence – though largely unsuspected (most of us thinking its Middle-East assignment long-term) – the 'Second Front' planners must long have rated it essential as a 'cutting edge' for their own operations. A secrecy which had now left me to learn of the

Division's recall only by the most first hand of all methods – actually joining it!

The discovery served as a shot in my arm of adrenalin. Unfortunately, the effect was short-lived. There was something of a 'Cambridge syndrome' to the situation; another of those legends without visibly realistic back-up. No sign anywhere of tanks, or armoured cars, or artillery support, or any of the trappings of an armoured task force. And as for my new colleagues – which of them had, in fact, been in the desert campaigns? Some, doubtless – but which? Not a grain of sand on any of their boot-soles, and no-one mentioning past exploits at all. They looked ordinary, and behaved just as ordinarily. Desert Rats or no Desert Rats of the past, nothing yet was happening in the present, here at Swaffham.

It says much for the week upon week of the place's crawling boredom, that I recall nothing of the town itself, save the mournful, chilly interior of what must have been a church hall, in which I was attending a meeting of the local gramophone society. Rather scratchily performed on a barely adequate machine, I was there initiated into the first of Schubert's piano trios; my wonderment at the inevitable flow of its seeming effortless lyricism easily transcending both the ugliness and discomfort of the indoor scenery. My reference book extols the picturesqueness which must have been available outside – the little market square, with its 'pedlar of Swaffham' monument and 'domed rotunda' of a market cross, the fifteenth century church of Saints Peter and Paul, the Georgian houses, and suchlike. But I was still young enough to be anaesthetised against quiet, country attractions of the sort; much preferring to have been whiling away this additional waiting time amongst the hustle and bustle of faraway London.

As it was, Time itself now became the anonymous one, as 1943, with only a week or so to go, fairly dawdled into 1944. Christmas, at any rate, managed some sort of residual identity, with the aid of a week's leave for marking the event; though, unless I was mistaken, there was the smack of a 'farewell edition' to it, this time round. The New Year had nothing with which to greet us except the same staple diet of routine Camp chores, interminable jogging sessions of physical training, the occasional lecture on this or that, and (for such mechanical illiterates as myself) periods of driving tuition – mostly self-conducted, in the impossibly high cabin of one of the three-tonners, with scrunching and scraping of worn gear-levers to disillusion all but the most determined.

January – then into February – then into March. How unbelievably were the struggling weeks turning into monsters of months! But, at last, came April with our next ration of home leave; and, this time, we all of us knew it would be our last before 'the happening'. No specific pronouncement had been made on the subject, but there remained not the slightest doubt. I had sensed an indefinable change in the atmosphere a couple of weeks earlier, in fact, when I made purchase in the local stationer's of a small, hard-backed memo-book. It still rests before me as I write, its blue cover and red spine weather-worn, yet not really betraying its years, and its pages confirming my original hope of their comparative immortality – living on, I thought, into at any rate a short future of which I might not be part. With what might be considered unwarranted grandiosity of concept, I had resolved to keep a diary of future events!

The substance for a first entry was not long delayed. My terseness of the moment, with words clipped to the bone, conceals the veritable avalanche of excited commotion which only now had been overwhelming the Camp site with accelerations of packing, loading, stuffing away and mopping up, in readiness for the exodus. No longer was there time for more considered thought.

Sunday, 16 April, 1944. Left Swaffham by lorry convoy (about 46 lorries). Reveille – 5.30 am. Breakfast – 6.15 am. Finally arrived at Middleton, Sussex (or, more properly, Elmer-on-Sea) at half past eight in the evening.

Chapter 15

It is yet further irony that, at this near juncture of finding the answer to the riddle of 'real' warfare, I should have been bamboozling myself for the future with another puzzle. Or, rather, it must have been the Army authorities to blame, in the first place, since the precision of that 'or, more properly, Elmer-on-Sea' could only have come straight from their 'movement-direction-order' of the day. The trouble now (as I have discovered from meticulous magnification of every available South Coast atlas) is – where has 'Elmer' gone? It is nowhere to be found, even in the smallest of prints. If, of course (most improbably), I were to revisit the area, I might find it still tucked comfortably away around the corner of one of Middleton's outskirts; but, from this distance, it seems most probably, over the years, to have become fatally submerged by the English Channel.

Reassuringly, however, I find that Middleton itself is still acknowledged by every one of the atlases, which also confirm that the whole area in which we now found ourselves was as close to the Channel (and France) as ever possible without actually treading water. Bognor Regis was right next door, and, intrigued by its 'Regis' embellishment – with royal undertones of George the Fifth's recuperation there from illness – I took an early opportunity to make its acquaintance; expecting a rather superior kind of place but finding it, instead, disappointingly and coldly drab, and (necessarily, I suppose) devoid of much life outside of khaki. More in context, there was the realisation that Portsmouth and Gosport were each little further afield. While the proposed area of France for invasion was, of course, closest-locked of all secrets, it needed little brainpower to pinpoint probable departure points for the operation. I thought that we couldn't, indeed, have much further to travel to get to 'the boats'.

And there was no secret now of what was about to happen. The whole region was teeming with troops and equipment.

Tuesday 18 April. In the afternoon, land-mines (being exploded by RE personnel for safety purposes) brought part of the plaster down from the ceiling of the Orderly Room – 'Private Rendezvous Hotel Middleton.'

Wednesday 3 May. Looking out towards the sea tonight, saw, away on the horizon, a miniature fleet of invasion barges. Felt quite awe-stricken for a second or two. Thought 'History in the making!' and all that sort of thing. Meanwhile, air activity over the coast here seems to increase day by day. As we watched tonight, there would be about forty aircraft zooming about in the sky, in all directions.

Thursday 4 May. Invasion rehearsal on the beach here, by Commandos and other troops. Smoke screens, etc.

With all this realistic battle-practice going on around us, day by day and much of it at close quarters, the timing and direction of our next move became ever more of a certainty. In a few weeks, we would be crossing the Channel, headed for France. Nothing could now intervene. For the first time, the sequence of coming events was entirely predictable. Or was it? Out of the blue and with strange urgency, six of us found ourselves dispatched northwards again, to resume surroundings of, by now, unaccustomed peace and quiet, in the area surrounding horse-racing's Newmarket!

The other five were 'storemen', leaving me as the only 'clerk' partaking of this mysterious emergency. As with most other military switches of intention, it was entirely unexplained, even to letting us know whether the transfer was temporary or permanent. ('Simply, do as you're told!' was the most petrified in rigidity of all the Training Camp dogmas.) As a result, it felt as if, scooped out of the heat of the frying pan that was Middleton, I was being served up uncooked on to a lukewarm plate, for no other reason than to cool down again.

In line with what was, I suppose, my 'organised retreat' from those last-minute front line preparations down south, the Unit to which I had now been posted was designed to lie further to the rear of the supply-line chain than had ever been the role of '107'. 'ADOS [Assistant Director of Ordnance Services] 30 Corps Troops' was revealed to be in charge of a much more substantial affair, saddled with holding the bulk stores from which smaller, more mobile branches of the Corps would be replenishing their stocks in a battle situation. I supposed that, because of its own resultant bulk, it would not be so early in the queue for France, but, clearly, there was a panic around the place to get everything fully shipshape before the start of things. If I had needed proof of the importance of this, it came only a day or so after my arrival when, as dusk fell (and after a normal day's work), we started a mammoth job of checking all the stores against record cards and the like. Knowing that the work simply *had* to be finished by early the next day, we toiled on throughout the night, only 'dotting the last i's and crossing the last t's' at almost eight o'clock in the morning. Despite my having near-vomited with tiredness around two after midnight, the diary preens itself in recording that, at downing of tools, I had seemingly recovered to the freshness of paint!

Assuredly, the activity here could be as frenetic as Middleton's. On the other hand, the overall ambience seemed a throwback to Swaffham. How uneventfully quiet it was out of doors! Even further in spirit than the miles from those landmines and Commandos and invasion barges of the mounting climax way down on the coast. Present surroundings had the slight edge on Swaffham, nonetheless, with Cambridge close enough at hand, I found, for the spending of a few hours 'time off' in renewal of my friendship with the place. Perhaps that recent taste of battle atmosphere had infected me with carelessness. Or had it been mostly ignorance, when circumventing the niceties of a 'leave of absence' pass? I was shown, at any rate, that my curse of permanent innocence to my features might, just occasionally, be of advantage. Accosted sternly by red-capped Military Police, I was let off with a caution.

In a way, the incident symbolised my disorientation by recent developments. I no longer had much idea of what would happen next, or even with whom I might be sharing the experience. At Middleton, amid first-hand demonstrations of the likely latter stages of the War, I had almost got to the boarding of one of the landing crafts; whereas, up here, I was back amongst the planning and preparation stages of the affair, with the renewed availability of civilian entertainments and enjoyments contributing to my general befuddlement. I find myself recording, for example, the imminent arrival in Cambridge of Myra Hess with her veritable jewel of a piano recital, as well as sadness at train timings making it impossible for me. There was, nevertheless, a slender aesthetic straw for grasping at Newmarket itself, when I discovered the meeting place of its gramophone society. Clinging to my last shred of artistic pretensions, I shuffled into a school hall, miserable enough in its own right, which had managed to achieve absolute pathos by the level of its existing audience – five solitary individuals who provided, I suppose, a damning verdict on the possibility of recapturing a lost world of yesteryear. (Yet I was still able to marvel that the RAF man who was running the recital should come from Jarrow, on Tyneside, and even to revel in his subsequent offering to us – a broadcast of Beethoven's 'Choral' Symphony, on the school's wireless set.)

In these circumstances, the next fortnight was largely indistinguishable from a couple of months, and when the Newmarket concern had finally collected itself together to the point of readiness for the road, I had the sense of being quite well rooted into it; securely enough, certainly, to consider it my permanent niche in the design of things for the coming campaign. This appeared to be confirmed on Wednesday the 3rd of May, when the six of us moved down to Middleton in concert with the rest of them; leaving Newmarket at 11.30 in the morning, yet ('owing to one or two mishaps'!) not reaching the South Coast until ten that night. Not for the first time, however, I was wrong in my assumptions. ADOS 30 Corps Troops transpired to be as much of a red herring as Burma had, previously.

> *Monday 5 June.* Rejoined 107 Armoured Ordnance Sub-Park. Sorry to leave the ADOS Unit. In the morning, collected various things from the QM Stores, such as vomit-bags, life-belt, and anti-louse shirts and drawers. Started work after dinner and (as now usual with '107') did not finish until nine at night. Lots still to be done – checking off account cards with the actual stores in the binned lorries. Tremendous number of spare parts, etc.

Following this entry, my diary mentions, significantly, that 'Arthur Protheroe, who was on guard at night, reported the sky absolutely crammed with aircraft. He couldn't see them of course in the dark, but there was the sound of them, and their lights.'

We were, without doubt, firmly back again in that frying pan, with events around us (and above us) moving swiftly to a conclusion – or, more properly, their long-awaited beginning! When dawn broke, I was to have an item of quite momentous excitement to proclaim.

Tuesday 6 June. Heard this morning that the invasion of the Continent has begun. All day the air activity over this coast area has been terrific. About eight o'clock in the evening, very large fleets of planes towing gliders went over continually, for half an hour or more; and in the meantime squadrons of fighters were coming over, from both directions. Goodness only knows how many aircraft I've seen today. Finished work just in time to hear the King's speech on the wireless, at nine o'clock. (NB We *start* work nowadays at half seven in the morning!)

From now onwards, the recurrent bane of 'waiting' took on a different complexion to the varieties which had pursued me spasmodically throughout the War years. Though there was more of it than ever – continuous, you could say, from one day to the next – it turned into a series of expectations of something developing within hours, rather than days or weeks. And when, yet again, nothing came about, the fact that everyone else was in the same boat (or, more precisely, ready for jumping into the first one available) stifled all frustration. In any event, we knew full well the reason for the continuing hold-ups – the weather! Who could ignore it? – the sheer, concentrated malevolence of the brute, in its present mood! For half a century, the history books have highlighted the ferocity which almost wrecked the whole affair at birth, yet no description has exaggerated. The very clamour of those gales – lashing the Channel into an extra, boiling vortex of a German defence – advertised the near-impossibility of safe landing Commandos, let alone 'sitting ducks' of back-up troops like us. This made the new chores of waterproofing the underbellies of all our vehicles so obviously vital that grumbles, over muscle-strains or sheer exhaustion, became trivialities of the past. With each day came new, distracting possibilities of the weather suddenly clearing, to set us on our way. Just as important was the squeezing of spare time available to us for doubting our chances of ultimate survival; and the newspaper reports of successes in the initial onslaught made romantic and reassuring interpretations for us of the start of the bloodletting.

At the time, the storms were seemingly never ending, but, in reality, it was only a matter of days before they had subsided to the mere misery of the cold, drizzling rain of Friday the 9th of June. That day introduced a further twist to my preconceptions. From recently imagining myself a permanent member of the ADOS squad, my present, revised belief was surely better founded – that I was now finally settled into the cohesion of the self-contained, single entity that was '107'; both for the crossing and the campaign to follow. I was, on the contrary, to record that 'Numbers 1 and 3 Sections of the Unit left us today for the "big trek". We cheered them as they set off in the morning, knowing that, in all probability, we'll not see them in France at all. Queer, as we're all the same Unit and all that!'

The remainder of us were told that we would follow them in a week's time; dependent, of course, upon the scale of disruption which the weather had actually wreaked upon first schedules. Encouragingly, the British climate soon developed second thoughts, relapsing into a state of such friendliness as to suggest the end of further delays for which it would take the blame.

Wednesday 14 June. At ADOS, pay-day was every Wednesday, whereas here it is once a fortnight on Fridays. However, today was an exception. We were paid at five this afternoon, in French coinage. Two hundred francs per man – and in addition I got ten-shillings-worth of English money exchanged for 100 francs. Last night we were working until after eleven o'clock, but today we finished at six. Everything now ready for the road; lorries lined up ready to move off, office equipment packed up, etc. My own personal kit, too, is pretty-well ready for dumping on to the lorry. Went over to Bognor at night, and collected soap, tooth-paste, shoe polish, etc. from the NAAFI. Walked back to Middleton, as it was lovely weather. When I arrived back at the billet, heard that after all we'll *not* be moving off tomorrow. Slept quite well, considering that the bed was harder than usual: we handed in palliasses and bolsters to the QM Stores early this morning. My lifebelt, however, made quite a useful pillow.

Thursday came and went, without a glimmer of green light for the possibility of moving off, even next day. Friday, in fact, arrived (after a second night of acclimatisation to rock-hard floorboards) with all the appearance of resigning us to stultified readiness for quite a few more days. It must have been fully tea-time, before we learned of the extra-early wakening which had been scheduled for us for the

Of Straw And Stripes

Saturday morning.

Saturday 17 June. Am writing this just before leaving Middleton – at 5.30 in the morning. It's still quite dark, and an air-raid siren has sounded just as we're due to move off; probably some German pilotless plane coming over. (They've been using them now, apparently, for some three days.)

Monday, 19 June. Arrived at the marshalling area on Saturday – with one or two mishaps to truck on the way. We collected our special ration packs etc. from the stores yesterday, and are now only awaiting the signal 'Go!' Owing to a last-minute change of plans last night, I had to switch my kit from the three-tonner 'Chev' on which I was travelling to the big crane-lorry. Thus I and five others will be going over in a different 'boat' to the rest of the Unit.

By now, my unadulterated ignorance of the colossal organisation needed for modern warfare (even just to start it off) had been fully exposed; my fond imagination, in relation to our journey out of Middleton, that it would, somehow, lead straight on to the landing crafts – which, in turn, would simply zip straight off with us. Across the Channel in a flash, as it were. The idea that there could be yet another intermediate stage of a so-called 'marshalling area', had never occurred to me. Hadn't we, after all, been 'marshalled' already? What else could that order at Swaffham to head south have been? Incredibly, I realised that we were to endure a further species (however brief) of the 'waiting game'!

The extent of my misconceptions was graphically illustrated by the size of territory needed for this final processing of Second-Front reinforcements. And by what appeared a countless accumulation of substantial bell-tents – infinitely more impressive than all the wigwams, put together, from the simulated Red Indian villages of Hollywood Westerns.

A few of them became the Unit's home for the week to follow. Gradually, I came to appreciate the extraordinary depth and detail to the vast organisation now surrounding us; some of it, not at all limited to essentials, even extending to the near-Utopian luxury (in these circumstances) of entertainment itself! A particularly battered-looking version of a Nissen hut transpired, on entry, to be a more than acceptable cinema – as well, apparently, as the venue for occasional gramophone recitals; whilst a positive marquee of a larger tent housed a troupe of ENSA performers, enlivening rapt audiences with a show entitled *All Aboard*. For many passing through on their way to France, these may have been the last relaxations they were ever to enjoy; and in a place like this, with spare time no longer rationed, the emphasis was evidently on leaving as little of it as possible unoccupied, against the supreme danger of too much thinking. (Psychologically, there was also the 'dangling-carrot' of an effect that, when the fighting was over, such refreshments would be waiting for us once again, as normalities.)

Wednesday 21 June. Another day of complete leisure, spoilt for most of us by the fact that, having changed much of our English currency into French (for we were given the impression we'd be here no longer than a couple of days), we're 'stony broke'. I myself, at any rate, can't order a penny cup of tea at the NAAFI without first feeling doubtfully in my money-pocket. Finished reading *The Under Dog*, by Agatha Christie. A rather disappointing book. (News – Cherbourg Peninsula now cut off, Americans only 3½ miles from Cherbourg itself. Russians seem to have defeated the main Finnish Army.)

Sunday 25 June. The remainder of the Unit (with the exception of the four or five who are travelling over with me by a different boat) left the Camp for the port of embarkation. They set off about eleven at night, after being provided with a decent hot supper. Our tent looked and felt empty: I was now the only occupant.

Perhaps poor Mrs Christie was unfortunate in the writers with whom she was being compared. Out of the elevation of the soul which a background of warfare brings to private thoughts – prodded by the constant, nagging imagination of a much earlier death than Nature ever intended – can come the urge to sample the better outpourings of the human spirit before it's all too late. Or so it was for me. One of the few luxuries tucked away in my kitbag, from the very beginning, had been the Everyman edition of *A Century of English Essays*. Here and now, inside this unlikely bell-tent of mine, there must surely have been some sort of ghostly literary influence pacing the grass floor. At any rate, I suddenly found myself to have frolicked merrily through large chunks of Charles Lamb, Dr Johnson, Leigh Hunt and William Hazlitt, in quick succession. I could sense my soul – or was it my morale? – rising to new heights. Some meaning to life temporarily returned: all by myself in the big tent, that final night, I managed a surprising amount of sleep.

From next day onwards, the waiting game – the months, the years of it – was a thing of the past.

Monday 26 June. I'm writing this at ten o'clock in the evening. We're in a landing barge, vehicles and all, and we've just this minute set steam from Portsmouth, heading for the open sea and France. We left the marshalling area this afternoon at about two o'clock; an uneventful journey altogether. Having had an invigorating hot supper, I'm just about to get into my sleeping bag and try to get some rest. I've my three vomit-bags conveniently at hand – hope I don't need them! – and my life-belt is harnessed round my chest in regulation style. Regardless of my unusual environment, I've just been reading Charles Lamb's *In praise of chimney-sweepers.* Also (rather ironical as it may prove) Hazlitt's *On the feeling of immortality in youth.* And now I'll finish this writing, and take my last view of the shores of England for a while . . .

Chapter 16

Tuesday 27 June (11.30 a.m.). We are now lying just off the coast of France, waiting for instructions to go in to the beach and land. The sea has turned choppy, and this landing craft is now rolling around in such a way as to suggest I'll be having *another* bout of sea-sickness! We had an uneventful journey last night, and I managed to get almost a normal night's rest, curled up in the driving compartment of this lorry. It was when I got up this morning, however, that I had my first qualms. Thus I've had to avoid even thinking of eatables, so far today.

In the normal course of events, the advent of nausea is hardly a calming influence; but the effect of even the common variety, let alone the sea's additional twisting of its screw, leaves little spare capacity for worrying about other things (even the distinct possibility of sudden death). A trivial enough inconvenience long-term, it exercises a monopoly of purgatory while it lasts. When boarding that barge, a hail of bullets and mortar-bombs had seemed likely to greet us when we eventually got across the Channel. Yet, now, as our vehicles – completely unopposed, in actual fact – were rolling unharmed off the craft, through shallow water and up on to the beach, any relief I might otherwise have had was overridden by the continuing instabilities of my stomach.

They didn't, however, prevent my recognising signs of the furious activities evidently endured by this stretch of the coastline over the past few days. Innumerable tyre-treads scarred the slope of muddied grass leading upwards; and, as my crane-lorry strained its way heavily to top level, I began to see the scores of miniature (nine-inch) wooden 'markers' now encrusting the sides of the roadway. Each demonstrated the general direction of a unit or regiment which had already established its claim on this small sliver of France. Amongst them, there was never a sight more welcoming than the picture of that perky little jerboa of ours, pointing its particular way onwards for us. This was organisation, I thought, at its very best!

But it was no time for considered thought. The background of sound to which we were now introduced needed none, in any event. It arrived as almost unbroken, near-distance salvos from batteries of heavy artillery; which were to provide for us, from now on, their constant, atmospheric reminder of the nearness of the front line, as well as the congested and slippery nature of this mere fingerhold on Europe.

That first day was taken up by just collecting ourselves into some sort of order, in expectation of a further move to where we would be setting up shop as a supply centre for the forward troops. So far as trivialities like sleeping quarters were concerned, it was first-hand experience in making do; and eventually – every one of us now foraging for himself – I settled down for the night beneath one of the ten-tonners, as good a potential raincoat as I could conjure up. As it happened, the weather kept dry. Instead, on waking, I found my battledress blouse incurably saturated by what must have been a heavy shower of oil, from the brute's stormcloud of a leaking sump! Circumstances, however, graded even that as trivial, and, in any event, we were soon transferring ourselves to a more permanent location.

> *Thursday 29 June.* We're now stationed just outside of Bayeux, in Normandy. Our Unit is functioning in what seems to be a typically long and narrow field. I say 'typically', for several things seem to be 'long and narrow' round here. For example, the nearby main road is a straight and a long one, and fairly narrow into the bargain; and it's lined on both sides by rows of tall, 'narrow' (if you can use the word) trees. The cattle which are continually grazing around, and conscientiously munching up our camouflages of leaves and twigs as quickly as we put them up, are, however, fat and well-nourished-looking beasts.

I am prepared to swear to that particular field being the greenest and freshest, the most lush and the sweetest-smelling piece of turf I've ever encountered. As it turned out, I had oceans of time to decide upon its virtues, since it remained our one and only operating base for exactly a month, while we waited expectantly for our next movement orders. Indeed, in common with the rest of the British forces, we were to be restricted to this small Normandy beach-head, as a whole, for an eternity

Of Straw And Stripes

of ten weeks; a tenancy which the map now insists can only have been a lurking nightmare of terror for the lot of us – breeding from ever-increasing pessimism against the safety of the outcome.

Which is nonsense. It was nothing of the sort. By now, we had absolute faith that this veritable crusade of a war would soon end with a suitable welter of overwhelming German defeats. The difficult bit was done; we were established on European soil (however little a patch of it); and Germany was there before us for the taking – a matter of weeks or months at most. Certainly, that persistent, cannon-fire timpani, night by night, rammed home the realities of life versus death, but it never sounded anything like the rolling of execution drums. On the contrary, it encouraged our imaginations; an advance sample, it seemed, of the climactic orchestral crescendo which would usher in the last act of the whole affair – the 'attack to finish all attacks' (and most of the other hostilities to boot). The petrified nature of our Normandy adventure puzzled us at times, but that was all. Obviously, we concluded, there must be the need to build up even more overpowering reserves of weaponry and stores. We were all much too busy for pessimism.

No propaganda that had ever been thought up could have produced morale of this vintage. Rather was it the evidence of our eyes and senses. We already had first-hand comprehension of the colossal scale of troops and material being flung into the Invasion; but it was the 'negative' side of things – the non-events – which taught most significantly the changing balance of the War. Where, for example, was the German Luftwaffe? Hardly one of its planes to be seen, near or far! (How well must those hordes of RAF fighters, throbbing the skies above Middleton, have done their jobs!) A year back, a percentage of supply units such as ours could have expected to be dive-bombed out of existence, or disrupted into uselessness; whereas here we were, safe, sound, relatively untouched, and with only the impossibly long hours of hard, slogging work as our immediate enemies!

Yet they were cruel taskmasters. Were we, in fact, up to lasting the pace? The thought – repetitious after the first hectic week or so – was stupid, for we had of course no option: short of the shame of falling forward in a dead faint, there was nothing for it but to keep going. Better (we secretly imagined) than falling properly dead against enemy machine-gun nests. Or was it? In a strange way, it was indeed a subsidiary trial of strengths, not with the Germans, but with the drivers of the smaller, front-line OFPs, who now regularly assailed us with their requisitions for ever more urgent spares and replacements. At any rate, there couldn't be a doubt of how vital a cog we were already, in this, the Army's corporate, strength-building machine. At the same time, however, our own strength was being systematically sapped, not in the materials (the engine assemblies and the like) which the storemen were pouring by the truckload out of our 'binned lorries' – replenishments were swiftly collectable from Base Depot – but in the sheer stamina of human flesh. Of Churchill's 'blood, sweat and tears', we had so far been spared the bloody part of it, but our sweat was being measured in gallons, and at times I wasn't quite so sure about the tears, either.

Whilst diaries of my (time-rationed) wartime sort had to concentrate on facts – with thoughts and opinions put to one side as luxuries – letters home could only be the reverse, since censorship was always around to obliterate any juicy morsel of the slightest interest to the enemy. Unexpectedly, I had first-hand confirmation of every one of those I wrote to my sister Hilda; when, at her death some years ago, I found them all securely preserved amongst her most personal belongings. They still exude all the pent-up emotions of the War; self-confessions more extrovert by far than would have come from me in normal times, often naively immature into the bargain to the point of juvenility. Most of all, however, they sparkle with reassuring light-heartedness; especially those written from Europe, when I find myself dismissing hardships as ephemeral trivia, or not even mentioning them. During our very first day in that Normandy field, I was, for example, seemingly overflowing with cheerfulness.

> Dear Hilda – I received a whole bunch of letters, mostly from you, this teatime; and, spreading myself out luxuriantly on the grass, I spent a glorious half-hour wading through them. This was the first time I had heard from any of you for almost a month, and believe me it *does* make a difference! I'm writing this sat in the open air, fresh-smelling grass all around me, my knees serving me as a desk, and an empty petrol can as my seat. In front of me is a lorry in which I've only just finished making myself an improvised bed for tonight. I've tried to lessen the hardness of the floor by using a combination of one blanket, a greatcoat, and a change of underwear padded between them as a mattress.

In the course of the incredible five pages to this particular, pencilled effort, I make no other mention of myself except – in the second half of it (written the following day, with four further letters from home under my belt) – to record the newly sanctioned information of our being 'somewhere in France'. (Not, I imagine, an especially startling revelation, given the preemptive reporting of the newspapers.) I was evidently more obsessed with keeping my family's hearth fires blazing away as brilliantly and free from care as sentimentality would now have me believe normal. Most of my letter, for that matter, comes through as positive 'reverse propaganda'; very much of a 'pep-talk', you could say – written as if it were I and not they who had been left behind in the safety of England. An epidemic back there of head-colds and days off work provoked my concern for 'taking care of themselves' (with the boost of a tonic), while my sister, in particular, found herself firmly admonished to 'get more rest and relaxation', as well as to quench that conscience of hers at still being a civilian. Roughing it out here was only the luck of the draw; I would have felt guiltless the 'other way round'; and so on, and so on. Undiluted sermonising, all of it, in which old age can now recognise the supreme patronage of youth!

Whatever the degree of happy leisure which the multiplicity of families back home, each tending their hallowed hearth on our corporate behalf, may have inferred from these literary masquerades – for I'm sure the others wrote in the same vein – there is my factual journal, still in front of me, to redress the balance. It is in no doubt: the pressure of the work hour by hour, and the sheer length of it day by day, was each as heinous as the other. So much so, that our moments of spare time, precious to a fault, were often entirely negatived by the very writing of the letters themselves – which can never have conveyed anything of our yawns or that constant background tapestry of the gunfire.

It says much, indeed, for the level of stamina which had been forced into us that whilst, on the 13th of July, there is an entry recording the arrival around us of three or four subsidiary OFP units, bringing some easing of the pressure in peak periods, I still thought our stipulated 'hours' worthy of mention as unchanged and unchangeable facts of life. They ran from eight in the morning until nine at night, with only the main mid-day meal to justify a break of any consequence. Admittedly, mind you, we now rejoiced in the luxury of a newly arranged roster of 'early nights', a turn for one of which arrived every four or five days. This temporary escape could be made no earlier than quarter past six into the evening; but it continued to assume the aura of a quite unbelievable treat!

The work was one long, patterned routine. The requisitions came in; were checked for availability; were authorised; were passed to the storemen for issue. Then more requisitions, and yet more again. (On one morning alone, I have it that we received no fewer than two hundred – of what had become veritable paper-locusts!) Everlastingly intermingled with all this was the 'immediate' (somehow – anyhow) making of time-space for the ordering of replacements. It was a non-heroic side of mechanised warfare which would never make the history books.

At the same time, we weren't in danger of descending into boredom. The constant, throbbing anticipation of something decisive about to start saw to that. As early as three days after our Normandy arrival, I was noting: 'This evening, a very large fleet of planes went out towards the enemy lines. Looks as if a big attack from us will shortly be developing.' And then, switching to an item of seeming equal importance: 'Oh, for just one slice of bread with our meals! It would seem the height of luxury! Biscuits, still, in the meantime and yet more biscuits.'

In hindsight, it was an incredibly mixed bag. On the one hand, there was the impressive background of current world news. On the 13th of July (after a full fortnight of pressurised silence), my diary's adrenalin was flowing from the latest instalment of it. 'Caen taken two days ago. Russians surging forward along the whole front, and now threatening Brest Litovsk, after having stormed and captured Minsk.' Ten days later, I was mentioning even headier stuff: '. . . the attempted assassination of Hitler, together with radio reports of internal trouble in Germany, and lightning Russian advances towards the borders of East Prussia.'

Sandwiched between these encouragements is an occasional reminder that the heroic side of affairs might not, after all, have been so very far away. 'A single German plane which came over, a few nights back, dropped a land-mine quite near to us, sending part of a petrol dump up in flames. Shrapnel from ack-ack guns continues to be rather dangerous at nights. Tents don't offer much protection.'

None of this pointed to the past. Yet, on another level, the signs were there of the astonishing diversity and fine detail of planning which had preceded the Invasion, with terms of reference evidently unrestricted to basics. Even at the start, coming over on the landing-craft, those mere bagatelles of tins of soup, dished out in profusion, had been intriguing. Pull the ring-handle on the lid, and each would magically central-heat in seconds to a near boiling point which – never mind the heart – warmed the very cockles of the stomach! Never since has there been anything in the shops to match them, possibly because the necessity has vanished.

But by far the most astonishing piece of unexpectedness (for this early stage of the campaign) was the availability amongst us of 'entertainment'. Always provided, that is, that its precise location at any point of time could be pinpointed; and, rather more improbably, at one which coincided with the sanction of an extension to the 'early night' roster, for the purpose of the search.

Wednesday 13 July. Last night I was down, with fifteen or twenty others, to go to a concert party given by 30 Corps and Army Troops Sub-Park, only about a mile from here. It was due to begin at eight o'clock, but by the time our lorry had lost the way and taken the wrong turning once or twice, we found ourselves by mistake at a concert being given by Rear HQ, 50 Division (which had started about *seven* o'clock). Thus we missed half the show, but what we did see was first-class, almost up to professional standard.

In juxtaposition to the daily grind, enjoyment of anything faintly resembling escapism was, I suppose, bound to have swollen to something like our present exaggerated exuberance. Here, a nursery rhyme would have excited applause; and it went without saying, therefore, that the glory of bawdy nonsense on offer was cheered uproariously onwards to its inevitable encores. Unfortunately, while this 'War adrenalin' served to heighten pleasures of the sort, I never sensed it alleviating any of life's mundane unpleasantnesses – such as that visit to the Field Dressing Station at Bayeux, or the toothache from one of my molars which had forced me into it. Just like the sea-sickness of the crossing, neither was improved in the slightest by thought of more serious potential disasters.

Whilst, amid its preoccupation with war-wounds, the Army did cater for dental treatment, it was necessarily of the emergency variety only.

Of Straw And Stripes

There was only the one cure for my trouble. Out it came, without ceremony; and out I came into the fresh air, to walk back to Camp. Perhaps it was expecting too much to have nothing but the residual throbbing of my gums to bother me. But I have it recorded that 'of course, this Normandy weather of rain when you'd least expect it had to decide to reveal itself in true, typical vein. I was wet through to the skin when I arrived at Camp; where I found a *very* seasonable letter from Hilda, describing how *she* had got similarly soaked only a few days before. This wasn't really much comfort, however.'

Neither was the necessity to get dried out as quickly as possible, for the resumption of a work-load which by the 17th of July, I report:

> ... has again become simply terrific. It develops into a battle for who is the master – you or it. Seems that Seventh Armoured will be on the move in a few days time. Is this going to be the big push, I wonder? The Workshops etc seem to be getting themselves nicely stocked up with spares. Only hope things ease off when the Div. does get moving. No-one can keep up this amount of work and these long hours indefinitely!

Had I but known, the unexpected length of our continued imprisonment in Normandy – in contradiction of the sweeping German defeats now materialising on far-off battlefronts, and of recent American successes in the nearby Cherbourg Peninsula – was to put my assertion severely to the test.

Chapter 17

Now, by this time, you will be thinking that Army life (post-Borehamwood) must have become vacuum-like. Bereft, that is, of surrounding humanity – or, at any rate, specimens of it which were fit even to lick the boots of the Gilgallons or the Watsons, Pratts or Kemishes alike of this world. Or, in her case (and putting it more decorously), just to polish the shoes of that most beguiling girl Edith Lees. Certainly, in my innermost thoughts, there could be no-one to take *her* place. She was an unfinished part of my life that would now, alas, never ever be realised.

The War itself was the vital ingredient of each half of our personal equation: I see that, now. Peculiarly, the unholy global strife bred spare-time romances never otherwise possible; meetings that could never have occurred; emotions which would have been muted in normal conditions. With 'Fate' seemingly so often involved, and irresistibly so. But, where I was concerned, there was also the irresistible grinding into me of the belief that I was down at the very bottom of the heap in everything; a nobody – least equipped of all around for making a way for myself in the Services, and one who had succeeded no better in civilian life. In that County Court Office, my office-boy ranking had seemed terminal; and here I was again, surrounded by people sporting 'stripes' of all varieties, to show up the unchangeable starkness of my own sleeves. I had no faith whatsoever in my future. Or in being able to maintain an interest in me, *in absentia*, of a thoroughly attractive and normal young woman like Eddie. Certainly, we corresponded; but the letters soon tailed off – perhaps surprisingly, from my side of the affair not hers. The final death-knell – little could she have realised – came from the cheerily conveyed information of her acceptance as candidate for an ATS Officers' Training Course. That was effectively to nail me down into a coffin of absolute inferiority; ruinous to an unsure youngster like me.

Not that there was much of a conscious decision about it. What difference, after all? For, by now, variety of gender was an obsolete concept for us, girls and women having become generally unrecognisable commodities – apart, that is, from the occasional reminder of a Betty Grable pin-up, displayed jealously here and there for the maintenance of individual sanities. The total removal of the previous delectable, leavening distraction of those ATS might have been expected, I suppose, to highlight such new personalities as were surely somewhere around. Certain was it that – when found – only they could now constitute the staple food of memory.

As so often, reality was the other way round to supposition. It became evident that it was the catalyst of femininity within The Grange which had sparked interest in the rest of it, even in its menfolk. By contrast, this present all-male diet, unrelieved, seemed devoid of all individuality to the verge of cloned dullness. It was Richmond all over again; only worse, since there was no promise this time of any future, more stimulating posting.

Monday 23 July. Just returned from a half-day visit to Bayeux. Not really worth the trip: much too many troops in much too small a town. I decided all this last week, funnily enough, but somehow felt that *this* time there would be something worth buying in the shops. What a hope! All I managed to buy on my last visit there was a couple of picture postcards of Bayeux Cathedral – but at any rate there *was* the Cathedral itself to explore. (And the NAAFI Canteen -- about a mile and a half the other side of Bayeux – to find.) Whereas, today, nothing fresh remained to amuse me. Surging crowds of khaki, khaki, and still more khaki.

It was just as well for all of us that we were mostly worked off our feet. Sheer tiredness was a much better antidote than bromide against sex-frustration. The general roughness of life helped, additionally, by elevating occasional, trivial comforts into the category of Heaven-sent, rapturous, distracting luxuries. Such as, that same evening, the unexpected arrival of Hygiene, in the shape of a hot shower-bath! This was, I recorded, 'the result of the efforts of one or two of the more ingenious of the Unit, who, a day or so ago, erected an intricate, mechanical contraption in the middle of the field – a sight infallibly reminiscent of one of Heath Robinson's dreams. Anyhow, the main point is that it *does* work, and that the water *is* hot.' For once, in contrast

Of Straw And Stripes

to the undisturbedly grubby state of my long-johns, I was able to sleep that night minus every drop of my normal residual body-sweat.

This welcome refreshment was a 'one-off', as they say, so far as I was concerned. I had had my turn, and there weren't many of those going around, since, amongst other things, heating the water involved a certain degree of filching from our petrol supplies for the necessary combustion. There was, however, nothing at all wrong with the creature's functioning. A large tin box, suspended over the 'bathroom', had had a series of holes bored through one of its sides, enabling the pulling of a rope to heel it over and evacuate the contents most deliciously downwards through the apertures. What has since beaten my less than scientific brain is the theory which was behind the non-spillage, through those side-vents, *before* the thing was tilted! At any rate, its efficiency was perfect; worthy indeed, we thought, of any respectable peacetime patent for commercial success. Perhaps, in fact, it was this demonstration of hidden brainpower which finally persuaded me. There must be more around me than mere anonymity – masculine though the exceptions might necessarily be.

Yet, of the new characters which gradually eased themselves into my memory cells, the first – more of a push, in their case – were simply the possessors of those all-important 'stripes'; contributors of nothing at all, I'm sure, to the invention, save, perhaps, the blindness of their eyes to small amounts of disappearing petrol. 'Tug' Wilson had three of the precious decorations and 'Taffy' Evans two, making it a near impossibility to blank out either man for very long. (The stampings of boots on drill-square concrete might be of the past, together with the bellowed commands which had prompted them, and the surfeit of required saluting of commissioned ranks – now reserved chiefly for 'pay parades', when there was at any rate a reward for it! – but it was still of supreme importance to do as one was told; with stripes as telling as ever they had been.)

There can be no doubt that, of the two men, only Wilson was anything of a military stereotype. A smallish individual – I can't remember any sergeant greatly above average height – he had all the solid, bouncing, muscled bombast that seemed to go with the triple insignia. He had only just been promoted; and, in my innocent naiveté, I vaguely wondered why. What was his particular talent? How, indeed, did anyone get to be promoted to anything? I was again on the outside, looking in, with years yet before I could finally credit his secret; the most important

Of Straw And Stripes

ingredient of all – that absolute, bigoted, belief in himself, the unquestioned, inner certainty of being so much better than everyone else. Having said that, he breezed cheerfulness with it; positively effervescing as he bustled around all over the place, a half-smile on his face even with his most unwelcome orders. The idea of not 'jumping to' any of them being quite unthinkable, he was, I suppose, the unstoppable force amongst us; the principle reason for any sergeant's existence. And I remember him now, at the end of the road, almost with affection.

Whereas, in his case, there had been nothing at all dislikable or distrustable about our Corporal Taffy from the very beginning. Admittedly, the protective paperwork of his administrative stint was there to save him (and us) from the need for any further salvos of verbal fireworks on top of Tug's. But, in any event, by nature he was one of the few NCOs I ever came across who asked rather than demanded; the persuasive authority of his deep, calm, cultured, Welsh lilt invariably proving sufficient in itself – quite as effective as the standard, more explosive Army techniques.

Of course, it helps to have a presence to complement the voice, and Taffy didn't fall short. Beneath that generous topping of flowing waves of brown hair were strongly-chiselled features, softened by slight chubbiness, whilst his well-built, thickset frame carried just a suspicion of tubbiness to match; the whole adding up to an aura of educated dignity quite unsuited to his stripes – more the prototype of a commissioned officer than the mere bagatelle of a corporal. Whereas Tug Wilson was typical of many an Army sergeant since seen at the cinema in comedies about the Services, the only reminder of Taffy, shortly after the War, has been the film portrayal of the younger edition of Colonel Blimp. Which is not to suppose that circumstances were always conducive to maintaining this level of serene poise.

Saturday 12 August. Yesterday evening, someone remarked to me that we'd just had the funniest 'pay parade' he'd ever known. It was certainly unusual. Imagine us, if you can, crouching in a ditch, officers and men, while German shells, whistling overhead from one of their long-range guns, made us temporarily doubt the importance of those scraps of paper called French francs. Not more than six shells altogether dropped around us, but they were quite sufficient to shake up our nerves for the time being. Anyhow,

Of Straw And Stripes

I received my pay – correct to the franc – 'in the ditch', and everyone lived happily ever after.

I suppose that this terminal exactitude (you might call it) to the episode credited Taffy (whose principal periodic showpieces were the pay rituals) with the retention of, at any rate, a *crouched* variety of poise. But not one of us, certainly, with the least degree of serenity!

However generally admired, these twin temperaments, I think it highly improbable that either had been heard of, let alone comprehended or aspired to, by young Richard ('Dickie') Watts, a carefree twenty-year-old who was destined to be my unlikely friend and travelling companion in that extraordinary journey (just the two of us, only weeks ahead) across the whole belly of Europe. Come to think, he could have been a close relative of Dick Watson, though more loose-limbed and lanky again, and (without an iota of Dick's ambiguity of outward appearance) quite undisguisable in his youthfulness – often near-childish and, at the same time, gloriously irresponsible. He was a country lad from an extremely small village near Oxford, so he told me. A place with a large proportion of its hundred or so inhabitants seemingly bearing the same surname as himself! If, as I have since thought, this implied a sheer bigotry of inbreeding over the centuries, there was also the soothing logic of what must have been, throughout, a happy and contented lifestyle to the whole village; magnetic enough, presumably, to have stifled even the notion of anyone leaving.

Dickie was a strong advertisement for this theory. A more cheerful radiance than the constant flaunting of that flashing smile of his was past imagination. Or was it a broad grin? No! – on reflection, he was mostly laughing outright at something or other; even if, on occasion, it seemed almost a matter of laughing along with Life itself. A commodity with which he seemed always to be on the very best of terms.

Whilst I found this customary exuberance infectious – refreshingly so – there was another side to his coin. My frustration from that revelation of such dazzling brilliance in the teeth he so persistently displayed lingers even yet. Though I had already suspected as much, they gave the final lie to much of what Mother had drummed into me as a child. Her kindly wisdom that the purity of dental whiteness could only emerge from vigorous applications of a toothbrush, her unshakeable prediction of their doomed decay if teeth were but left to themselves for a single day – neither had produced anything more optimistic for me than a light shade of cream, as well as the recent history of a spent molar yanked out so unceremoniously at Bayeux.

Dickie's personal display of dental excellence was, on the other hand, something else altogether. Nothing could be whiter than *his* white; and, whenever I was to chide him for a typically lengthy disregard of his toothbrush, he would light-heartedly ridicule my concern as so much balderdash. Annoyingly, the pristine colour (or non-colour, I suppose) of his teeth insisted, obstinately and exactly, on always remaining the same, even allowing for the slight periodic fading of its top veneer of gleam; whilst, in any event (when he did decide to look for his brush), a mere touch of toothpaste seemed to prove his whole point, with its magical restoration of all the original sparkle.

Now, envy being (as I've always thought of it) a kind of mental infection, it isn't something of which to be proud, and pride itself makes me insist on only rarely having suffered an attack. But I would be dishonest not to admit to a further spasm directed at Dickie. It was in the realm of those impossibilities of mine which turned to basic, everyday, slices of bread-and-butter where he was concerned. His mere slip of a body could perform miracles of vaulting, and jumping, and – most awesome of all – shinning up the tallest of trees with an ease which bordered on disdain. To this day, I'm uncertain of the animal to rival him. A monkey? More probably, when speeding up a tree, a particularly large squirrel. Either way, he was quite out of my league.

For that matter, I cannot think of anything whatsoever which we ever had in common: you could say that he was all body, and I was all mind. Theoretically, indeed, we should have got on each other's nerves; but boredom never entered into it, and I found the other side of life which I witnessed bubbling and bouncing out of him educationally entertaining. We never had a wrong word between us. In a strange way, he gave me hope for the future of mankind. Which, paradoxically, was the reverse of my acquaintanceship with Edney.

That was his surname. What he had been labelled individually, under the blessing of Christ, I am not at all sure. There is a faint suspicion of its having been 'John', but the very doubt illustrates the indefinable aura of being, somehow, out of the ordinary which the man emanated. Plain 'Edney' was what he answered to, at any rate; any embellishment seeming an unnecessary overstatement. And, like Dickie, he was tall and slim, though with a sinewy wiriness which contradicted the relaxed flexibility of the Oxford lad. Securely bespectacled, besides being a follower of the growing fashion around me of shaving the head to total baldness (presumably pursuing hygiene), he presented a remarkable resemblance, I thought, to Gandhi himself. Yet, on first contact – how opposite a pole position to Dickie's! – there were so many facets of his inner persona matching my own, that we should surely have been twin souls throughout.

But the successful mix of personalities lies deeper than amalgamating their credit and debit accounts. Certainly, Edney was brightly literate – very well educated and expensively so, in all probability – with an evident grounding in the kind of culture which appealed to me; a love of classical music in particular (always a welcome contrast to the rough and tumble of Army life). He had widespread opinions, and a measure of humour with which to wash them down into my digestive organs. Yet it wasn't long before I found his talk superficial; too much so for anything so exaggerated as my first level of interest. At the same time, I was recognising the matching surface veneer of the man himself. A protection which allowed him little self criticism, and nothing at all in the way of self-directed wit.

Nevertheless, he got on famously with the rest of the Unit. Not in the least concerned with the depth of his soul, they simply accepted him as a hail-fellow-well-met type who radiated bonhomie to all and sundry. Our hierarchy must have rated him as highly; since, before I knew, he had replaced me as Taffy Evans's assistant on the preferential orderly room work proper to my trade of 'clerk regimental' – shoving me out, instead, amongst the run-of-the-mill 'technical clerks' dealing with routine issues of stores. (Yet another ramming of me, I thought, into my 'proper place' in the deepest available cellar!)

Having thus suffered the overwhelming rebuff of his first, unobtrusive, trial of strength with me, I began to realise the tough mental muscle which undoubtedly nestled beneath his bookish, studious top layer. It made his past history more believable by far; that astonishing involvement in the Spanish Civil War, of all things, only a year or so back! How bloodily involved, he had never made plain. (For all I know there may have been clerks employed there, too.) But merely to have volunteered, in the first place, for the Republican cause against Hitler's clone, General Franco, pushed him light-years further away from my league than the more humanly understandable Dickie Watts ever was. Spain, in its way, had served as advance practice for the present maelstrom; and Edney, I suspect, must – almost bigotedly – have regarded the outbreak of the latter as a goal in itself; the ultimate end of his Spanish tunnel, rather than the beginning of this one of mine – one-tracked, back to civilian life. He was much too single-minded for only an amateur soldier like me.

Maybe it's because, at my present, far-distant point in history, I have the sense of never really 'solving' Edney, that there is a touch of sad nostalgia to his memory. Could it be that I put him too roughly and quickly from my mind as trivially unimportant? Or was the situation in reverse? Either way, he rapidly fades from present viewing of the scene. What, indeed, eventually happened to him? I only know that he wasn't anywhere in sight later on, when, finally unearthed from that cellar of mine, I found myself promoted first to Taffy's job, and, after that, to Tug Wilson's itself!

Chapter 18

If any phase of any war comes to have sense to it, or even a recognisable pattern, it can only be from the pages of some history book. On the field of conflict, there is sight ahead of a hundred yards or so (given clear daylight), with actual understanding of what is going on beyond that horizon – and why – chained to possibility at the level of zero. At the end of this particular War, the wholesale capture of secret German documents resurrected the frenzied, hypnotic commands of Hitler to his Normandy troops against any retreat whatsoever – as little as twelve inches, by implication, constituting unthinkable treachery to the Fatherland. All we sensed at the time, of course, was that, over there in the distance amidst that continuing rumble of battle, there must be the most determined of blockages to the progress of British armour.

The nearest we ever got to the wider scheme of things up front was the 'informed rumour' which would occasionally percolate through to us from that direction. Usually circulating around the early dusk of an evening, it invariably whispered of a big British offensive in the small hours of the following morning. Always convincing, and detailed to the extent of quoting the precise starting-time – I can recall one instance of '2.30 a.m.', and 'three in the morning, exactly' in the others – each bore the true aura of Forward HQ's staff college itself; and when, successively, each then progressed to the disappointment of a damp squib, it was only, we knew, because of some (wisely considered) cancellation of the operation at the last moment. Never was there the possibility of the message having been bogus: this way, I suppose, we allowed hope for the next rumour to be true.

That said, there were several less challengeable signs around of readiness for the big assault upon the Germans – that expected attempt at a complete breakthrough towards the end of the War itself. (Or would it be more of a 'breakout', to start with, from this prison of Normandy?) I have a note, for example (23rd of July), of 'General Montgomery, in some message or other to 30 Corps, [having said] that, should Rommel stand in his present positions and fight the battle out here, the War can be won in the next few weeks. If he doesn't, it should be over in any case by October this year.' This was over-optimism which did morale no harm at all; and, to add to the expectancy, certain disturbances to the hitherto strictly static nature of the Unit were soon to confirm our sense of the climax which was in the offing.

They started with what now has all the semblance of a preliminary, feinted, shadow-boxed jab; back and forward in a flash. Well, not quite so lightningly quick as that – there were four days between the sudden move of us to eight miles past Bayeux, in the direction of Caen, and the finding of ourselves back at our original site – yet, in relation to the heavy transit of bodies and lorries and stores, it must surely rate speedy in its own variety of reflex action! Maybe, it had just been an exercise to prove the effectiveness of our mobility after all these weeks of static permanence. On balance, however, I rate it more the result of some front-line strategy which simply hadn't materialised. There were never to be 'captured documents' to explain trifles like this. Nevertheless, it took a day or so for the proper recapture of our corporate breath, the indents for stores and spare part replacements piling in upon us more relentlessly than ever from the interruption.

Very soon, the 'world news' which my diary was continuing to store, as background evidence for future, more considered reading, predicted further movements from now on as no more than part and parcel of normal life. By the beginning of August, the Russians were at the approaches to East Prussia and Warsaw, and only eighty miles from the border of German Silesia; while the Americans, still 'going great guns' and exploiting their breakthrough into Brittany, had almost reached St Nazaire. Moreover – most significant of all – the enemy was now 'conducting an organised withdrawal on the Caen sector'. Substance for the following entry was not long delayed.

Tuesday 8 August. Likely to be on the move again tomorrow morning, this time definitely 'on the advance'. Place we're going was held by the Jerries only five days ago, and today our advance party reports that a pocket of resistance is giving trouble only some 2,000 yards away. Landmines still knocking around; shells etc. Not too pretty a picture, from the sound of it. But we'll see for ourselves tomorrow. We'll have to pass through Tilly and Villers-Bocage in all probability, so we'll see how they've been knocked around. Very badly indeed, so they say. (World news: Americans, having reached Brest, now making good progress in the direction of Paris. British and Americans now approximately the same distance from the city.)

By dusk of the next day, I was close to exhaustion, yet apparently managing to push myself to quite voluminous comments on the finishing education we had just received. Recalling that my sister and brother Andrew (with his wife) were that day starting a two-week holiday up at Dundee, I mused that it might

... interest them, in after years, to know that, as they were swapping greetings with our Scottish branch of the family, I and the Unit were ploughing our way through Villers-Bocage. Villers, with its heaps of rubble all plaintively trying to tell that they once formed part of a place that was *habitable*; that they were once shops, and streets, and houses. Villers, with its main street giving off clouds of white dust such as to convince that you were back in the days of the Wild West and its covered-wagon trails. Yes, it was a sight to see! Fields which at first seemed ploughed in preparation for next season's crops proved, on closer inspection, to be pitted with RAF bomb-craters every three or four feet. Trees, too, standing drunkenly here and there, their branches askew, like the hair of a person just out of bed in the morning, or, more properly, the tousled head of a heavyweight boxer who, after ten gruelling rounds, staggers punchdrunk around the ring, refusing to admit complete defeat. Yes, Villers-Bocage *was*, and now is not. In slang, it has had it. And now, after a very tiring, very hot, broiling day, I'm turning into bed. We're now stationed, after our trek, in an orchard – the apples aren't yet ripe, worse luck! – almost due south of Villers.

The Normandy climate – only just now, it seemed, the wettest of wet, an unrecommendable mix of mud and misery – was now at the opposite end of the spectrum, an unmitigated sweatbox of stifling heat. There were to be two full weeks to go before we needed again to dislodge ourselves but, amidst the renewed slog of our work-load, I had no time for further writings, except for one brief explosion of despair at the continued assaults upon us of the wasps and horseflies. It was

Of Straw And Stripes

my first experience of the latter, but, though I never *saw* even one of them, the quality of each bite was undoubtedly equal to sudden transfixion of the skin by a meat skewer! As for the wasps, there was an immediate need for the thickest of blindfolds against the dangers of non-hygiene. Rejection of every food item over which they had crawled in their dozens would have resulted in our slow but inevitable starvation. So it was that we learned to treat their probable addition of germs as merely a natural garnish to the rest of the meal. (And never, we found, in the least a harmful one.)

Insects, as part of the enemy, hadn't as yet entered my concept of any respectable battle scenario – except, perhaps, way out in the Burma jungles of that ancient, aborted posting notice of mine. At any rate, mere horseflies and wasps were only minor nuisances as insects go, weren't they? How much worse, had I but known, was the variety which would soon pester us out of our lives in open conflict. On the 20th of August, however, all else paled into triviality in juxtaposition with – as my diary described them – 'the sudden, sensational developments in Normandy'. Before we knew it, these were rattling around our amazed comprehensions with all the speed of light. I was, for example, recording the German Seventh Army as completely broken, part of it encircled near Falaise, and the remainder in full flight to the River Seine, where escape barges were frantically massing. The Allied Air Forces, taking a terrible toll, had already obliterated 3,000 enemy vehicles and 300 of its tanks in only three days. Further afield, the Russians, dealing with German counter-attacks near Warsaw and on the East Prussian border, had put a further 500 tanks out of action.

The battle for Caen now being won, I was soon, in the privileged condition of complete safety, to be inspecting the defunct battlefield. On Wednesday the 23rd of August, I walked round the part of the city which now lasted, I wrote . . .

> . . . only as a collection of bomb-pitted skeletons of houses. I saw great destruction; yet the place is much better than Villers, of which you could scarcely say that even one skeleton remained. Certainly, there is one half of Caen which appears untouched; to judge, that is, from the brief glimpse we had of it as we whirled through in the gathering dusk of Sunday evening [20th August].

Of Straw And Stripes

In support of this supposition, I added my own postscript to Caen's ruins, by also squeezing in a visit to its cathedral, which I 'found almost undamaged. There were two holes in the roof, but that seemed all; and even the glass chandeliers were untouched.' The ghastly, shattered neighbourhood of the place may have given it even greater beauty, to my eyes, than it might otherwise have shown, but I drooled over it, in comparison with its close relation at Bayeux. Though lacking the latter's 'ornamentation, the gilt, and the bright scarlets of the stained glasses', I judged that 'it gained much by its sober, subdued, grey-stoned atmosphere.' It was pleasant to know that worth could still survive carnage; a hopeful sign that Europe might survive the War better than as a mere wasteland.

That previous Sunday, we had left our Villers-Bocage camp at 8 p.m., arriving at Mondeville (one of the outer suburbs of Caen) by ten o'clock.

> It being too dark for pitching tents, most of us slept underneath the lorries. Rain wasn't too pleasant, and neither was the noise and shrapnel from some nearby AA guns. But it wasn't long before we found out the *real* snag of the place – mosquitoes! Since then we've all tried remedies like spraying out our tents with paraffin, and coating our faces and arms with anti-mosquito cream, but the numbers of them are too large for anything like this to be effective. Net result – an average of only two or three hours sleep each night, and great red blibes right over my arms and legs. Some of the chaps have been *really* badly bitten.

Those vicious little devils need more than a line or two of typescript to do them justice; or, rather, to give rein to what they still deserve from me by way of vituperative loathing. They couldn't really have been insects at all! More like endless fleets of miniature German helicopters, with rotor-blades – or were they, indeed, just wings? – which whirred mercilessly and sadistically, just above my skin, in careful selection of an area suitably juicy as a landing pad. And when each buzzing stopped – much in imitation of Hitler's new weapon, the flying bomb – the silence was then dread warning enough. Yet another disaster was at hand, albeit one with the usual delayed effect to it – for their actual bite was just a pinprick of any respectable horsefly's. Did I *feel* it much at all, for that matter? It was a question of fuming helplessly at the disfigurement probably in course of infliction – and then having to wait for the light of morning and a mirror to confirm it. All of this, moreover, amidst the sweatiest, the dampest, the clammiest atmosphere that any mosquito could have dreamed for, even in the nearby swampland which had bred it in the first place.

For, without warning, the climate above us had once again reverted to type; the intense, baking sunshine which had emphasised the dryness of the heat giving way to copious lashings of water, cascading almost nonstop from an uncompromising sky. There was rain and yet more rain; mud and yet more mud. The most wretched conditions of all since we parted company with England. On the first morning of our stay at Mondeville, for example,

> ... we had to get sorted out while the rain was absolutely pelting down. Of course, my groundsheet was in my kit-bag; my kit-bag just had to be on the ten-tonner; two motorcycles, moreover, just had to be lying on top of the kit-bag. Was I wet! The Office penthouses took a deal of putting up, as the rain had temporarily shrunk them; and, when they were up, we had to dig little channels round them to stop the water flooding in and making things really impossible.

That day, I was (sardonically) sure of having had 'the time of our lives'!

After this, you might say, anything would have been an improvement. And indeed, less than a week later – after what was to prove the last of our shadow-boxing capers – we were exuberant over what we considered the sudden, heavenly luxuriance of our new camp, sited this time near the village of Pont L'Eveque, in the general direction of the River Seine. Oh, the clean looks, the clean smell of it all! Back once more in the accustomed cubby-hole of an apple-orchard, this one offered a convincing charade of being so far from bombs, or shells, or the rubble of their havoc, as never to have heard of the concept of war – any war, anywhere – in the first place. And, most importantly, with not a single mosquito in sight (or sound), and only a wasp or two in isolation.

The nearby scene – only yesterday, it seemed, a more than suitable companion piece for the violence of the battlefronts – was now one for turning the quickening pulse of their escalating developments into near-fictional unbelievability. Assimilating the renewed sense of civilisation offered by this new and peaceful sanctuary, how could we properly take in the assertion that all of the Allied front in Northern France was now on the move; or that its advance troops were already nearing Belgian territory? Any more rationally than the reports of Germans, desperately defending, having started to flood both Belgium and Holland? By contrast, on the 1st of September, I was able to register nothing more exciting than a quiet afternoon visit, with Dickie, to nearby Beuzeville; 'a small place, yet surprisingly undamaged by the upheavals and destructions of recent weeks. Plenty of jewellers' shops and cafés – little else. We had a look round, a hot meal, and then a leisurely stroll back to Camp. The good sunny weather made it a pleasant change from Army routine, however.' We were all somewhat confused.

> *Tuesday 5 September.* The front line advances at still faster a pace, and yet, for some reason unknown, we remain here waiting for our marching orders to come through. 7th Armoured Div. is so far from us now that we haven't received a single indent for stores during the whole of the past four days! For all I know, it's probably over the Dutch border by now . . . (World news: Brussels liberated in the past few days, together with Antwerp. British forces operating well over the Dutch border, closing in on the Pas de Calais area, etc.)

In point of fact, we had little to wait before the stultified nature of our current involvement was ended. It was Friday the 8th of September which was to prove the swan-song to our stay in Normandy. Only the day before, no doubt in celebratory foresight, the Fates had prescribed a touch of comic relief for Dick and me, as preparation for what was to come. My diary records:

> I can imagine nothing more welcome or more thoroughly delicious than the bright sunshine which is, at this moment, gloriously spreading over our Camp. Last night, however, we had a deluge of rain, and when I woke this morning, it was to find the inside of the 'bivvy' almost flooded out at one end with pools of rainwater. Problem – how to dry ourselves out. (We had soon fixed the troublesome end so that no *more* swamps would accumulate.) Dick soon had an amazing brainstorm of an idea; which was to

sprinkle a little petrol on the water, set light to it, and so help it evaporate. 'There's nothing to worry about!' he assured me. 'Now, you don't honestly think I'd be fool enough to set us all on fire, do you? I'm only using very little petrol, you know . . .' And so on, until I was thoroughly convinced that his was the very genius of an idea. Well, five minutes later, the scene was almost typical of a vivid film melodrama, where the he-man staggers through sheets of flame to perform the magnificent rescue of an even more magnificent heroine. Except that in our case there was no heroine, and that saving our own skins and property seemed much more important than any deeds of valour. However, no real damage was done, and the flames very soon died a natural death in the sizzling and now stagnant pools of water.

If this little anecdote carries with it a first impact of extreme improbability, touching on actual untruth, it must come from my 'bivvy' seeming to have had the billowing size of one of those Marshalling Area bell-tents, rather than that of the dictionary's 'very small tent'. It was, most certainly, not one of the regular, miniature, one-man variety with which, a week or so after our landing, we had all been issued. Unpromisingly tiny – with a height of barely three feet above ground level – these were, in fact, snug little affairs; that is, as soon as the art of sliding into them was perfected. And with each of us, in his own manner, striving to improvise extra amounts of snugness, I had soon settled for the combination of a spade and a stretcher! The spade enabled me to dig a shallow 'grave', three inches deep, into which the Army stretcher (thick cloth over a stout frame) was carefully lowered. Only then, over and around it, did I erect the bivvy. It was hard and vigorous work which, however, more than paid off in the sumptuousness suddenly and magically acquired by hitherto unsympathetic Army blankets. The whole operation, needless to say, depended upon the existence of the stretcher itself. Where exactly I found it is by now an unsolvable mystery, but it quickly and indisputably became part of my essential earthly possessions, with Dickie's 'ten-tonner' always there for its effortless transit to our next location.

Nevertheless, while this basic item of furniture made for comfortable enough sleep, there had been nothing which could cure the complete lack of space in such a dwarf of a tent. Even turning over to one's other side on that stretcher-bed was a work of art, and sitting upright a clear impossibility. To my way of thinking – Dick's, too – that huge lorry of his, following our last change of location, had developed a sad, impotent look to it. Resting there uselessly at the side of the orchard – lying fallow you could say, until its next test of strength – part of it at least cried out for more continuous use. Why not, then, we plotted, create a kind of 'super-bivvy' out of it? Nothing more than the detachable superstructure would be needed. Lifted down complete with its weatherproof tarpaulin and planted securely on the grass, it could serve both Dick and me as a perfectly reasonable bungalow of sorts. Never mind the sitting bit of the argument, we might even be able to stand up in it as well; and without so much as brushing the thing's roof, either.

It was, therefore, this bloatedly oversized travesty of any recognisable shape of 'bivouac' which so nearly went up in flames that day. The resulting, somewhat smoke-stained ageing of the tarpaulin didn't, however, prevent the prompt resumption of its proper role as the rain-proof skin of the Chevrolet's restored skeleton – prior to the heavy loading of the lorry against the imminence of our next move. On that Friday evening, back again in my own small tent and verging on sleep, there was the sense that, this time, it couldn't again be just a mile or two this way or that. The sparring was over. Time, now, for a leap across the ring into the opponent's very corner. Of the extraordinary length which that leap was shortly to achieve, I had no inkling.

Chapter 19

Sunday 10 September. Written during a halt by the roadside. It's about half past nine in the morning, the sun shining, and everything looking very bright and cheerful. We travelled a hundred miles yesterday; crossed the Seine, and halted for the night at a little village on the road from Rouen to Amiens. Had quite a good night's sleep there, in a barn, and then, wakening to a very frosty morning, we had a substantial breakfast and continued on our way. Some of the three-tonners are temporarily held up until further petrol supplies arrive, but these ten-tonners seem able to go until Doomsday before refuelling. (We started off with 160 gallons of diesel in the tanks, and we've still about 120 of them left.) Rather a painful business, however, ascending hills and slopes, for, with 14 to 15 tons 'on the back', we're badly overloaded.

My journal, by implication, overstates the smoothness of our progress thus far. A hundred miles was nothing compared with the perils of the first twenty yards. Dickie, endeavouring to coax his juggernaut through the orchard's narrow egress, succeeded only in lowering one of the rear wheels into the very bottom of a ditch. Heeling over suddenly and frighteningly, I had split-second resignation to the whole lot of it (including the two of us) actually capsizing – to the inevitability of a more prolonged stay in Normandy than any planner could have intended. At any rate, whilst not so finite a disaster as all that, it was a full hour's job to get the monster on a level keel again and chugging out on to the road. In the meantime, the remainder of the Unit had proceeded on their way without similar mishap, and we were relieved, as much as in anything else, when we finally succeeded in catching them up. This short experience in individualistic pathfinding was excellent practice, had we but known, for what was later to develop.

I am not in the least denying, mind you, that things went slickly enough for us that day, once we had joined the rest of the lorries. I was then able to marvel at the open, unblemished, civilised countryside through which we were moving. Understandably, I must have expected signs, here and there, of the German divisions which had been broken during the inferno of the Battle of Caen; derelict tanks and artillery pieces, perhaps, lying by the roadside; the occasional flurry, even, of unsurrendered German troops, sniping away at us – European equivalents, surely, of those Japanese in the treetops of the Far-Eastern jungles. But there wasn't a trace. No enemy material. No Germans at all (live or dead alike). No defence lines. No 'lines' whatsoever. Just oceans of glorious, fresh-aired space. What, I wondered for a flash, had become of the War itself? Had there suddenly been an armistice, of which Top Brass had forgotten to tell us? This scenario, outside Normandy, was as contradictory of the continuing War bulletins as ever had been its apple orchard.

Alternately jolted and rocked and bumped along, as I sat uselessly in the vehicle's lofty passenger seat – even the impossible, front-wheel stepladder of a hubcap (for getting into the thing) was dauntingly chest-high – I had all the time in the world to indulge myself in this kind of fantasy. An occupation which was dangerous, since its hypnotic effect was a somewhat over-relaxed confidence in staying power of the lorry itself. The latter, after all, had more than proved its stamina and balance by surviving the 'ditch test', there was fuel in plenty in the tanks, and its tyres were so colossally stout as to make any idea of a puncture far-fetched nonsense. What therefore, within any reasonable possibility, could now go wrong? The answer arrived during the second day of the 'grand trek'; that same Sunday, the 10th – not very many hours, in fact, after I had completed my breakfast-time (gloriously ignorant) contribution to the diary.

My follow-up entry, unfortunately, was to be of 'a chapter of accidents, the main cause of which was the snapping, one after the other, of the lorry's fan-belts. So that, when we'd unscrewed the fan and [each time] with difficulty levered on a new belt, the rest of the Unit was miles upon miles ahead. We're still hoping to catch them up, one of these days!'

A seemingly impossible pipe-dream, as it turned out, and one from which it took several days for the two of us to waken.

Supplementing this account of Sunday's minor disasters was one of Monday morning's postponement of a much more immediate worry,

Of Straw And Stripes

with the considerate provision of cups of coffee and sandwiches by the tenants of a nearby house – Dick and myself 'both feeling rather empty, as we'd had no supper last night.' Following which, just after midday, came the acknowledgement of a kind of personal chaos.

> Lost in Belgium! Sounds exciting, doesn't it? But in actual fact it's exasperating. We passed through Brussels this morning, and arrived here in Antwerp just before dinner-time. After wangling some rations from a military unit near the road where we're parked, I'm just about to try and seek out some Provost chap or other who (I have a rather vain hope) may be able to tell us where Seventh Armoured Div is, or, better still, our own Unit. What a farce, to send men off on a long convoy trip like this without telling them precisely the spot to which they're going! The Army system all over again! (Our route was Arras – Tournai – Renaux; but, after that, only the vague information of the new Camp being somewhere round about Antwerp and Gent.

The following morning, Tuesday the 12th, found us

> ... just in the middle of having breakfast off our two and only tins of 'bully', [and about to be] off in the direction of Gent. One thing seems certain: no-one around Antwerp seems to know the vaguest whereabouts of the Division. From what I can gather, they must be operating more south than Antwerp. Or are they? Dick and I are properly in a fog. Last night, however, we managed to fill up at an RASC station with a hundred gallons of diesel, so that we're good for many more miles yet.

Following this feeding to saturation point of our huge, mechanised packhorse (for so I had come to think of it), we had settled down for the night not, on this occasion, using the shelter of the vehicle's bulk, but lying unprotectedly outside, sucking in an atmosphere which was both fresh and balmy; the grass our mattress, for a blanket, the sky. We were quite isolated, not really near to Antwerp itself, but only just south of the estuary which adjoins it. Across the water, as I slipped gradually into sleep, came faint, distant rumblings of heavy artillery as sole disturbances of the otherwise awesome, all-pervading silence. It was as if the Creator was trying to illustrate for me the terminal agonies of the War. Nearing its last phases, maybe, but with frenzied paroxysms in plenty still doubtlessly in the pipeline. When my sleep finally arrived, it was to calm an inexplicable sense in me of sad nostalgia. The sunshine which eventually stirred me brought, however, the relief of a world magically returned to optimism – and the comforting sight of Dickie all ready to 'rev up' for our continuing explorations. As it turned out, only a few more were now needed.

> *Wednesday 13 September.* Gent, yesterday afternoon, proved much more successful than Antwerp. In the morning, just before we arrived at Dendermonde, we began to see the old familiar 'Desert Rat' signs by the roadside, and, after much fruitless driving around – nearly destroying one of the smaller bridges with the weight of the lorry – we caught up with our Unit near a place called Buggenhoute. Thus, all's well that ends well.

Our experiences of the past days now assuming a more acceptable place in the general scheme of things, I was quick to register for posterity the scenes and events through which we had travelled. The words seem to have poured from my pen.

> Belgium seems a grand country from what we've seen of it; a clean, healthy and fertile country. During our journeying we've had almost forced on us, from the very friendly civvies, tomatoes (of a size and quality seldom seen in England), pears, apples, grapes, walnuts, plums, cups of coffee, free beers and free wine. There can be no mistaking the look of happiness and relief on everyone's face. They really *are* overjoyed to be rid of the Germans; a fact confirmed by all with whom I spoke. Flemish, I must say is 'double Dutch' [sic] to me, but most of the Belgians speak some degree of French, and quite a few perfect English. If you pick out the best dressed man he's almost certain to understand French.
> And, incidentally, such a display of patriotism as I've never yet seen. Flags in their hundreds are draped from most of the windows in Brussels and Antwerp and, for that matter, mostly everywhere else. Red, and yellow, and black, and yet more reds and yellows and blacks, until your very mind seems imprinted with the colours. Notices, too, in the shop windows – 'We thank

our long-expected liberators for their speedy freeing of our dear country,' and so on, all of them with the same intention of gratitude.

Meanwhile, I hear that the Allies are now five miles inside the Reich itself. It recalls the evening when, in the pitch darkness of a moonless night, that French gendarme stepped out of the gloomy mist and waved our waggon on over the Belgian frontier. 'But yes,' he had said in his broken English, '*mais oui, messieurs*, the way it is good, *n'est-ce-pas*? *Mais oui,* the way it is good!' And, from what I've seen, the way is, and should be, very good for all mankind . . .

In today's somewhat more blasé society, much of this may be for downgrading to the precipitate over-sentimentalising of a naive youngster. But wartime lets leash torrents of honest, unrestrainable emotion – of the sort which long years of peace (with battle-horrors cushioned for the new generations by safety of distance) can so easily emasculate into sophisticated veneers of present irrelevance. For me, the sentiment, the emotion of the time, lingers still.

Chapter 20

The more that I look back on the War years, the more spasmodic, jerky, and unpredictably jumbled up do they now appear. There have been countless, perfectly cohesive, adventure yarns written around sections of them; but, taken as a whole, they show up as shapeless, certainly so far as the needs go of any saleable fictional saga. To be able to identify a specific starting point to the story, and then trace gradual and progressive heightening of tension, to the traditional crescendo of a once-and-for-all ending, would need the most complex unravelling and pruning of all the stops and starts, the expectations and frustrations. A black nightmare of sorts for any current novelist with designs upon them.

Back there on the spot, as you could say – right in the midst of things – I suppose that we were in the closest position of all to the brilliance of this phase of the grand design for being blinded by it. All those weeks of Normandy and its orchards, peering through each in turn of its assorted tunnels, we had always seen, at the far end, the ferocious struggle for Caen and the hoped-for break-through. When the latter materialised, it was perhaps natural to magnify it into just about *the* climax to the whole War. So that, when it came to our own turn to join in the slicing through of the German lines, the peaceful vacuum we found facing our lorries (with the matching friendliness of the civilians who so often crowded round them) raised hopes of finding a Germany already suing for peace; maybe, even with the formalities of an armistice close to signature. With the wisdom of their hindsight, the history books have long since agreed with this instinctive logic; and we ordinary souls – who didn't credit that the bigotry of one man (dismissive of all logic) could still have either the insistence or the power for prolonging the War – were rudely disillusioned when we perceived not a trace of peacemaking in the offing. What, I wondered, had become of Monty's forecast of an early end to the whole affair? Evidently, Herr Hitler must have dismissed that from his mind as easily

Of Straw And Stripes

as the logic.

Nevertheless, even if we had seemed to be chasing will-o'-the-wisp Germans during this prodigious excursion across Europe, we soon discovered that our 'prey' – apart, that is, from the Unit itself – must really (all the time) have been the work load which we had briefly mislaid back there in France in the last of the orchards. At Buggenhoute, the rest of them had evidently recovered it full two days ago, and Dick and I were accordingly flung into the general frenzy as soon as ever we had unloaded our basic needs from the ten-tonner. It was, from then on, much 'the same as before', the shoals of indents arriving for top priority action signifying not only that the Division was indeed in the near neighbourhood, but seemingly in strenuous conflict with strong German forces of a more seriously factual nature than I had begun to suspect.

It reminded me to feel fortunate that, out of all the changed balances of strength reached by this stage of the War, there had been such a huge switch in the sphere of operations which could have affected us the most. Left with anything substantial from its previously overwhelming muscle, the German Luftwaffe would have been strafing and bombing supply units such as ours all the way from France onwards. At best, we would now be counting our losses; that is, if we had managed to make it at all – or in any condition resembling coherence. As it was, we were intact and unharmed whilst, as that unexpected bonus, there had been the continuous accolades, offered up to us all along the way, as the supreme heroes we most certainly were not. (Slogged hours of hard work, however stamina-sapping, have never yet qualified as deeds of valour.) Nevertheless, if nothing else, we were receiving free education, and at first hand, of the glaringly unequal effects of the War on different parts of Europe.

> *Friday 15 September.* Yesterday evening, some of us went into Brussels. It is a city whose brightly decorated restaurants, gently playing orchestras, smartly groomed young men, and fashionably clad young women seem already to have forgotten the War. Indeed, they appear perhaps never to have really appreciated that there has been a War going on. The shop windows still reveal luxuries almost forgotten in England – wrist watches, fountain pens, wireless sets – and the cafés still offer you ice creams of a choiceness known surely only to Italians of pre-War days.

Of Straw And Stripes

But it's unfair to think of the part of Brussels that we saw (corresponding, I suppose, to London's West End) as typical of Belgium. Just as unfair as occupants of the Regent Palace Hotel being representative of the working masses of the Durham coalfields. Anyhow, the dance-halls and theatres are certainly working overtime, and British troops are being fussed over with great enthusiasm, especially by the seemingly well-to-do Belgian girls.

A Belgian commercial traveller, however, with whom we had started chatting, just outside one of the brightly lit ballrooms – the blackout is only partial, here – told us how queer it all seemed to him, who had seen these same crowds laughing and joking with the German officers and men only a fortnight ago. 'Ah! but you know what these young people are!' he said – he spoke perfect English, having had, in pre-War days, occasion to visit London once a fortnight on business – 'They do not understand.' He told us he had served in the Belgian Army in the last War, and that, in his job before this one, he had had much to do in Germany as well as England. Indeed, he said he spoke German almost as fluently as English. 'Many of the Germans, too,' he admitted, 'I found very agreeable, friendly people.'

From what he said, and what we had heard before, we were able to piece together the true condition of Belgium during the German occupation. It permitted of a system of extensive and outrageously priced black markets. If you had the money – probably eighty out of every hundred hadn't, as another Belgian had previously suggested – you could get most of what you required. The wealthy, then, were not much affected by the Germans. The Gestapo didn't interfere too much, and there were even luxuries for you 'under the counter', provided you put your hand deeply enough into your money-pocket.

Out of these vivid impressions of the city and its inhabitants, I still retain my accompanying sense of their being incomplete, and very possibly lop-sided. Europe, above all else, emphasised the millstone of a hindrance which language hangs round the neck of anyone seeking to recognise common truths in common-folk. We talked, of necessity, only to the educated. Ordinary workers, the labouring classes, could speak not a smattering of English to us, nor, for that matter, anything of French, either. Yet it didn't need much imagination to grasp that they had been the ones to bear the brunt of prevailing hardships. And others amongst us, on occasion, were to meet up with English-speakers who had been *personally* educated of the Gestapo's brutality. On the whole, nevertheless, it was crystal clear that Belgium had suffered loads less destruction (material or economic alike) than had France – parts of which, I wrote, 'suggest a country that has yet to recover from her many deep scars of the War. Belgium almost seems, by comparison, *pre*-War – happy and smiling still, so to speak, in spite of all her misfortunes.'

There were, indeed, so many pleasures for savouring in the Brussels of that time, such a variety of entertainments for enjoying, that the place should, by rights, still sparkle for me as the supreme of all wartime tonics; right in the centre of battle-territory, an absolute Utopia of a refreshing oasis for mind and body alike. Before long, there was a 48-hour leave scheme in place for us to benefit from it. But that sharp kick-back of a reminder of cold reality is as jarring now as then; a young friend's romantic naïveté which I saw turned into sour delusion.

I cannot blame him for having fallen into the trap. Most of the Belgian girls whom I saw mincing delicately through the throngs of the City streets were quite beautiful creatures. Dressed the smartest of smart, there was nothing in the least 'tarty' or cheap about these innocent-looking seductresses: any serviceman would have preened himself just to be seen arm-in-arm with one of them. While we never got to meet this particular girl, she had obviously and instantly entranced him with her charms. Indeed, from his occasional lapse into love-sick comments, the affair seemed dangerously nearing the idea of a permanent liaison for after the War (or even earlier), when, suddenly and unavoidably, he was called away from the Unit; an absence which lasted for several weeks. As it happened, however, we weren't left with even the vestige of a puzzle for solving. Before departure, his deep distress (and embarrassment) had overflowed into an indication of what had gone wrong; a far cry from the aura of romance for which we had teased him. It was a purely medical question. As a kind of macabre pre-engagement present, he had received an unmistakable dose of gonorrhoea. Was this a gift (I now wonder) which was only second-hand, at that? From some German soldier, perhaps, just weeks before? It isn't a savoury recollection . . .

From now on, as if to support the premature retastings of civilian lifestyles which Brussels offered, my diary gives frequent evidence of near-asphyxiation beneath the increasing inrush of news bulletins; most of them from battlefields able to flaunt more and more of Allied triumphal success. A collection of cut-out newspaper headlines would have been easier to maintain; but, of course, nothing of this kind of printed matter ever came our way. We got most of our information from 'Forces Network' radio broadcasts, and there was always the Division's (cyclostyled) news-sheet, the *Jerboa Journal*, to ram home the main thrust of events.

Now, it has to be said that, amongst all the bombastic lead-up to the start of the War, the building by the Germans of the 'Siegfried Line' had at once established it as the unambiguous symbol of their strength of arms. Strangely, though it was a colossus in the way of defence fortifications, it also epitomised the resolute, aggressive attitude of the whole Reich. Whilst the quick collapse of the corresponding French system, their 'Maginot Line', was now a matter of history – sliced through as easily as cheese by a carving knife – *blitzkriegs* and such hadn't previously been dreamed of; and ever since, the belief had lingered that this German Line would never be overwhelmed in like fashion. The 'Siegfried' had continued to lurk there on the sidelines, with hanging out of Tin-Pan-Alley's 'washing' a most unlikely proposition. Even our triumphs of Normandy couldn't reduce the brooding menace of it – as permanently undismissable as the associated Wagnerian music so beloved by Hitler. When, therefore (half-way through September), the news arrived of four separate penetrations of the Line, it was as much an onslaught on our in-built conceptions as upon this outer bulwark of Germany itself. The Americans' resulting advance of full twelve miles into Reich territory suddenly turned not nearly so incredible – now raised to the category, you could say, of 'only to be expected!'. Adrenalin was fast coursing through our veins; and, with the report of an Allied airborne landing in Holland for added stimulation, I promptly noted down 'the definite feeling of expectancy [which was now] in the air.' (Failure of the Dutch development only reached us much later; the fortunate delay of a 'damper' which might have spoiled the general euphoria.)

Even so, to flick forward but a page or two of my log-book is to recall the surprisingly low level of expectancy to which we soon returned. There is, too, a touch of the same vague sadness which I had experienced that evening under the stars at Ostend. It was longer lasting

Of Straw And Stripes

this time, but just as lacking in any obvious explanation. It may, of course, have been merely autumn to blame, with the gloom of its evenings, following the departure of summer's vibrant mix of heat and sunshine. There was certainly the conviction that, by all the rights of reason, this should have been the autumn, as well, of the whole European War; its winter almost upon us; the end to all the horrors and the killings – surely, more wasteful and meaningless now than ever before? Yet, who could tell how protracted might be its own death-agonies? Instinct pointed perversely to there being, maybe, no clear-cut ending at all; simply the stretching out of it to the very last gasp. (Even then, Japan was still in the background as an even lengthier insulation against normal life.) Whatever the reason, pessimism threatened my spare moments.

Thursday 28 September. The dark nights have arrived on us all of a sudden, and, though it is only half past eight in the evening as I write, it has to be with the aid of a flickering candle flame. Tonight, the first time for three or four days, it is calm. The gales and swirling rains seem to have spent their force for the time being, and we should be without the usual fears of being awakened by a collapsing tent. The stillness outside is emphasised by the faint music coming from the wireless of a nearby lorry. A minute ago it was the sound of a soft and caressing violin solo, and now I can hear the trumpeter in Glenn Miller's band doing his very best in the way of what *he* calls entertainment. And so, in ten minutes time, I will be getting into bed – early, as is now usual with me, for there's little to do, and not sufficient light with which to read. Out will go the candle, and for the next eight or nine hours it will be the accustomed contest between warmth of the bed and its deliciousness of sleep, and the draughts that will always contrive, by some means or other, in finding their way down my neck.

This subdued, un-Warlike setting was symptomatic of the Unit's 'spectator role', well behind the front line action, which it had now resumed (presumably, its properly efficient position for the rest of the campaign). Adulating mobs with thrusted gifts were unrealities of the past; and the general pattern of life, come to think, was not so very different from our Normandy days, save for the fact that, for some time now, we hadn't seen a single apple let alone a whole orchard. Yet I am in danger of forgetting a more basic change. The concept of our being constitutionally static commodities was also well into the past; constantly moving on from place to place being a way of life which we now took for granted, almost with gypsy mentality. Buggenhoute had given way to a village by the name of Haacht, and that, too, was now well behind us, with the industrial town of Bourg-Leopold our current campsite – still in Belgian territory, but only just.

The stark contrast of present scenery with the fresh, rural panoramas of past weeks, was epitomised by the coarse grasses and heathers which now had to serve our tents as fitted carpets – and, at that, only just covering their underlays of inky-black soil. Away on the horizon, meanwhile, stood a substantial, tall-chimneyed factory, presumably responsible for the fine grey dust which had long since descended upon everything around. To go with the unprepossessing landscape, there was also a temporary change to our rations for adding to the general cheerlessness. Almost three quarters of them now came from captured German supplies. 'Cheese that you squeeze from tubes, like toothpaste; biscuits that would test even a dog's teeth, and others (a kind of tougher Ryvita) which are at any rate more palatable than our own; jam in near-solid form, which the cooks serve by 'cutting you a slice'; and butter (so-called) with an ersatz flavour which nothing could possibly camouflage.' We all rejoiced that such German 'delicacies' were not, apparently, available on any longer-term basis than a few days.

Before we left Bourg-Leopold, there had been two events of considerably greater impact than anything the town itself had to offer. The first, momentarily, was almost in the same class of earth-shattering importance as the crushing of the Siegfried Line, since the recent lengthy log-jam of mail from England had proved the most insidious of slow tortures for each one of us. And this, you see, was where it all finally burst through to us – a glorious flood of ordinary news about ordinary places and ordinary people. Amazingly so, in next to no time a negligible trickle so forcibly gushed out as to turn things completely around. It was only on the 28th of September that I had been bemoaning of 'three days ago [receiving] two letters from Hilda over a fortnight old, and the following day another which had taken only three days over the journey,' and wondering where all the post in between had wandered off to. Following which, on the 30th of September, there comes the

Of Straw And Stripes

delighted answer. 'Yes, decidedly yes! (in reference to our mail problems, I mean); in that yesterday I received altogether seven letters and a package of magazines – which left me, on the whole, in a rather more satisfied frame of mind.' Even for me, it is hard now to re-believe the full, insatiable craving which we undoubtedly had for domestic news; as addictive as the hardest of drugs, just as badly requiring regular shots in our arm. Strangely, while censorship stopped us communicating anything of the slightest strategic importance which might surround us, letters from England, largely unrestricted, were savoured above all for their trivialities, the run-of-the-mill, routine stuff with which they were usually and liberally padded. The continuing food of our nostalgia for civilian times; stimulating the memory from losing touch altogether with that faraway world.

Of course, while the availability of genuine 'home comforts' was usually in the range of fantasy (the odd bundle of British magazines being swiftly ephemeral), there was no embargo on our finding 'ersatz' versions of them to keep us going; and it was on this same day that 'Slim' Stribling's own particular contribution to so worthy a cause first made its appearance. Slim was a young friend of mine – and of Dickie's – among the driver-mechanics of the Unit. All of a sudden, we found ourselves with a brand-new tent, and of superior 'officers' quality' at that.

He had, my diary confirms,

> ... wangled it from Heaven knows where and brought it back in his lorry. And so, there were the three of us (Dick, Slim and I) busily engaged in getting it set up, as dusk was deepening over the Camp. It wasn't long, however, before we had almost an army of willing civilian helpers – well, five or six of them at any rate – who provided a useful saw, helped us cut the uprights and the stakes, and finally even to peg the whole thing down. And certainly, at the finish, it turned out a great improvement on our old bivvy – as it keeps out most of the draughts and also, apparently, *all* of the rain. In addition to the fact that it shows none of the other's partiality to being knocked all askew by the more boisterous breaths of the gales.

For exactly six nights, therefore, the three of us enjoyed the supreme luxury of sleeping as fully commissioned officers. After that, however, the episode became twisted with irony, since Bourg-Leopold proved the last location, prior to the onset of the colder weather, at which we ever needed canvas for a bedroom.

Chapter 21

After the indigenous grime of Bourg-Leopold, Valkenswaard entered our life more acceptably; assisted, I suppose, by instinctive sympathy from the eventual sight of its War-scars, an over-abundance of bomb and artillery damage and assorted rubble. But that was only when we had had time to settle down.

> *Thursday 5 October.* The only things which impressed me, I believe, after we had crossed the border into Holland yesterday, were the facts that the local electric power supply had been destroyed by the Germans, and that the harness of the tradesmen's horses in the streets jingled with the music of small bells, such as I recollect of our milkman's horse, years ago (before the man became, like the rest of the world, 'mechanised' and drove around vastly more streamlined and efficient, yet vastly less interesting to his customers).
> For the first time, we are billeted indoors; in a dance-hall, in fact, and quite comfortable, too, by comparison to a tent. At the same time, there's certainly more noise than we've been used to, as the adjoining café runs a substitute dance each night, complete with the usual bar, beers, jostling throng of men and girls, and even a solitary accordionist; very necessary for helping along the general jollity. Last night, the improvised oil-lamps seemed trying – very much in vain – to damp down the spirit of things to their own lack of brilliance; but they tell me the electricity comes on again today, and that should be a great help.

Even so, there was already no need to doubt the windproof stability of my sleeping quarters. Which didn't, unfortunately, prevent cold air stealing over the floorboards as if the brickwork simply didn't exist; whilst the floorboards themselves were evidently of like disposition to those briefly sampled at Middleton. With the same exception of shoe-clad feet, they maintained every bit as iron-hard an objection to close contact with the human frame, and insisted on some immediate brainwave if, from now on, I was to counter the absence of that trusty stretcher of mine. It was, therefore, against all probability that a vein of hidden practicality finally surfaced in me; sufficient, at any rate, for future 'makings of my bed' from much less wasteful a blue-print than I had ever before used. No doubt, the certainty that I would have to 'lie on it' was the ingredient which so effectively stirred my imagination.

The trick was in turning the standard ration of four Army blankets into a combination of nine thicknesses of them. Wiggling myself down inside the completed cocoon – a sort of prodigiously overpadded sleeping-bag – I became used to the comfort and supreme warmth (whatever the outside temperature) of the two layers on which I would be lying and of no fewer than seven on top of me! And it was quickly done, too. The first two of the blankets were laid crossways, one on top of the other, with each end folded inwards (in interleaved fashion), the third folded lengthwise and laid on top of them, while the fourth, the 'tuck-in' security guard, as it were, went over all the rest, to prevent even the suspicion of a draught getting through. All that remained was to have a couple of towels positioned to cushion my hips, together with something or other to improvise as a pillow, and the result was sheer luxury; equal to anything, I was convinced, which the Hylton or Savoy Hotels could have offered back in London. So far as I know, my patent was never purloined by any of the others, whose ignorance of it can only, I hope, have been their bliss. But I remember my 'invention' as potentially suitable for the North Pole itself; and ever since, I have retained a fond – if rather more distant – understanding of the virtues of floorboards in general. I, if no-one else, can always appreciate their secret versatility.

Valkenswaard was an inoffensive place, but unremarkable to the point of near-stultification. Perhaps that was why the Powers-that-be, in their accustomed pig-headedness, kept us there for a solid two months of unrelieved routine. Though, to be honest, not entirely so.

Monday 9 October. Sitting in the ENSA Garrison Theatre at Eindhoven this afternoon, listening to Solomon playing the Rachmaninov G minor Prelude as pompously, the 'Cathédrale Engloutie' of Debussy as mystically, and Chopin's A major Polonaise as triumphantly as ever I could have wished to hear

Of Straw And Stripes

them in 'civvy-street' – well, the very theatre seemed as English as the performer, and our uniforms and the whole idea of this War some far-fetched, grotesque joke. Altogether, it was a thoroughly enjoyable afternoon; though we missed half the programme in the process of trying to find the concert-hall. But *something* always has to go wrong: that has come to be the hallmark of being in the British Army.

Music appeared to linger with us all the way back to Camp, as being seated in the back of Lieutenant Hatch's jeep suggested a suitable accompaniment from the whirlwind music of Tchaikovsky's 'Francesca da Rimini'. Sufferers from the sleepiness of travelling on London tubes would do well to try the extreme contrast of one of these jeeps. The wind buffets into your face and down your ears, squeezes past your collar and round your shoulders, and makes it impossible to open your eyes wider than to squint vaguely at the hedges and the people whirling mistily by you on both sides. You shake your head, and gasp, and think you're in some half-way stage between real life and fantasy.

Disembarking, somewhat breathlessly, from this early experiment with the sound barrier was to return to an Army environment growing ever more schizophrenic. Its variables were of unpredictable arrival – the hopeful salvos of triumphal battle-news from the troops we were serving being leavened by spells in which time was dragged along by boredom. Sparkling jewels like Eindhoven, on the other hand – rare finds, indeed – seldom entitled us to more than a few hours of their tantalising charades of premature demobilisation. And now and again, thrown into all of this to remind us of the true facts of life, would come a short, sharp demonstration of the front line's violence; not nearly so distant as we may well have grown to dismissing it.

Wednesday 15 November. Yesterday afternoon, at half past three, we heard in the distance the rumblings of an artillery barrage, apparently of heavy guns. Last night, the billet was still occasionally shaking from the shock of them, and the firing continued intermittently throughout the night. This morning, we learned that a new attack has been launched by formations of our Second Army east of Eindhoven.

Of Straw And Stripes

It was three weeks before that we had first heard of renewed Allied advances from the Nijmegen salient. If true, this would be an end to the prolonged lull in the fighting which had followed the disastrous mauling of the Arnhem airborne landings. The ever-present, ever-changing rumours then circulating had propagated that (as I recorded it) 'if successful, [this offensive] should lead to our final, decisive major attack; the main obstacle, at the moment, [seeming to be] the difficulty of completely freeing the Scheldt Estuary, for enabling Antwerp to be used as a major port and base.' And now, even while these shock waves of massive gunfire were still persisting, authoritative news of the final clearance of Germans, both from the port and its approaches, started to leak through. 'Full operation of Antwerp's facilities within the week!' These were to be War headlines for us with a vengeance; just the stuff for turning boredom in a flash into sky-high morale!

That fanfare of artillery, as it transpired, was the start of a series of limited advances which set the whole of the Western Front on the move again. That is to say, with what seemed the solitary exception of '107'. As November refrigerated into December, we remained as firmly at Valkenswaard as if set in cement, our latest flurry of excitement quickly evaporating into yet another trough on the Unit's 'bumpy' graph of mood-changes. Even the throbbing enlivenment of those next-door dances had become (unexplainably) a thing of the past – adding to the twilight persuasion of frost that bed was a better choice than reading or writing alike.

How hard it was now, to credit the quite different scene which had lain in front of me only five or six weeks earlier, when, my name having blissfully come out of the hat, I had been retasting Brussels. Moreover, with no restriction to just the 'smacking of my lips' – this time, a full-coursed, 48-hour meal for me of the whole place. Since my first fleeting visit, there had been a considerable Services take-over of its amenities; including, amongst several of its like, the 'Hotel Splendid' – in whose considerable luxuries I was able to saturate myself to my heart's content.

It would have been stupid to miss out on economical comforts of this quality – accommodation as free as the air itself, and meals of almost equal cheapness. Little call, then (from this direction), for the collection of Belgian francs and Dutch guilders with which most of us had stuffed our pockets, in readiness for a rare opportunity to spend some of them. No payment at all, either, for any of the top-class entertainments on offer at the theatres. Indeed, with what now appears a strangely topsy-turvy sense of financial values, I suspect us, by this time, of taking that side of affairs for granted. Way back in London, after all, there had already been shoals of hostels and meals costing little more than a pittance, with theatre doors wide open to khaki-allocated free tickets. Almost universally forgotten, by now, must have been the expensiveness of these things in their natural dispositions.

There was, at any rate, nothing wrong with our sense of how sparkling were the stage shows to which we were being treated. ('Value-for-no-money-at-all', I suppose you might have called it.) On the first night, I revelled in a slick revue at one of the ABC Theatres, and on the second, I had 'an even better seat at the ENSA Garrison Theatre, where, among others in a good cast, Ivor Moreton and Dave Kaye were appearing; with their "Tiger Ragamuffin" style, of dizzy fingers and notes of the very hottest variety cascading at top speed from the keyboards.' Harry Roy's danceband, from whom the two performers were seemingly on temporary leave for the purposes of the show, would have been proud to claim relationship with them. Well up to the standard, I thought, of 'Tiger Rag', their maestro's speciality band number of those days.

While, no doubt, we would have been taken aback if asked to pay anything towards these enjoyments, we weren't averse to squandering money elsewhere on goods which nowadays would be considered as light on excellence as they were heavy on price. At the time, I had to concede that . . .

> . . . the multitude of shops, with their well-stocked windows and their courteous service inside, prove too tempting for the majority of us; and the fact of our pockets being well filled with guilders and francs make these black-market prices less audacious and breathtaking than they *should* seem. At any rate, I myself have spent goodness-knows-how-many francs on a wristwatch, a fountain pen, a pocket French-Flemish dictionary, and – the most welcome sight in any of the shop-windows – some very passable Christmas cards! Of course, they celebrate 'Saint Nicholas' here in Belgium much earlier than England (on December 6th, if I remember rightly) and so the Christmas displays are well to the fore even now in the big stores – with numerous of the Belgian counterparts to 'Santa Claus' already diffusing Christmas spirit to long queues of kiddies, waiting to see them in the bazaars.

Of Straw And Stripes

But here we were, now, slumped down in the trough of this darker, more barren landscape, with Brussels reduced to the vague, surrealist memory of a yesterday's world. Just as much of yesterday as if, during those couple of days, I hadn't so much been demobbed (in my own mind) as never conscripted in the first place. There had been nothing particularly of 'foreignness' about the Brussels shops, or its streetlights, or its streets and buildings – or its pedestrians, for that matter; except, I suppose, for the occasional clattering of their clogs on the pavements (much the same, though not so prevalent, as from the feet of the working-class folk in Holland).

Of course, boredom in the Army was just as uncertain as everything else; and when, after only a week of December, we unexpectedly received movement orders, they raised expectations that Valkenswaard's stagnation would be dispelled once and for all by a positive advance, to match up with that of the front line. How hard to comprehend, then, when we found ourselves tracking *backwards* once more into Belgium. Moreover, to a location not far from our previous campsite. This time, it was to be a place called Lommel, whose only initial claim to excitement was the familiar ring to its name; rhyming, surely, that famous bugbear of a German general from the Division's Western Desert campaign (and the enemy's mastermind for this one, too, back in Normandy).

Nevertheless, as it so happened, any threat of boredom continuing to plague us was put decidedly on hold, for our 'movement in reverse' seems to have tempted the Gods to reinforce the sense of it being a retreat with disturbing developments at the front-line itself.

Friday 22 December. Three or four days ago, came news that (whichever way you looked at it) fairly made us sit up and realise that the Jerries are anything but completely defeated. To have broken through the American First Army and advanced some forty-five miles, on a seventy-mile front, is more sensational than anything *we've* accomplished in the past month or two. However, today's six o'clock news stated that the flanks of this new German drive are being held, and that the actual spearhead of the attack has now been slowed down: it looks as though we're beginning to find our feet again after the first surprise of the break-through.

Everyone you meet, these past few days, appears 'browned-off'; thoroughly depressed – partly due to the War news (and the

Of Straw And Stripes

feeling, I suppose, that it may interfere with the Blighty Leave Scheme, which is scheduled to begin on the 1st of January, and, too, to the fact that there's been another temporary dislocation of our mail deliveries. This last is very probably the result of our being switched from one Corps to another with such confusing rapidity. Up at Valkenswaard, for example, we were in 12 Corps; then we were transferred to 30 Corps, on coming down to Lommel; and now, they would have it, we're officially back in 12 Corps again. Makes you wish, at times, that someone would make his mind up about 7th Armoured Div.

In the meantime, preparations are all ready, here, for the celebrating of Christmas in traditionally drunken Army style. In all probability, we'll be on the move again on Boxing Day, or the day after; so I suppose we'd better not eat and drink *too* well, but rather just wisely, on Christmas Day.

This was a case of my diary grossly underplaying the seriousness of the situation. None of us, privately, did so at the time. Unchallenged understanding, flashing lightning-quickly around us, was to the effect that, if the Front worsened still further, supply units like '107' might not only have to remember the rudimentary weapons training of those distant Training Camps, but, without much warning, practise most of it upon flesh-and-blood Germans.

This strong possibility festered right up to Christmas, and beyond to the New Year itself. None of us talked much about it, and, indeed, we did our best to counter pessimism by feigning minimum concern with the news bulletins. Beneath the surface, however, things had for the moment changed. No longer was it just the impatience of uncertainty, as to how quickly we could finish off the War: there were now the faintest gleams of doubt – how certain was it that we would win it? (A thought, mind you, to which no-one would have owned up.)

It was, of course all the more difficult to downgrade the nature of the present War news when it was backlit, so vividly and contrastedly, by the pleasant domesticity of our billets at Lommel. These had materialised, at the very last moment, out of an initial prospect of reverting to tent-shelter only; a Spartan existence for which we weren't at all, by now, properly 'hardened off'. But, at the end of the day (literally), we had finished up in the relative comfort of local inhabitants' homes, two or three of us in each – my own allocation to one of the farmhouses making impromptu hosts out of a married couple and their three young children. Despite my inability to communicate in anything more subtle than sign-language – they spoke only Flemish – I found the general atmosphere of the place very friendly indeed; turning the whole idea of the nearby 'Battle of the Bulge' (as it later became known) into something of a warped fantasy.

Monday 1 January 1945. I was rather expecting to be asleep when the New Year arrived, having been in bed for a day and a half with a bit of a temperature and a chill on my stomach. But the sound of a German plane, strafing very near our billet, woke me; and, some two or three minutes later, the clock downstairs was cheerfully and ironically chiming out the strokes of twelve o'clock – a time, usually, for merriment and rejoicing, optimism and good intentions, as yet another unpredictable year takes its allotted place on the calendar. My feelings on this occasion were too sleepy to be other than very confused. The present state of the War makes me wonder – what *should* they have been?

Chapter 22

Flicking through the remaining pages of my journal reminds me that, in actual fact, the end of the European War was reasonably close, by now. Would that I had had even a glimmer of foresight of it at the time! The only certainty about the twelfth stroke of that clock, as it echoed up the staircase to me, was that 1945, the year it flaunted, would quickly create a third anniversary for my first indoctrination into khaki. After which – the indeterminate way things were going – it might eventually be marking six long years of continuous warfare, with still more to come. Since I was soon to be drifting off again into sleep, there was little immediate capacity for considered thought, but daylight brought a pronounced sense of depression; of being stuck in the mud of a no-man's-land where struggling either forward or backward was unlikely to result in a recognisable end-product. In this welter of gloom, admittedly, my state of health didn't help at all.

And this, more trivially, was also a disillusionment. Almost in the same league as the lengthening of hostilities. Active service hadn't brought much of benefit to the 'also ran' type of conscript like me, except, I had soon realised, amazingly good health. Coughs and colds and snuffles and sneezes – when was I any longer getting them? Or hearing any of the others wallowing in the symptoms? 'Toughness' was surely the word for it. Nothing need now be avoided. Extremes of cold and heat, draughts, rain-drenched clothing, even water dripping down the back of one's neck; none of these had their old properties. I – we, all of us – had sudden and total immunity! Something, indeed, to relish taking back with me to England: people there would want to know the secret. So, really (I suppose), did I.

Before long, however, it started to unravel of its own accord, with Valkenswaard the main catalyst in a simple subtraction sum. It was at Valkenswaard, after all, that the magic had started to dissipate, leaving us to regress rapidly into our previous acquaintanceships with the common cold and its various close cousins. Subtract it from the other components, and the nature of our temporary inoculation was shown up as nothing tougher or more scientific than 'fresh air and tents' (in which, as I recollected, the air had been fully as 'open' as outside). As an extremely small, and usually isolated, community, we must severely have discouraged such germs as were already inside us with the scarcity of bodies in which to breed, or to which there might be emigration possibilities. I can, on the other hand, easily believe that hundreds of thousands of the Dutch variety of the tiny brutes must have been queuing up amid the steaming entertainments of those next-door dances; all desperate to get going on prime virgin material like us. So, here I was, at my own personal climax of their ravages, with the seeming contradiction of a 'feverish chill' and a distinct sensation of having sunk to the deepest dregs of human misery. On balance, things could only improve.

Wednesday, 3 January. Working in a brewery and sleeping in a hospital! Sounds rather like 'going from bad to worse', doesn't it? Whereas, in fact, it's a case of from good to even better. I still felt rather groggy yesterday, when the Unit moved from Lommel to this present town, called Genk – a journey of some two hours; but since then I've lost much of the sickness and feel almost well again. Anyhow, as I've said, conditions are good. The vacant rooms in the set of offices at the Brewery are well-heated, and we've all our 'Control and Provision' clerking kit moved in there now. Moreover, the unused maternity (!) ward at the hospital makes a grand billet. Three or four of us to each room, spring beds, good lighting – what more could you ask for? This is too good to last . . .

Monday 8 January. All day it has been snowing – whimsically; furiously, and then half-heartedly and even wearily in its careless scatterings of snowflakes here and there. But the snow has kept on right through the morning and the afternoon, and now, even the tiniest twigs on the trees are finely powdered with the mystical delicacy of its whiteness. Winter is here in force, and apparently intends to stay.

More bad news from the Western Front! After the stabilisation of the German salient in Belgium, it is reported today that the Jerries have now broken through in force on the Venlo Front.

Sounds serious but I've heard no news so far, except the bald statement of the fact.

Perhaps fortunately for the long-term future of the European continent, reality, up there at the battle-front, was reacting more optimistically than were the cells of my mind. With the assistance, apparently, of concentrated and overwhelming bombing from the Allied Air-forces, the 'Bulge', already contained, was in process of being totally eliminated by the middle of January. Indeed, by the time of my next entry, there were additional tidings for making even me renewedly resilient.

Friday 19 January. Who *said* the War news was bad? The weather may be, I'll admit – after three days of gradually thawing slipperiness, gusts of cold wind have been swishing around, chaotically mixed up with showers of the wettest of snowflakes – but these latest reports from the Russian Front are stimulating, to say the least. Advancing rapidly on I-forget-how-many fronts, they've taken Warsaw and Cracow, and are actually fighting on the German Silesian border. An advance, in this area, of some seventy miles in a week's fighting!

This was a bonus of success which confounded, both in scale and speed, the hostility of the conditions.

Much more savage, by all accounts, than here, where I could certainly vouch for the treacherous, half-thawing state of the ice which still survived. Jumping down from the back of one of the three-tonners, I succeeded only in a clumsy 'slipped-landing', directly on to my left kneecap; a stupidity which left me, as I noted, 'hobbling around stiffly, like the most incurable of cripples, for fully a week afterwards.' Reluctant as I always was to seek proper medical attention, I dismissed it as a 'nothing-which-wouldn't-soon-wear-off' affair; whereas, though I was never to confess them to a soul, the symptoms persisted for almost a year. Sitting for any length of time would always start up a dull aching of the joint – easily bearable, yet gradually inculcating a doubt which was infinitely more uncomfortable: would the trouble *ever* clear up? Had I but known, this seeming triviality of a mishap was a rehearsal for the much more serious near-disaster later to befall me.

For the present, at any rate, there was much to offset it. You might even say that a touch of Normandy was in the air – on the heels of the encouraging turn in the War, some partial recovery of that original, pulsating conviction of impending triumph; a renaissance stimulated by the unexpected discovery of freely available 'entertainment'. Closer at hand, moreover, and with greater choice, than any which had previously come our way. On the 25th of January, I was rejoicing that

> ... the nearby villages [to Genk] of Winterslag and Waterschei both have cinemas which follow the usual custom of showing English-speaking films with French and Flemish sub-titles. And a half-hour trip by tram to Hasselt (no charge for soldiers!) brings you to two or three more cinemas, an ENSA Garrison Theatre, where I saw a really good show last week, a YMCA canteen, and even a traditional NAAFI.

It was, I think, mainly its tramcars which gave Genk such a visual flavour of un-Englishness. Come to that, trams to this day remain one of the distinctively foreign impressions for the mind after a holiday on the Continent; though, with their obsolescence long ago in most parts of England, the difference is now the more obvious. Even at that time, however, the European vehicles were noticeably different in being only single-deckers, the British double-decked crossbreeds never seemingly having migrated anywhere at all. But there was more than that about the Genk transport system. I was intrigued to see only 'a single set of tramlines running down one side of the main street, on which, by some miraculous arrangement of timetables, trams are to be seen alternately running in either direction – and, now and again, steam-engines pulling goods wagons!'

Mixed in with the plethora of exciting War bulletins, there were, here and there, more sombre hints of why, at this stage of a seeming hopelessly lost cause, there should still be such determination on the part of the Germans for prolonging it. It must, I thought, be linked with those accursed 'secret weapons' of Hitler's most recent ranted oratory. Revealed by now (both of them) and increasingly coming into play, they would certainly revel in more time for germinating their full potential of terror.

Wednesday 31 January. The thaw had come suddenly, overnight; and this morning it was almost complete, with drippings from above and squelchings underfoot, and even the evergreens in front of the hospital looking naked and sombre in colour, by contrast to their dazzling whiteness of the past few weeks.

As the dilapidated-looking goods train came puffing painfully up the street, in easy sight of the big window of our office, there were of course our usual cries of 'She's a-coming through! Thar she blows!' and other such elementary Wild-Western wit. And then, observed someone: 'We haven't had our doodlebug for today yet! Well past its time!' Which remark results, it should be noted, from this area having become of late almost a 'doodlebug alley', so to speak. Three or four of the flying bombs now come over each day with rather alarming regularity. Yesterday morning, for example, we had a very good view of one as it chugged its way overhead, away into the distance, its exhaust belching out flames in vicious style as it went. This fiery trail is often all you can see of it, especially at night. You hear the unmistakable sound of it (like a particularly noisy motor-bike), and, straining your eyes upwards into the darkness, you see only a steadily moving light, going quite slowly (almost like a candle-flame) into the dark mists of the distance. And the noise of it gradually dies away, and you breathe again – until sometimes a dull thud, far off, reminds you of the unfortunates who must have been in the danger area, when its engine finally cut out and sent it hurtling relentlessly downwards.

I recalled the first time I had been able to view one of these atrocities with any real clarity. Incongruously enough, it had been from the back of the lorry carrying us into Brussels for that now-distant two day 'pleasure break'. Flying reasonably low, it had passed directly above us, with the bright sunlight serving as a more than adequate spotlight. Not that there had seemed anything so very remarkable about it. Except for that spectacular tail of belched fire, I might have been witnessing the try-out of some oversized toy-plane, operated (before his time) by a nearby enthusiast with a remarkably powerful remote control. Yet, when I think again, that would have been an impossible fantasy, with the picture almost immediately ornamented by exploding anti-aircraft shells only feet from either side of the thing; so near and yet so far! Reverberating noisily into the distance, it had soon effected so remote a disappearance that we were never, in fact, to hear the inevitability of its final 'thud'.

While Hitler's 'V-1' weapon – which is was what the scientists had christened this first of his 'secrets' – assumed nicknames almost from the start, its follow-up, the giant rocket-bomb 'V-2', never got round to acquiring even one. This was probably because the 'flying bomb', most prominently and deliberately visible to the human eye, soon became an acquaintance of sorts (even if only of the most hated variety), while the 'V-2' remained anonymous and unseen throughout its ghastly task of indiscriminate havoc. Presumably, the unfortunate victims knew nothing of it either, right up to the instant of their death. In point of fact, the only direct evidence I ever had of its existence was on Boxing Day of 1944, at Lommel, while we were watching a local football match. My diary recalled that

> . . . it must have been well below freezing that day, and, miles upon miles away, I could clearly see the white, curiously crooked and zig-zagged trail of the rocket (something like a perpendicular 'graph', in fits and starts) as it went quickly up into the frosty pale-blue of the sky. Queer to think that there was no question of my hearing any explosion in the distance – that it had a journey still to go of hundreds of miles before doing its devilish work!

Nevertheless, it would have taken more than these few dozen assorted robots to kill the euphoria now hauling us, ever so smartly, out of this latest of our troughs. There were signs that, at last, winter was beginning to lose its bite; and, if the campaign itself continued in this new imbalance, there wouldn't be sufficient of Germany left for battlefields, let alone battles, before very long – even if the Führer, with his warped and blood-stained philosophy, might still contrive to think so.

If we ourselves had needed further convincing, it came with our next posting, on the 7th of March, to a Dutch town called Weert, where our education on the ready conversion of everything in our path to 'billets' was completed by an irresistible taking-over of the local railway station, both for our sleeping quarters (in the waiting rooms, next to the platform), and for functioning of both Office and 'Receipts and Issues Bay' – the two of which fitted snugly enough into the adjoining goods station. Evidently intent on giving the enforced hand-over of the station an aura of proper consent, two nearby windmills maintained tradition by continuing to stand guard over it, one on each side, both quite intact of War damage, and with (as I noted down) 'their sails turning sluggishly or spiritedly, according to the whims of the wind.' They did in fact, when I think, radiate some measure of calm, imaginary approval to our occupation.

Not only that: hardly had we settled in to the town than the vibes of the whole area were pulsating into us; the sense that we were only a small part of a nearly completed build-up of colossal Allied force – the preparation quite clearly for 'something big'. It was soon general information within the Unit that the entire Seventh Armoured Division stood massed within the range of four or five miles from here, and there was an accepted understanding of the obvious; that we were poised to form the spearhead to an all-out attack on the remains of the German army. Certainly, Weert wasn't at all just one more 'stage coach stop' along our way. The atmosphere was as crackling with electricity as in those ancient days, way back at Middleton; the history to come, every bit as inevitable.

Meanwhile, as if to stress its greater neutrality than, maybe, those windmills, the actual weather – not to be accused, so to speak, of supplying a slippery floor to the ring for the last round of the fight – was improving astonishingly. After two weeks, indeed, the cold mud and drizzling rain of our arrival at Weert had warmed into a fair impersonation of summer sunshine itself (leap-frogging spring in the process). The timing (on the 21st of March) of the issue to us of brand-new small bivvies was thus given some seasonal logic, though I suspect the pleasant turn to the weather of being only coincidental. More apparent was the hint of increasingly nomadic routine to our future; turning the discovery of further eligible railway stations, hospitals or breweries into extremely unlikely Acts of God. One way or the other, preparations were in hand for all contingencies.

Chapter 23

From this point onwards, events largely take over from thoughts; for which they left little time.

Thursday 22 March. For the past three or four days, we have been expecting to move again. Our new location is apparently not far from Venlo; where, according to all reports, there's little worth seeing except piles of landmines – minus detonator, we hope, in all cases! – lying by the roadside to testify to the good work of the Royal Engineers.

The weather remains perfect: everyone's hoping it will remain so for the 'big offensive'. The newspapers have been telling us for the past week that 'AGRO HOUR IS AT HAND' for the armies of Field-Marshal Montgomery. As, for that matter, have the German radio commentators, and there are certainly signs now of movement in this concentration area. Tonight, as I was walking along towards the 'Jerboa Club' (where I'm now seated, busily writing this), there was a long line of three-tonner lorries speeding along the road out of Weert, carrying troops of the Highland Division. Altogether, there is quite a steady flow of transport on the roads just now, all day long. Everyone knows something big is about to happen. It's just a question of 'When?' (World news: Allied Armies now massing along the West Bank of the Rhine, almost all the way from Holland to Strasbourg. General Patton's 3rd American Army is completing the rout of the Germans west of the Rhine on the southern part of the Front.)

Saturday 24 March. It was difficult getting to sleep last night. Great numbers of aircraft were roaring overhead, and, even after dark, convoys of lorries still rumbled through Weert. Today, the one o'clock news quotes the Germans as saying that Monty has at last begun his offensive. There's no confirmation of this from

Of Straw And Stripes

Allied sources, but no-one round here *needs* confirmation: that the attack has begun is now obvious to everyone. Tremendous fleets of transport planes and gliders have been passing overhead all morning, and at one time the sky seemed literally full of them – your eyes followed them away into the grey haze of the distance, where they appeared numberless as swarms of mosquitoes. First came wave after wave of paratroop transports, and then, very shortly afterwards, the towplanes and gliders, in such numbers as to make the previous spectacle a mere nothing by comparison.

At nine o'clock that same night, the welter of exciting developments merited my follow-up entry of

... the news [continuing] to be very good. At points, our men are now three miles in from the new Rhine bridgehead. And it is announced that the first men to cross were personnel of what the radio announcer termed 'the famous 5th Royal Tank Regiment' (one of the two tank regiments comprising the armour of 7th Armoured Division). Well, '5 RTR' have certainly had a good share of the supplies issued from this Sub-Park of late, which all goes to show that even an unadventurous behind-the-lines unit like ours is doing a useful part in the tremendous supply organisation for the offensive.

Friday 30 March. The present is very reminiscent of the time when the 2nd Army was streaking across Belgium, shortly after the Battle of the Falaise Gap. Then, we were at Bonneville in France, and, for a time, the Div was so far ahead of us that we'd lost touch with it for issuing stores. Well, the same thing is happening now, except with different place-names, of course. We're stationed near a little village called Brockhuisel, which in turn isn't far from Venlo, quite close to the German border. And the Division (officially quoted on the wireless as 'the famous Desert Rats') is now in the thick of Montgomery's spearhead breaking out of the Rhine bridgehead at Wesel. No-one knows where the 2nd Army advance-guards are – there has been a security blackout on this Front for days – but there's no doubting that things are going very well, as the sensational tank advances by the American 1st and 3rd Armies, further south, confirm.

Optimism is running high, and the discomforts of life under canvas (crawling into bed so as not to bring the bivvy down on top of you) are forgotten in the general expectation of 'End of the War in weeks now, eh?' Everyone goes around putting his own estimate of when the end will come. Pessimists are almost non-existent.

Thursday 5 April – written at Bocholt, Germany. It's drizzling miserably with rain. Though they left before us, the other half of the Unit hasn't yet arrived at this new location; and here am I, writing this in the driving compartment of one of the three-tonners so as to keep dry. (Reminds me of a similar entry I made while we were near Bourg-Leopold.) Why is it that, almost always when we've moved camp since those Normandy days, it has had to start raining? At other times, we've had good weather for weeks on end – as at Weert; but only after the rain had showered down on us on the very first day!

Anyhow, we crossed the River Maas this morning, and the Rhine shortly after dinner-time. Notice that I didn't say 'after *dinner*': the Cookhouse has still to arrive. So here we are, 'awaiting developments'. And, generally, feeling rather damp and wretched into the bargain.

The German towns through which we've passed have been terribly knocked about; almost on the same scale as Villers-Bocage. Most of the German civilians we've seen have been women, many of them wheeling handcarts which carry their only remaining belongings. You can't feel too sorry for them, having seen the like in France – and, to some extent, in England (during the air-raids). No doubt, however, they're beginning to feel sorry for *themselves*.

A far cry, you could say, from our own buoyant morale. There was no shortage, either, of fresh ammunition for our self-esteem; finally convinced as we now were of '107's' central role amongst the essential cogs to British Armour's supply lines. We were in a fortunate, yet sometimes frustrating position – neither sufficiently far forward to experience at first hand what was progressing at the cutting edge of things (with the accompanying probability, of course, of not living to tell the tale), nor far enough to the rear for relaxing into more reasoned,

Of Straw And Stripes

wide-angle assessment of events, as merely part of the 'audience'. Yet there were ample signs around of the speed with which the size of the battleground was now being squeezed from all sides.

Monday 9 April. Just before lunchtime today, there was a babble of wholly unintelligible German going on, in the doorway of the outhouse which we're using here as combined office and sleeping quarters. Two excited German women were trying to explain something, and the more we explained to them that we couldn't understand, the faster yet became their talk and the more mysterious their meaning. Eventually, however, we got the idea that they wanted us to come and take charge of a small band of Jerry soldiers who were wanting to surrender. At any rate, it was evident that they wanted us to come with them to a nearby house. So Sergeant Wilson, Wilf Ford and I loaded our Stens and set out to find the cause of the bother. Well, we might have known their frightened looks weren't connected with *Germans*: five or six Russian soldiers it was who were 'putting the wind up 'em'. They'd been freed only recently from a prisoner-of-war camp at Munster, and were demanding food from this farmhouse. My own sympathies were all with the Russians, and we fixed them up for rations at our own Cookhouse, before sending them on their – haphazard, I should think – way. Goes to show, though, how the Jerries feel about Russians: they know of the atrocities wrought on them, and there's no doubt that they are more scared and uncertain about 'Joe Stalin's men' than of either the Americans or the British.

Half the Unit moved off this morning to our next location, near Osnabrück. We'll follow them probably on Wednesday. 7th Armoured, meanwhile, were last reported on the wireless to be almost on the outskirts of Bremen. Question still is – how much longer can the Jerries hold out? I wonder.

Thoroughly hardened off into migrations of all shades of distance and direction, we now took for granted the reliability of predictions of future ones. These had increasingly proved more accurate than any of those at the start of the campaign. Surely enough, therefore, on Wednesday the 11th we duly resumed our gypsy culture with

... quite a substantial journey. Something over eighty miles from Bocholt brought us in the neighbourhood of Osnabrück, and near to the town of Wallenhorst. After a dry, glaring, dusty day of travelling, I felt as dirty and sweaty and tired as I've done for some time; but, even when Office kit had been unloaded, bivvy put up, and myself very hastily washed, I still had to perform my share of that mind-breaking guard duty. In the course of which a chap from Monty's HQ came in at about half one in the morning, looking for a sub-park where he might be able to collect a Leyland engine. This was for the Field-Marshal's own personal caravan, which had apparently conked out unexpectedly. But we couldn't help, not being scaled for much Leyland stuff.

At Wallenhorst, we were to start a new trend in campsites. Railway stations and such might be in short supply, but this was at any rate a promising enough brickyard! The kilns and the low-lying, slated sheds identified its past principle usage, though more recently, it would appear, the place had been a storage centre for half-completed articles of furniture, made at a nearby factory. Certainly, we noticed plenty of good timber knocking around. 'Altogether,' I registered, 'it's not a bad location. The surrounding countryside's very beautiful, too!'

Ordinary washing was only superficial so far as getting all traces of the journey's grime and sweat from our bodies; but, a few days later, following an unpromisingly dusty and jolting transportation into Osnabrück itself, we emerged from the Mobile Bath Unit there with the gloriously clean metamorphosis effected by its hot shower! Indescribable luxury! It was, however, I admitted, 'anything but a luxury travelling on these German roads. Pot-holes abound, and it's just a question of whether the lorry will be shaken to pieces before your own inadequate system of bones and joints gives way under the strain.' Still, opportunities like that shower had to be grabbed before they got away: it was problematical when we would next see such a glorious gushing of sparkling clean water ...

Friday 20 April. I've only a hazy idea of where we are now 'on the map': things are moving too rapidly. Close on a hundred miles we travelled yesterday, to arrive at a place called Rethen – vaguely, some distance north-east of Hanover; roughly, I would say, half-way from the Rhine to Berlin. The Div, however, is now very

Of Straw And Stripes

close to Hamburg, and I wouldn't be at all surprised if we eventually wound up in Denmark. Things are going so well, now, on the battlefronts, that examination of the map shows only a comparatively small portion of Germany which hasn't yet been occupied.

We've just been informed that we're on the move again tomorrow; only three or four miles, though, I gather. Wild rumours are now going the rounds about the Unit being static after this; of half our transit trucks being sent back to the depots, and so on. But the person who believes that sort of thing piecemeal has only himself to blame for invariable disillusionment.

As I get to the point of reproducing my comments of the following day, there is within me an overwhelming, if not immediately logical, sense of whimsical sadness. It is as if a candle is about to be snuffed out on a whole subdivision of my life.

Saturday 21 April. Probably the last entry in this diary – for I'm leaving the Unit early tomorrow morning for 'Blighty' leave – must be to state that, very occasionally, Army rumours *do* come true. For we *are* now static, for a month probably or more, and half of our trucks, together with twenty-five of our chaps, *are* leaving on Monday to form a new, temporary Stores Collecting Unit – to help out the RASC, who are very hard-pressed with work. I must be getting too suspicious: this forecast sounded one of the most fantastic I'd heard for a long time, yet it happens to be the one that had good foundation in fact.

Today has been one long downpour of rain. We were all soaked through by about nine o'clock, so that, when there were sudden showers again this afternoon, we were much too damp and miserable even to notice them. However, our new Camp (another brickworks!) is compact, if small, and we've our offices in a set of workshops which were filled with debris and rubble when we arrived. These now reward us for hours of 'excavations' (almost) by presenting something that *looks* like neatness and tidiness and, most important, waterproofness.

And now – leave . . .

Chapter 24

The expansive, benevolent smile which suffused the rounded contours of Taffy Evans's face, as he handed me my leave pass, told it all. No question but that the European War was, at last, all but finished. Only some incredible explosion of black magic from the Devil himself could now extend it for more than a week or so. And, indeed, before the end of my trip back to England, Adolf Hitler, on the 30th of April, had committed suicide in his Berlin bunker, leaving Montgomery – at Lüneburg Heath, on the 4th of May – to accept surrender of the enemy forces in North-West Germany, Holland and Denmark, and General Eisenhower, three days later at Rheims, to savour the capitulation of the entire German fighting machine.

Nothing, you might say, but good news in prospect; a happy ending to the story; the return of peaceful, normal existence in the not so distant future; no storm clouds in sight. Little did I know, as five or six of us climbed into the back of the small fifteen-hundredweight truck which was to take us to the train terminal, how close I was to my own end, never mind the War's.

It was a nightmare which I was lucky to survive. Yet there was more to it of extreme *bad* fortune, for me to have been thrust into the situation in the first place. 'Catapulted' might be a better word; as our little truck, speeding ambitiously along the main road, suddenly skidded viciously across and off the side of it – crashing headlong into the unyielding solidity of a nearby tree, and hurling me, with all the speed of light, back on to the centre of the road surface. Two of my companions landed, more paddedly, on top of me.

The first slice of luck was that the concrete didn't first make contact with my skull, and the second – even more miraculous – that no vehicle had been travelling close enough behind to run unstoppably over the three of us, when I would doubtless never (ever!) have been able to sense anything of what had happened. But that was as far as luck was prepared to go: I lay there, still as death itself, for quite a few moments, trying desperately to comprehend.

My instincts were surprisingly – unbelievably – calm. In the face of this rushed chaos, and even before testing my limbs, I distinctly remember giving myself a firm talking-to. 'Remember, Bill,' went my silent self-prescription, 'shock's the real side-danger of any accident! Relax, can't you? Relax! For God's sake, guard against tension!' Whereupon my mind, not at all in disagreement, did its best to pass on the advice to my body – only for the latter to reject it out of hand; allowing itself instead a sudden, simulated dose of palsy in the violence of shaking which now racked me. A suitable accompaniment, I suppose, to the undoubted chattering of my teeth.

Presumably on the supposition that, since my limbs could display this amount of uncontrolled activity, they might still be capable of something more functional, I was soon struggling to lever myself perpendicular. And, with some help from anxious colleagues, I did then manage a few yards, staggered only precariously yet in fair imitation of proper steps. This, I instantly took to represent full recovery, asserting to all and sundry that there wasn't a scrap of residual damage. 'Ready to press on!' I insisted – being absolutely determined that no Army hospital in Christendom was going to block my route back to England.

At this point of my hindsight, I have been about to claim as little recollection of the eventual continuation of my journey as of that earlier trauma, three years back, from Catterick to Tyneside for my poor Mother's funeral. Certainly, there is nothing of sharp clarity, now, of the stop-gap transport which obviously managed it for us, more successfully, to the railway station; or of the train travel itself to the ship; or even, after docking in England, of the means by which I arrived at last in front of Andrew's front door in South Shields. But to put forward total amnesia for the whole sequence would, I realise, merely perpetuate the clearcut lie which I kept repeating at the time, all along the way. What was no more forgettable then than it is now was the persistent *pain*; those alarming, knife-sharp jabs of it which kept cutting clean across my left collarbone – on which, in my clumsily grotesque, asymmetrical attempt at a forward roll as I was thrown across the road, the concrete had seemingly wreaked some sort of havoc. Increasingly, no amount of pretence to others could conceal it from myself. The slightest flexing of any of the fingers of my left hand was sufficient to trigger a fresh spasm; and I began to suspect the shoulder, in fact, to be broken.

Almost as soon as he opened the door to me, I imagine that my brother must have been aghast at the mere sight of my distressed condition. After he had assisted me in peeling off the shirt and top half of the 'long-johns' which were concealing the true state of my bare skin, he was nothing short of appalled. The mirror was enlightenment for me, too; for it showed the whole of my chest and upper stomach, together with my left shoulder and left arm's upper segment, to be painted as in oils with the densest and darkest blue-purple of a bruise that I had ever seen, or thought possible.

Now, I cannot be sure of it, but Andrew's first reaction must have been to whisk me down to the local hospital's Casualty Department, even though I would have done my best to kill off the idea at birth. To have stifled my leave at this stage, when, against all those difficulties, I had actually reached England, would have been the worst disaster of all! In the event, however – probably interpreting the look in my eyes – he came up with a much more acceptable proposal. Or, more realistically, with what was his only other option. At any rate, I soon found myself being rushed along, willy-nilly, to the home of the gentleman who was physiotherapist to the town's Rugby Club.

Never an enthusiast of the game (playing or watching alike), it was the first time I had met with either himself or the particular avenue of his medical expertise. Ever since, however, I extol it to the heavens; for, so far as I am concerned, that house was one of pure magic: almost as soon as he set his diagnostic eyes on me, optimism prevailed. For a start, it was clear that the ravages of my 'top half' were turning not a single hair of his head (as they say). Evidently, nothing special at all about them; to him, just an everyday job of work. (Maybe the general blood-and-thunder of the War had, indeed, filtered into the local rugby matches?) At any rate, by the time he set properly to work on me – having satisfied himself that my bones were, in fact, intact – I already sensed he might well be about to put most of me to rights. Perhaps, as well as the pain inside that bruise, he might even be able to lighten its colour-shade? (Of the time-scale for its complete disappearance, I was more realistic.) For the moment, however, I could only submit to what seemed like a ferocious attack by him upon my upper body-frame.

For all the world, he might have been in course of repairing an imaginary harp, formed by my left collarbone with the shoulder's sinews as its strings. Digging his fingers deep into my flesh, he seemed to be trying to pull one or more of them back into place; a struggle which lasted for several minutes on end. Then, just as I was wondering if my exhausted constitution could stand very much more of this, he paused, breathing heavily, before changing to a determined belabouring of the whole of the bruised area with hard, flat-handed smacks. Another decided pause, a further ration of similar flagellation, and the treatment was evidently complete.

As I dressed, ready to accompany Andrew back home, I felt almost like some recalcitrant pirate, on board his Jolly Roger of a vessel after a savage punishment of cat-o'-nine-tails flogging. A comparison, nevertheless, which I soon recognised as inapt since, far from having to endure untold lingering pain, those pestering knife-stabs of my own variety of it were, even now – Heaven be praised! – things of the past. Miraculously, that harp seemed in tune again.

Thus it was that, satisfactorily patched up, I celebrated the European War's final week with my first back home since the Invasion; assimilating the dying embers of the campaign from the unaccustomed and peculiar position of being just another member of their distant audience.

Chapter 25

On my return to those brickworks of ours in Germany, I found everything to be exactly the same and everything to be entirely different. Not only had I seen the light at the end of my tunnel more clearly than ever; I had, only just now, been crawling all the way through it, and out at the other end into its full brilliance. Having then to squeeze myself, this time backwards, along the whole length again of the pipe-line, had been a disorientating labour.

In one way, I was sad to be back, but not nearly so deeply as I might have expected. The real – wistful – sadness, I had left behind me in England; that sense of the irrevocable years which had slipped from my grasp since long-term immersion in its peacetime normalities; the complete break with the past which the War had effected. Most especially with *my* past which had, after all, never left its starting blocks, as you might say, towards any proper potential whatsoever. Being late in completion of my physical growth, I had been able to find not a single relic among my civilian clothes which still fitted me; none of my shoes which didn't now cramp my toes, and no shirt collar without the acquired ability (and seeming determination) to strangle the rest of me. Nor had I been able to recapture any belief that the town of my birth – with buildings and streets condensed yet further in size and importance from my last sight of them – could have much future significance.

The present renewal of my exile was not, then, in itself so great a concern. The real trouble was that disturbing vacuum, newly intrusive into my concept of the War's overall 'story'. Having been brought up on tales of the First War, I had possibly in mind the triumphant end of that one; the final (and almost immediate, I had thought) anaesthetising of past miseries by 'The Armistice', with its jingoistic offshoot of 'Johnnie comes marching home again!' against a backcloth of ecstatic civilians, wildly cheering 'the boys' back to home comforts. In retrospect, a quite unarguable '. . . and everyone lived happily ever

Of Straw And Stripes

after!' scenario; the clearest of all possible clearcut endings to the whole affair. Whereas, what was I supposed to rate this current page of my history book? Higher than just the end of an episode in a long-running serial? I had no ground for thinking more positively; for that other war, in the Far-East against Japan, still stretched out alarmingly into an unscripted future, of which I would most certainly be part.

In the meantime, there were some strange aspects of 'post-War' Europe – how novel the category! – to hold my attention. Our continuing work-load, for example. It had evidently been at full throttle all through my English adventure, and I was to find it equally intense for several weeks to come. This very sameness was what surprised me the most; almost prompting doubt as to whether the War was, indeed, finally 'done and dusted'. If we weren't still blasting away at some remnants or other of the Wehrmacht, there must obviously be quite a queue of battle-scarred metal on parade at those overstrained workshops of the REME – all of it needing repairs or servicing. Back, ideally (I supposed), to the stuff's pre-battle, pristine condition. Perhaps, ready for the Japanese?

Nevertheless, whatsoever their source, these stacks of voracious requisitions had to be cleared, and we duly continued, therefore, with the work-patterns which had functioned so unexpectedly smoothly throughout the campaign. Loaded lorries strained their way creakingly to and fro, just as before; outgoing with our issues of spares and replacement assemblies, and incoming with the replenishments for them from Second Echelon warehouses. The Office-truck's filing cabinets were still tenanted, as precisely as ever, by those originally suspect record cards, very well-thumbed indeed by now, but quite unruffled by all the rugged journeying to which they had been condemned – and, most certainly, never once found spilled across the floor in missorted confusion, as I had first envisaged. For that matter, just as reliably accurate, too, in their present stocktakings as in the first ones they registered, after the Normandy landing. As for ourselves, in operating our well-oiled procedures, we had minds which had become almost automatons, needing the very minimum of thought or supervision.

Or did they? During the hostilities, no doubt; yet, currently – well, this was where I found the similarities tailing off. Certainly, the work remained uncomplicated, but the accustomed 'life-and-death' motivation for it of a nearby, seethingly active 'Front Line' had all of a sudden vanished into thin air. A revised atmosphere in which no fumes from firing artillery, no scraps of flying shrapnel, no exploding bombs, or mortars, or shells, or threats of any kind of premature body-extinction were anywhere still around; those catalysts which had hitherto given our lengthy shifts of mere hard work their comparative aura of luxury and privilege.

I will not go so far as to admit to any conscious weighing-up of the situation, but comparisons were obvious. Up to now, every gasp of additional effort had been for pushing the War towards its earliest possible end; whilst now, in these changed terms of reference, any extra push would only be accelerating this final 'clean-up' to the European part of things – and the arrival, by consequence, of the date when people like me would be for shipping out to the Far East.

The scenery hadn't changed at all. It was the viewpoint which was so different; my viewpoint, most of all. Even when walking away again from the family at the end of my leave, I sensed the awesome nature of the dividing line over which I was now to step. The immediate story of the War itself was, of course, quite finished: I accepted that part of the dividing line by leaving behind my precious little hard-backed book, the 'War Diary' which has been the basis of so many of these recollections. I tucked it away in a small vacant cranny on one of Andrew's bookshelves, in rather more comfort and snugness and safety than it had ever enjoyed at any time during the past year. Whether any of its contents were ever scrutinised by my brother – or anyone else, for that matter – I have no idea. Certainly, in all probability undisturbed, it remained amongst his book collection for many, many years, all the way up to his death, some time ago; when, appreciating the moss of historical curiosity which age would by then have deposited upon it, I rescued the thing during our sad sorting through of his affairs.

But this was 1945; my journal was bedded down already as part of the past; and the present was still with us, compulsorily to be lived into the future (wherever that was). If we had lost a trifle of our 'natural' motivation, there was always Tug Wilson – what, after all, are sergeants paid for? – to make up the balance; with rather more of brusqueness, now, than pleasant 'jollying-along' in the mixture which had always been his workaday personality. Taffy Evans, on the other hand, remained as serenely calm as ever he had been; one of the entirely identical parts of our new scenario. *His* viewpoint didn't seem one iota different: if anything, his smile was more pervasive than ever. (Considerably older than me, was it possible he now considered his chances in the

Of Straw And Stripes

demobilisation stakes?) Dickie Watts, similarly unaffected, continued to generate just as many of his flashing, ivory-white bouts of laughter. Maybe, in his case, he had actually got to *liking* Army life! For all of us, needless to say, it was simply a matter of 'getting on with it', the willing and the unenthusiastic alike. Since there was never the military acceptance of standard working hours, the work had to be cleared, one way or the other – and was.

And, at a pinch, I could still believe in its importance, however less vital might sound this revised concept of a 'Peace effort': what else could it be called? Plainly, there was, at any rate, some urgent need for all the 'issues' we were still grinding out into the empty bellies of those lorries. Which was more than could be said for our routine Camp security tasks – now perpetuated as nothing more believably crucial than monotonous chores. Guard duties, most of all.

Remembering that the closing formalities of the fighting were scarcely concluded, the attitude of certain of us had altered remarkably swiftly and sharply. Only a week ago, the ghost of Premature Death had still been floating around, never so very far away from any of us. Yet, now, that first, unspoken euphoria at its complete disappearance was already dissipated into the unremarkable normality of taking this for granted. Necessarily unrecognisable, at the time, as a universal part of people's behaviour patterns, it was the first display to me of what I have since seen as a tragedy seemingly built into the human mind at birth; its inability, that is, to enjoy, with any amount of continuing exuberance, new material luxuries or pleasanter modes of life – for more than a few days, at any rate. Afterwards, with the newcomers turned 'part of our furniture', viewpoints face front again, and most often upwards, as well; obliterating any idea of having won something which others, less privileged, don't yet have (and may never).

From this distance, mind you, it is difficult to reconstitute that sudden sense of inviolate security which enabled us, mentally, to relegate guard rosters and their like to the inconsequentiality of mere rituals. What real foundation did we have for it? Were there no spasmodic dangers about from, perhaps, the sort of 'fifth column' civilian resistance which had so plagued the Germans? And how about those pockets of the Wehrmacht to which news of the War's demise might never have percolated? (Smouldering ex-battlefields weren't, after all, the most systematic places for extinguishing every vestige of the flames.)

Well, the answer to each of those doubts lay in the way the conflict had finally come to rest; from the German side, that is. That 'proper' armistice which I suppose we had all been anticipating hadn't ever come about. And while Herr Hitler had had the option of committing suicide, his country had simply finished up in a condition of humiliating exhaustion, unable to push itself even one step further; closer, it might be, to complete collapse of the whole state than any previous history book of warfare would have on record. The very idea of civilian resistance was absurd. With no sign anywhere of it during the actual campaign, there were no Germans left around, now, except a few old men and a scattering of women and girls; most of the teen-age boys having been sucked long-since into the actual fighting. And most of the civilians we did see were already reduced to the depths of degradation – many of them scrubbing around, unashamedly, for stubs of cigarettes discarded by troops into street gutters; a search seemingly much preferred to the remote possibility of finding material (and energy) for making improvised weapons. Everyone we saw was, simply and obviously, tired of it all.

Visual confirmation that this state of affairs was not limited to just civilian relics arrived promptly – almost as if in response to one of our urgent requisitions for replacement stores – only a day or two after my return. Suddenly, a few of us were asked to help out at a location, very near our Camp site, where one of those suspected residual pockets of the Wehrmacht was, in fact, offering itself up for peaceful disposal.

Thus put to the test, our premature belief in the finality of the violence was found unmatched by any degree of confidence from Sten-guns left unloaded; and when, hurriedly, we arrived at the lower slope of a neighbourhood hillside, ours were fairly bristling with ammunition. Below us, was a disorganised mass of confused humanity, shuffling aimlessly around in a kind of corporate grey despondency; grey in the collective colour of the uniforms, and an even deeper shade of it from the collective colour of the faces – drawn, anxious, frightened (here and there), and, above all, as tired-looking as any of the civilians we had seen. Bodily exhausted – obviously; but mentally drained as well, to go by their eyes.

So *these* were Germans? Strangely, they were the first I had seen, face to face; not only during the hostilities, but ever! Over the years, of course, newsreels had more than filled my gap, with their repetitive demonstrations of the Wehrmacht forces at their most bombastic. For that matter, I thought, some out of this present mob might themselves have acted in the scenes I most gapingly remembered; that 'goose-stepped', strutting arrogance which had held so many of us, for so long, in total, subservient awe. Difficult, mind you, now to imagine it – such miserable, decrepit, harmless-looking individuals! Without their weapons – of which I could see none still around – that was all they had suddenly become.

Our part in the operation (if such it could be called) lasted only the half hour before a detachment of Allied infantry duly arrived to take over. It had, in fact, proved an uneventful episode; one of those rare instances of outward appearances telling the whole of the truth. Very fortunately for us, you might feel, since this representation of what was left of the German Army could hardly be called a 'pocket'; more of a 'rucksackful' at the very least – fully thousands of men, most probably the collected remainders of several different, broken units. Had only a few of them retained a spark of their previous Nazi fanaticisms, as well as a weapon or two, my remaining in a state of preservation for writing any of this would have been a miracle of the first order; particularly since – for some reason never since fathomed – I found myself, during four or five long minutes out of the spell, left all on my own (in as impressive a charade as ever I could muster at the time) patrolling that holy stretch of grass which surmounted all of them. Travelling back eventually to Camp, I was quite reinforced in my conviction that the European War was over and done with.

And I was realising, visibly, how comprehensively we had won it. Great Britain was already immersed in a welter of street celebrations of the victory; whereas I supposed that a continuation of what I had just witnessed would have to serve, for Germany, as sole commemoration of this War of its own creation. Back in London and other British towns and cities, even if their individual 'Johnnie' might still be overseas, each of the families already had him proudly marching home again ('Hurrah, hurrah!'); rejoicing in advance – by proxy, as it were, against this first lustre of the triumph wearing off before he could actually return. Here, on the other hand, the only corresponding ditty for concoction would have been 'When Jerry goes trudging home again – oh dear, oh dear!' Just a month ago, this kind of wisecrack would have generated fountains of bawdily refreshing humour amongst us. Unexpectedly, at this early stage, the memory of a sea of grey faces seemed already to be giving me less than expected of such satisfaction. Could it be the sheer unaccustomed quietude of this Peace? One way

Of Straw And Stripes

or another, the barren stupidity of the horrors was beginning to surface.

Necessarily, if I suggest a hushed nature to the Peace which had arrived, you will be right to assume that I am not being literal. The realities of Camp life remained as roughly bustling, as brusquely bawled, and as loudly clattering as ever they had been. It was the unusual calm of my 'inner ear' which I noticed the most. The noise of front-line battles had mostly been too distanced for actually sensitising any of our eardrums; but the certainty of its non-stop production had made it an almost companionable, continuous sound-track of the imagination. Now vanished, there were no longer restrictions on the depth to which one could *think*, during any wisps of real silence which might drift our way.

In point of fact, the only time we were fanned by a respectable breeze of it was on guard duty; that epitome for me, by now, of all the irrelevant boredoms which have ever descended upon mankind. (An indelible opinion which proves – if, indeed, proof is necessary – that the Army never succeeded in properly 'soldierising' me.)

Ordinarily, of course, during the tramping of these solitary safaris, the silence was nullified in its thought-liberating effect by the varying degrees of hypnotic sleepiness from which we would inevitably be suffering. Hypnotism, that is, from the combination of basic fatigue (from a normal day's hard work) and sheer monotony (from the 'nothingness' which surrounded us). So far as I was concerned, there were only two categories of guard duty, 'bad' and 'even worse'; the latter when, blighted by bad luck in the draw, it was to be the extra penance of the night's second watch: this had of necessity to start off, in the early dead of the morning, with that roughest of shaken cruelties – straight out of the warm sleep of one's bunk into an even deeper daze than otherwise of the cold reality which lay outdoors.

It was, nevertheless, during one of these more unfavoured of the permutations that, all of a sudden, the profundity of the tragedy of the whole War floated through to me. The scenario into which I had stumbled my way, from the comfort of the guardhouse, might have been made to measure for some genuine mystical experience, tremblingly awaiting me in the wings, as it were, ready for its entry. The black dregs of the night, drained into the sightlessness of early morning, had a suggestion of residual disaster to them; and the forbidding look of the sizable, warehouse-shaped building which loomed, vaguely yet persistently, out of the distant darknesses did nothing to soften the atmosphere.

Of course, I had seen much the same landscape before; lit (or, rather, unlit) much the same, and at much the same hour of the morning. But my mind, undisturbed at the time by anything particularly unusual, had only been ticking over at its very lowest throttle. This time, there were the very faintest of sounds – or was I merely imagining them? – coming, it seemed, from the direction of that same veritable mausoleum of a ghostly structure. Soon, they were discernable to the point of interesting me into a sharp condition of wide-awakeness.

Those first whispers of soundwaves, allowing for the distance of their journey, may well have started off as the loud shouts of a few individuals to one another: by the time they arrived, no-one could possibly have deciphered the speech-codes, or been absolutely sure of their emanating from human throats. But – however pianissimo – strains of music, trickling through this otherwise impenetrable darkness, were phenomena much too remarkable to remain similarly abstract; and my ears were soon identifying the far-off, reedy tone of an accordion, followed by the more seductive, silky caresses of a violin. Mixed in with both, were further traces of the supposed spoken contributions. Since the music seemed to have exclusively non-English flavours to it – Hungarian, Roumanian, Russian (a well-mixed potpourri of short, improvised snatches) – such talk as might be going on out there, I got to thinking, was likely to need complex translation, even at source and normal volume.

Whereas the very foreignness of the fragments of musical folk-lore I was receiving seemed only to have added to their impact. These were emotions which needed no translation at all – quite as universal as the air they had penetrated in reaching me. Sadness! That was the main message; though with a leavening, too, of hopelessness, of near despair; even more so, of nostalgias for unrecapturable long-agos. To be honest, my imagination must have embellished many of the music's bare essentials; for, by this time, I had realised just what, just whom, I was hearing.

So far as sadness was concerned, I was in course of being reminded of the saddest of all the aftermaths of the War; that living accumulation, sprawled across Europe, of the lasting disasters which long years of violence had wrought upon humanity. I remembered now what that great building had looked like in bright daylight. Not a trace to it, then, of the forbidding or the awesome; nothing to interest us into more than a glance, even if its recent neighbourhood activities had generated the odd snatch of informed rumour as to what was going on. Seemingly, it was a reflection of the civilian refugee problem; a local collection of them, out of the hundreds of thousands of similar Continental vagrants (inextricably mixed-up, nationally), who were all, by now, top priority for getting organised into temporary communes – against the twin nightmares of mass starvation and epidemic disease.

Out here, cocooned in the solemn eternity of the darkness, I was more affected by that distant poignancy of shreds of folk tunes than by all the sense of despondent disillusion which I had absorbed, only the other day, from the defeated Wehrmacht remnants as they surrendered to a highly suspect future. They, at least, would soon have been returning home. To shattered houses, no doubt, and families just as probably partly shattered. Yet with the chance to rebuild their lives, over periods of time; and some few of them lucky enough, into the bargain, to rejoin kinsfolk none of whom the War had damaged at all.

No such luck, I thought, for any of the unfortunates now confined over there, inside that great black edifice. For many of them, it would be the possibility of ever getting back to their own country, let alone anywhere near the town or village where they had lived out their pre-War days. As for the rest of their families, only the gas chambers of the German concentration camps might so often know the secrets. No more than a week or so before this, mind you, I would have been burdened with none of the horrors embedded in my last supposition. It had taken the final overrunning of German territory to expose them. While existence of the camps themselves had been common enough knowledge – presumably compatible with prisoner-of-war enclosures? – none of us had suspected one iota of what had gone on inside them. (Would we have believed it, even if told? The mass slaughter of millions of defenceless civilians? 'Grotesquely warped, Frankenstein-like fiction' – that would surely have been our instant ridicule of the whole idea. For that matter, half a century later, it remains incomprehensibly ghastly in the sheer scope of the evil.)

That said, it was the sombre, atmospheric parable of that one particular tour of guard duty – the only really vivid memory I have from the scores I lasted out during my years of service – which has stuck, limpet-like, in my mind, rather than any of the subsequent analyses of the history books. When the complete silence of the distance resumed, after twenty minutes or so, I could only assume that sleep had at last overtaken all of the motley inhabitants of the building. What had been keeping them awake, I wondered, at that unearthly hour of the morning? Unmitigated misery? Mere boredom? Or, more probably, just the break-down of any regular schedule of sleeping patterns, to accompany the rest of the meaninglessness of their lives? I never saw any of them; yet ever since (and somewhat unjustifiably) they have lingered vaguely on my conscience. How many of them ever managed to recapture even partial happiness? I have never managed much optimism about it. At the time, the routine return of the daylight and noise and bawdiness and hard work was surprisingly welcome. Too many opportunities for thinking deeply can be dangerous . . .

Chapter 26

If the object of this book had been to retell the story of the years of the War, the previous chapter should by rights have been the last one; with the status of my present words reduced to the briefest of epilogues. But I cannot credit any confusion. From the start, has this not been as obvious a self-indulgence as you will find? The reliving of *my* 'War-years' is a much more elastic affair; a different tale which, at this juncture, is still far from complete.

During the ensuing several weeks, there was at any rate no ambiguity about it. My continuing 'wartime' was still the world's as well; so long as the long-drawn-out struggle in the Far East showed no stronger signs of a final resolution than any hitherto. That was a miracle which, seemingly, was at the very pinnacle of impossibilities in any reasonable time-scale; the area over which the battles raged – the jungles, the tropical islands, the stretches of protectively dangerous ocean separating them – making for unending quantities of the same, steaming, stamina-sapping attrition, with no solutions within human vision. Not only that, but all of the conflict's 'extra time' was obviously to be as much a part of 'my War-years' as anything which had happened in Europe. It was an extension evidently made to measure for youngsters like me. If I had been in a kind of civilian limbo just before I was called-up, I was now as badly infected with the military mutation of the ailment. In my own, secret, highly personal way, I suppose that at the time I, too, felt like a refugee.

This was the very natural result of my mind's increasing juxtaposition of the near and the far-off. So close, still, seemed the England which I had only just been visiting, and how unpromisingly remote those unknown, exotic landscapes which – maybe only a month or two ahead – would be sweltering my guts out into the finalities of exhaustion. There were more than usual of the naggings at me of my particular variety of 'home thoughts from abroad'; but, perhaps significantly, these were no longer monopolised by my family. Occasional wisps of

Of Straw And Stripes

nostalgia for what now were revealed as the halcyon days and months and years which I had spent at that substitute home of an office, way back at Borehamwood, were now the more poignantly reminiscent. After all this exclusively male company – how entirely boring, in numbers, my own sex! – that assorted effervescence of ATS girls, at The Grange, was exaggerated to levels of glory I'm sure they would never have suspected of themselves. And what, in particular, of Eddie? I felt as much as ever the sense of that failure. All the more so, with my being the one who had veered off, taking with me with this clinging self-verdict of spinelessness. Had she, I wondered, finally achieved her commission? I was reminded that I was still right at the bottom of the heap. Not a single stripe; never the possibility (save for bottom-of-the-sleeve, long service 'first cousins'); no such ambition left by now, either.

Could it really be? Yet another visitation upon me of that insidious 'waiting disease'? I seemed to have been plagued with it for most of my life; what, in fact, had I *not* lain awaiting, in varying degrees of anxious uncertainty, at one time or another? The outbreak of the War; the delivery of my call-up notice; the luck-of-the-draw of that first posting; the eventual reality of the Invasion and my part in it; the interminably delayed end to Hitler; and, now – was all this merely 'to be continued' in the Japanese edition of the War? Certainly, pestering me unpleasantly from this moment on, were guesses of when the call-up notice for *that* one would be delivered. Events, you could say, were in danger of strict repetition.

At present, nevertheless, they were in a state of stagnation. Whilst this 'mopping-up' operation of what remained of Europe was still going on, nothing of real note was likely to transpire; nothing, at any rate, which could affect us, particularly, here at '107'. When, therefore, sudden news flashes came through that two of Japan's principal cities, first one and then (only a few days later) the other, had been wiped completely off the face of the earth, they sent every one of us reeling into a daze of unbelief. And when, to add to the impossibility, we were told that the destruction had been effected, not by gigantic and sustained bombing missions, but, in each instance, a single bomb dropped by a single plane, it was as if we were in course of being hoodwinked by some recently published work of exaggerated science fiction. Hitler's gas-chambers palled side by side with this! It took all of a few days more for the news to sink properly into us as reality; but, in as little time as that, the Japanese government had already decided to surrender, unconditionally.

Consequently, for us, the 'atomic bomb' – as it was apparently called (none of us having the slightest notion of the theory behind its invention) – was a miracle which had come straight from Heaven. Only much later was there the suspicion, and then the conviction, that it must, in fact, have been spawned on us from the entirely opposite direction. What time was this, anyhow, for starting out on any measure of moralisation? For years, violent death in battle – sometimes scores of thousands at a time – had been almost a normality, with Hitler, it now seemed, having presided as a bonus over *millions* of graves for undefended civilians. Not surprisingly, the inbred philosophy of 'them or us' still lingered as bigotedly as ever; and this development, after all, was to nullify any more such human devastation (spread, as it might well have been, over further years of misery). Who cared one hoot about recent calamities, whatever their size, out there in Japan? Just think! With this finishing-off – could we really believe it? – of *all* of the world's War, there could be nothing now of uncertainty left to concern us; save, maybe, the speed of arrival of our 'demob' papers: each set would constitute a final, personalised full-stop to the bloodstained story. Hurrah, indeed! All of us – all of us 'Johnnies'(as we were), marching at long last back home? It was the loveliest of all possible thoughts.

Unfortunately, this proved extremely short-lived euphoria; for those, that is, in which it had been aroused in the first place. I had to remember that, so far as several amongst us were concerned, a return to 'civvy-street' would signify the steepest of descents – from the now accustomed power and importance of their non-commissioned stripes, or even the sheer aristocracy of those commissioned 'pips' (the 'Captain Corbetts' of this world?), to that previous existence of inbred inequalities which they would have to resume at the bottom, more unequal than most of the others.

At any rate, I thought, that wasn't to concern me. Certainly, I would be for redepositing at the bottom rung of the Civil Service ladder ('clerical officer' indistinguishably replacing 'private'), but I was young enough – somewhere, somehow (surely!), that had to be an advantage? – for believing in a progressive civilian adventure still in front of me, one which could but merge, before long, into properly acceptable respectability. And, in common with the majority of my fellow-conscripts into Army life, I hadn't experienced, in that, even a vestige

Of Straw And Stripes

of a 'career' for comparison one way or the other.

Being thus firmly embedded in the cement of the lowest rank of all, most of us, in point of fact, had thus far existed in a world of complete equality. A strange state of affairs, you might think, since any military establishment, by the very nature of the brute, is bound to consist of an infinite collection of small dictatorships, each dominated by stripes, or pips, as the case may be. But the Training Camps' repeated soakings of us with liberal douches of brainwashing had turned the necessity for being dominated into just another fact of life. Moreover, with all of us crammed in any event into the same boat, domestic circumstances of the others weren't ever for arousing envy or frustration: they couldn't earn favours out here, not for us at the 'bottom of affairs'. In relation to our previous civilian existences, we were, by and large, anonymous.

The change, when it came, was gradual but insidious. After a month or so, it began to dawn on me just how heavy was the millstone, still round my neck, of my age, my lack of years; the newly revealed demobilisation schedules having shoved most of the others well ahead of me in the queue for getting out of khaki. I might not be rated of much importance as a soldier, but my continuing military imprisonment could have been in an Army 'glasshouse' for all the chance I had of an early escape.

The feeling, almost of resentment, festered all the more deeply when the proposed effects of the release graphs progressed from paper theory to visible gaps – appearing in what had been the unchanging stability of our Unit. To witness, successively, the permanent departure of many well accustomed faces was almost to experience, at this late stage, the impact of battle casualties. Just as irrevocably, I would never see any of them again.

Then, again, there were the replacements. These would often trickle in to us in surreptitious fashion – usually from the larger conglomeration of GHQ 2nd Echelon – first to astonish, and then exasperate us with their comparative mediocrity, particularly those who arrived with ready-made stripes on their arms; previous promotions for qualities completely hidden from us. The very idea of advancement, for '107' aboriginals like me, had long since migrated into the realms of the impossible for anyone short of positive brilliance of talent and personality. Obviously, we thought, it must have been altogether an easier climb in other places.

Not that all the grapes were sour. One of the newcomers came complete with SQMS insignias, no less, sewed to *his* sleeves; yet, in this instance, I sensed a distinct improvement on anyone of that level who had hitherto been allocated to us. Come to that, I have no recollection whatsoever of the individual whose place he must have taken; which may either signify the latter's complete lack of personality for registering long-term, or that the posting wasn't a replacement in the first place – perhaps (unusually), an actual addition to the complement as a whole. The new man's responsibilities were on the 'Stores' side of affairs, and I wouldn't therefore have expected to see much, if anything, of him in the normal running of the Unit. In the course of the early impression he made on everyone, however, he took care to get round to all of us, high and low alike, in his informal, conversational style of things – presumably, to get a close-up idea of abilities which he might find lurking around (for passing on to the 'pips' above him). 'Q' Davies! Him, I *do* recall. Quite young, tall and lanky in a leisured way, evidently well educated, he was anything but a typical NCO, particularly of what was usually the rank of a sergeant-major. Back at GHQ, during the campaign, there would have been more scope for the brainy, organisational kind of work for which he was most suited; but climbing to this height, on any variety of promotional rope-ladder, suggested considerably more grit and 'hard steel' to his character than ever he bothered to display on a day-to-day basis. But he had no need, getting all the respect and obedience in the world without any obvious effort on his part.

You may wonder why I am fussing so extravagantly over him. To be sure, he had little enough to do with us in the course of '107's' well-established routines. I was just one of the lowly peasants, against his lofty position on the fringe of that 'pipped' autocracy amongst us of the very few. But, behind the scenes, he must have been squeezing in a little agency work on my behalf. At any rate, when the turn came for departure of Taffy Evans, the most familiar face of them all, there was hardly time to savour the latter's terminal beaming smile, as he boarded the demob-truck on his way back to Wales, before I found myself astonishingly summoned to our very highest of presences – Major Cooke himself! – and handed the double stripes of a full Corporal for the stitching away of my sleeves' bare virginity.

Chapter 27

As I prepare to reassemble my final stretch of Army service into its due share of printed permanence, it occurs to me that Time has just about succeeded in thoroughly warping it – into more lop-sidedness than even the finished shape of the War itself. It has worked away at compressing, concertina-fashion, the period which followed such a ridiculous promoting of me; creating the very possible delusion that this 'beginning', as it were, was one shoved upon me right at the end of the whole affair.

That magical little 'War-diary' of mine has had much to do with this near-deception. Its absence, that is: sheltering placidly in Andrew's bookcase, hundreds of miles away, it was never replaced by me, the 'story' as such being over and done with, so far as I was concerned. Often, therefore, there has been nothing to jog my memory cells against the probable congestion of real months into imagined weeks; nor to rescue, from their total obliteration, those vague spells which weren't much out of the ordinary. (The concealed creases, you may agree, in the squeezed bellows of the concertina.)

The reality of it didn't altogether correspond. Mind you, that was warped, too, but into a quite differently proportioned shape. Far from the end being the miscreant, sinning of being too short, it was a matter of my 'finishing straight' stretching out much too exaggeratedly for what had gone before. No wonder the weeks and the months that were left passed so slowly: there were, after all, so many of them to be got through. Indeed, I was almost to be dealing in 'years'. The inflexible hindsight of that little military bible of my 'AB 64 (Part I)', still in front of me as I write, testifies to all of one and a half of them still to go, at the finish of the War, before I could finally wipe my feet clean of the Army.

Nevertheless, with the departure of the dangerous excitements of the past campaign – the news of nearby battles, *blitzkriegs*, pincer movements and the like (those constant doses of adrenalin which uncertainties about life and death and the very existence of a future had kept flowing through our arteries), a frustrating advance measure of civilian calm soon began to infiltrate our lives; reducing most events from now on to commonplace level, as well as lumping them inextricably together – quite without sharply defined sequence for any retrospective viewpoint such as this.

For example, when did we move to Itzehoe? Was it before or after my 'stripes'? I am not sure; even though, in itself, the slightest change of location was now unusual enough to stick firmly in anyone's memory (our previous culture of unexpected, nomadic wanderings having become the material of history). And Itzehoe I do remember well; a German town turned unresistingly into a British garrison and evidently not feeling any the worse for it. Strangely, to this day my mind still associates it principally with a cinema – and with a dog! Our dog, that is; or, rather, young Norman's. Private Rounce was one of those 'replacements' I have mentioned. As so often with them, he had arrived amongst us completely unheralded, a sudden yet, in his case, immediately acceptable companion. Fair-haired, bespectacled, quietly demeanoured, he was nevertheless more naturally suited to Army life than I. I almost believe that, like Dickie, he may actually have been learning to enjoy it! At any rate, he was one of those individuals who always managed to accumulate around them items of civilian luxury – whence, no-one could tell. And what could be more comfortingly luxurious (or of more mysterious origin) than a dog? Not much larger than a puppy when he first made his entrance, 'Rex' was a brownish-coloured, terrier-shaped, excitable mongrel for whom we soon established the strongest of affections.

It has to be said that, of the individual traits which children bring with them, straight out of the womb, mine must certainly have included the love of dogs. Terriers, seemingly, in particular; for that was the breed of which I was soon pestering Mother with my longings for a 'puppy-dog'. In an unguarded moment – perhaps with an eventual reduction in mind of my instinct to stroke every stray cat which might be patrolling the backlane, (whatever the animal's hygienic condition) – there had been capitulation, at last, from her kind-spoken 'Very shortly, Billy!' Soon, however, I got to discarding her emphasis of 'very', and then to disbelieving altogether so hopeful an adverb. It was a broken promise for which, to this day, I have never really forgiven the world at large, however much I concede the domestic upheavals which must

Of Straw And Stripes

have led to Mother's 'U-turn'.

Admittedly, this present dog belonged to someone else, but I saw as much of it, day by day, as if it had been my own. You could say that Rex was a friend of mine right from the start, and I like to think that the relationship was mutual. Indeed, I'm sure of it: if nothing else, that little typical episode by the side of the Itzehoe Garrison Cinema provided ample confirmation.

I remember myself tucked away into a long khaki ribbon of a queue to the door of the building; waiting, somewhat impatiently, for it to open for us into an evening of what was to be gloriously escapist film entertainment. Not unusually, there was the near certainty of a 'full house'. (Even one or two unoccupied seats would constitute unbelievable finds at most performances.) And as I stood there, just about propped up on all sides by a miscellany of shuffling fellow soldiers, I suddenly perceived none other than Rex himself padding vigorously along the skirting pavement – evidently cock-a-hoop over his own notion of escapism; out in the fresh air, all on his own. How on earth (I wondered) had he managed to get loose in the first place?

Being, in any event, free of those collar-and-lead restrictions which must normally be so frustrating to any dog of quality, Rex had obviously settled for simply following his instincts, wherever they led. So it was that, as he came roughly abreast of where I was cocooned inside the queue, he started what would seem to have been the sheer impossibility of sniffing me out from the distraction of all the strongly-sweated individuals who surrounded me. The fact that (despite my recent hygiene of a hot bath having worsened the odds) he succeeded in a matter of seconds, was my very first intimation that miracles can indeed happen.

Notwithstanding all the animal's clevernesses in finding me, it was, nevertheless, the almost human sentiment embodied in his enthusiasm for the task which has stuck the most tenaciously with me. Rex not only *wanted* to find me, he was absolutely delighted when he did. Oh! – those short, breathless 'Yaps!' of renewed admiration, the countless leapings and boundings and archings and wigglings, as I sidled to the edge of the queue to assist him, half-way, in his determination to muzzle in through the welter of legs.

It was just as well, as it turned out, that Norman had been, all the while, not so far behind his dog. (On the same walk, apparently – even if Rex might not have been willing to acknowledge the fact.) Otherwise,

Of Straw And Stripes

I suspect the dog's unshakable resolve might have stretched to designs upon the cinema itself, where he would doubtless have scurried disruptively around its seats to find lying-space next to mine, together with a share of my entertainment. As it was, ingrained hierarchy resumed in a trice; to leave the two of them – linked properly again by a reattached dog-lead – happily continuing their now indisputably joint expedition away into the distance.

Whether or not the fillip to my self-esteem from this explosion of Rex's devotions contributed to the film's quite delectable entertainment value is a moot point. Of course, there wasn't just myself to go by. The rest of them, too – packed brawn, sinew and muscle into the fuller than fullness of the hall – were gaping entranced at it throughout; the hypothetical fall of the traditional pin supposing, all the while, something in the nature of a thunderclap. Maybe, indeed, it was the single-mindedness of their enjoyment which has since swayed my brain into such sharp memory – not just of the film's title, but of the Hollywood 'stars' of the main roles, the plot's essentials – and, above all, the sheer hypnotic aura of the whole thing. Would a second viewing destroy its magic? I hope not; though – perhaps in unconscious protection of me – no television channel to date seems to have thought it suitable for even temporary resuscitation.

Times and circumstances, unlike the essentials of life, can often contradict everything which has gone before. Present concepts might judge what was put before us that day as incongruous, at the very least, for an audience of War-seasoned soldiers; tough as they come, most of them – long since coarsened into the basics of life and language; ready, surely, only for entertainment of obvious, earthy appeal? Something, at any rate, with fiery, explosive, fast-moving action to it? Only a few months later, more understandably, many of them would be immersed in as drunken soddenness of a Christmas celebration as would satisfy any present-day extremist. Dickie Watts, for example, was to be flat on his back in a street gutter at one point – very happily semi-comatose, with one of his drinking friends (who happened to be still capable of standing) just as happily pouring a stream of warm rum down on to his face in the general direction of his mouth!

These, however, were the other faces of them. Not a sign, here, of insobriety, unless you include the undoubtedly prevalent inebriation with the artistry of what we were viewing. Yet, surprisingly, we had found nothing on display of that expected blood-and-thunder thugduggery of a story-line, or of its customary condiments of bawdy titillations and the like. For that matter, there wasn't a single oath or curse or explosion of blasphemy to excite our ears during the whole of the film script. *The Constant Nymph*: that was the title of this strangely treasurable hour or so. A romantic tale of innocent, adolescent emotions, so remote from the sordid realities of recent times as to cascade refreshingly over the lot of us in the guise of the purest douche ever of spring water – such a relief amidst the continuing, sweltering over-heat of Army life.

I wonder. Since then, I have often wondered. Most doubtfully of all during the past few years, with their fashions in entertainment finally settled into such rigidly segregated compartments. How many counterparts of the wartime hunks of rugged masculinity in that Itzehoe audience would nowadays – even if dragged along – endure watching the gentle romantic appeal of a modern Charles Boyer (then, the French-born epitome of male screen lovers) or the demure, unsullied reactions to his good looks of a present-day Joan Fontaine (Hollywood's box-office counterbalance from their top reservoir of 'girl star quality')? Very few, I suspect. That film – if and when someone finds it! – must now repose in the 'mainly for women' enclosure. And any man concerned with his veneer of tough virility will be for side-stepping it altogether in favour of one of the 'violence at all costs' offerings which now monopolise box-offices.

If, thus put to the test, our own aesthetic sensibilities appear to have been considerably more subtle, it was simply that we had been allowed – compelled, rather – to wallow in the coarser levels of so-called 'excitements' for so many years. And the cruelties of actual bloodshed, and actual brutality, and actual explosions of bombs, or shells, or mortars needed nothing like that amount of time to remove them from any real enjoyment as viewed 'entertainment'. That (with the danger removed) had come to verge upon the boredom of a busman's holiday. As for the film's absence of explicit, consummated sex – that was where nothing could compete with reality; and there was never a shortage of willing fräuleins in the neighbourhood.

Exactly how long our Unit managed to cling to this static security which was Itzehoe I have, after this length of time, no idea. I'm not now even sure that we did leave, ever. Certainly, our stay was very extended: for all intents and purposes, I remember it as one of terminal immobility, as it were. And, on the whole, as reasonably pleasurable;

Of Straw And Stripes

apart, that is, from the nagging frustration of never being able to see the end of it. My promotion, of course, mitigated against boredom, whilst Taffy's duties – still centred around pay-parades and the like – I found surprisingly easy to assimilate, supplying these new chevrons of mine (carrying, as they did, no real need to bark out orders) with a friendly continuation of acceptability, back in that basement of affairs which I had only just left.

Unfortunately, just as military routines were adjusting to the strange lack of violence which now surrounded '107' on all sides, harsh tragedy – as always, securely hidden from the imagination – was about to knife into us, suddenly and searingly, in a disaster which still vaguely aches to this very day. It was almost as if the ephemerality of all life-forms, human and animal alike, was being restated from on high; a superfluous reminder, if ever there was one, on top of all the profligate blood-lettings of the War-years! By comparison, indeed, many may now dismiss a single incident like this as trivial. Never! – certainly, not for me. In one lightning stroke of horror, only feet from my eyes, the dog Rex was killed.

As well as Norman and I, there had been two or three of the others strolling nonchalantly along the pavement. All of us must still have been preoccupied with our light-hearted banter at that precise moment, when the start and finish alike of the animal's summary execution – seemingly ordained all along to take place in the road's gutter, just to the side of us – were being rushed through with such disguising speed as to dull our reflexes for seconds of incredulity.

Poor Rex's own version of Albert Pierrepoint, the heavy Army lorry whose wheels had ripped so savagely over his stomach, was already throbbing its way into distant streets; leaving in its wake nothing more than a small, shapeless, insignificant carcase, twitching still with the spasmodic convulsions of after-death, to go with the glazing of the eyes and the fountain of blood which continued to spout through those gaping jaws. This was just a heap of worthless butcher's offal, fit only for the dustbin. Where, now, I wondered, reposed the creature's joyousness and exuberance and emotional overflow with which he had for so long enlivened the fringes of our daily chores? Could there have been the miracle of a soul to this mere dog? I would have loved to believe so.

Never since then has he departed from my most essential memories. Overweighted importance, you may consider, to bequeath to someone

Of Straw And Stripes

else's pet animal; whom I hadn't myself trained, fed, exercised, or much of anything else for that matter, while he was alive. Norman it was, certainly (and rightly), who now picked up the remains and carried them preciously from the scene, and buried them with quiet respect at a spot near our Camp site. I was merely a grieving bystander; and, even then (as was obligatory in Army circles), most careful to reveal not a scrap of my real emotions to anyone else.

Nevertheless, bit by bit, that dog had undoubtedly nuzzled his way so determinedly and soothingly into the daily background of my life, as almost to own *me*, rather than the other way round. There was the vague instinct of his being part and parcel of my own 'lines of descent'; a lineage only finally completed and rationalised many years later, when, with demobilisations and the like long since faded to drab encyclopaedic material, I had become that absolutely impossible eventuality of mine, a happily married man; all of a sudden interested in resavouring my own childhood at first hand, when experiencing the small boy who was now, excitingly, our son and heir. In the process, I learned as much if not more about the two good people – especially Mother – who had led me through it, as well as they knew how, the first time round.

Resurrected as ghosts, which of them could possibly have failed to recognise this new treble voice? A first persuasive requisition – exactly as of old – for just any variety of 'pet', followed by the same, pleaded crystallising of it into the specifics of 'a puppy-dog, please!'. Not just the question but the answer seemed echoed in the past. No! That was our joint decision – softly transmitted, but non-hypocritically; an honest and firm one. Even so, our little lad was clearly as devastated by being put out of his misery right at the beginning, as I remembered myself when put *into* mine, right at the end.

This was mounting up to quite a sequence of throwbacks; a pattern moreover which, one way or the other, seemed bound to continue. Already, I had a sense of having inherited the undeserved stigma with which I myself had branded Mother, all those years ago; that supposed unreasoning apathy of hers towards children's need of four-legged friendships. And there were indeed to be more flashes from the past, the next one triggered by a sudden reversal of our original ruling – but this time pleasantly and leniently, by contrast. For all that, it remains the most debatable of all moot points, as to whether either of us did actually alter one iota of our first veto. Certainly, I've not the slightest recollection of a specific 'Yes!' – or even the vague implication of one

Of Straw And Stripes

– ever passing our lips; and I'm convinced, in fact, that the child himself must just about have achieved ventriloquism for the accomplishment of this particular U-turn.

The begetter of all this concern was a handsome black collie bitch belonging to neighbourhood acquaintances of ours. Apparently subject, during past months, to the courtship attentions of a nearby terrier (of undoubted stockily-muscled *un*handsomeness), she had finally admitted to the relationship by manufacturing a litter of six puppies – five tiny black collies and one equally minuscule white terrier; the latter giving the impression of having been thought up at the very last moment, just to make up the number.

I well remember where I was when the news of the 'happy event' suddenly erupted over me – at the counter of the local hardware store, buying 'do-it-yourself' items for my current ministrations of first aid to the needy parts of our house's structure. And here, rushing in, was little Keith, excitedly shouting up to my ear: 'Dad! Dad! There's a puppy been born! Can I have it? *Can* I? *Can* I, Dad?' Putting on what I imagined to be my most magisterial veneer, I was in course of gently reminding him of his Mum's dictum (that we were much too busy to have a dog to train, on top of everything else), when our offspring gushed out his exuberant interruption of her having said it was all up to me! At this, I realise that I must have lost every vestige of my veneer on the spot. Entirely speechless, I could only gape; whereupon the little lad, making his own translation of my open mouth, dashed back to tell Hilary that everything was satisfactorily agreed!

It was now obviously impossible to reverse (humanely) a *fait-accompli* of this magnitude. Before long, we were meekly allowing ourselves to be sucked into a close inspection of the puppies *en masse* for the purpose of the first choice which we had been offered. Unlike the subtleties involved in most decisions, this was at any rate a straightforward matter of black or white. Or was it? The little blighters were of very different temperaments, by the look of them; and both my wife and I were initially for choosing from black, the ones cuddling in placidly to their mother, in direct contrast to that excitable, wiggling and kicking smidgen of white; who, when his parent stood up at our approach, hung on in suspension to the teat with which she was presently feeding him – dangerously near, I feared, to treating it as solid food!

Having adventured this far, however, we were I suppose bound to leave the final choice to the boy himself; and, where he was concerned, there was only one of the litter for which he ever had eyes. I might have guessed: it was inevitable, after all. His unwavering casting vote went straight to the little terrier; and it was accordingly this veritable dynamo of a puppy who duly became a permanent member of our family only weeks later. Despite the evidence of my own eyes that he was the most clear-cut of mongrels, it wasn't long before I almost started to disbelieve it. Even then, you see, I had comprehended his proper pedigree. I must have; for, in near-dictatorial style, I insisted on being the chooser of a name for him. And, just as young Keith had been able to see only the one special puppy amongst the whole of the litter, I was hearing in my mind only the one possibility. Rex, of course! So Rex it was, for all of the twelve vigorous, pulsating years that he was with us.

But this is, unfairly, to leapfrog Time. Not always an advisable project (even if the necessary magic should happen to be around), it would indeed have been comforting to be able to do so, back there in the cold continuing conscription of Itzehoe. That the tragically-ended German dog was to have a future direct descendant over in England – with, presumably, no distinguishable language difficulties, between an animal's barking in German or English or whatsoever? – would have soothed away much of my secret agony at the happenings in that blood-spattered gutter. As it was, I was limited to a growing (albeit, non-material) belief in the proper ancestry of Itzehoe's Rex; surely, none other than the promised terrier-dog of my own childhood – so vividly cherished in imagination, yet taken from me before even the chance of its being born into reality. And that line of thought, far from dimming my trauma, encouraged it to linger with me afresh.

Chapter 28

After all this time, it would be easy to make myself believe (and make you believe, too) that what now still remained of my military experience was simply a 'lasting out of the sentence' as it dawdled by, with precious little of interest, and even less of reason, to any of it, now that the graphic adventure of the War had finished, and the background beyond the pale of our Camp site was ever increasingly civilian.

Certainly, the peculiarity of my now having both this compulsion and the time for it, for grieving over a common-or-garden road accident to a mongrel dog, confirms the degree to which 'civilianisation' – to coin a very necessary new word for these circumstances – had already seeped into me. Back in England, of course, the transition was proceeding nothing like so gradually. Already, there had been an absolute upheaval by way of resumed civilian politics; the Labour Party, so soon after the end of the fighting, sweeping Winston Churchill from office quite astonishingly, and in landslide fashion – the same man who had exercised the most supreme power of all for so long and so well, towards the winning of the War and the ability even to contemplate non-violent fripperies like general elections.

In point of fact, this particular change of government was so lightning-swift as almost to achieve a sense of violence in its own right. It seemed to surprise all of us; yet I have never understood why we shouldn't have taken it for granted, even in advance of the event. To my mind, not one subsequent historical analysis has identified the reason for the sheer cataclysm of the change; but I am as sure as ever. The hugely organised system of proxy-voting, put into being for the majority of us who were still in the Armed Services, had effectively turned us, you see, into a more than significant section of the electorate. In addition, the increasing number of British families already welcoming back freed soldiers via the demob-camps made the rest all the more anxious to be able to follow suit as soon as possible. And this was where that little matter of pre-election propaganda had fallen on extremely fertile grounds.

Of Straw And Stripes

Come to think, however, *was* there any whatsoever in the first place? Nothing, at all events, which was blazoned loudly and directly to us in the strict traditions of vote-touting. The Forces Radio Network was mostly concerned with entertainment, and the newspapers of those days with specific reporting of news. And, by the very nature of military cultures, there were neither the necessary soapboxes around nor the people with permitted political bigotries to stand upon them. How, then, could it have been that all of us were not so much *persuaded* of the merits of the Labour Party, but had been rock-hard sure about them, from the very start of the argument? No-one, for that matter, ever thought it a matter for much discussion, let alone dispute of any strength.

We weren't, of course, deliberating a political manifesto; nothing so extensive or deep as that. History may have made it appear that the whole mass of us were determined to have a 'brave new world' of employment for all, a National Health Service to go with it, more equality of opportunity, and much more again of that sort of Utopianism. Not a bit of it! Just to get out of the Forces and back home was the bravest of all worlds just in itself, and that was all we wanted. Very possibly, the lingering memory of Labour's pre-War stance of pacifism – with the similarity of Chamberlain's long since annulled by the belligerence of Churchill – had turned catalyst for our universal certainty that any Labour administration would have us back in 'civvies' before we had time to salute. This proved the first of several 'touch-ups' to my finishing education with which I was furnished during the finale to my Army career. Never since have I accepted pre-election promises; nor, especially, any of the general and ill-defined impressions which they often generate. It is obvious now that, whatever the government, demobilisation would have proceeded on exactly the same course, and in exactly the same time-scale. You could say that the politics of post-War Britain switched direction overnight on the basis of one stupidly misplaced line of expectation by soldiers and their families.

I dare say, mind you, that had the smoke from this gargantuan pipe-dream not stifled any apparent necessity for deeper judgement, a very sizable number of us – though far short of landslide, or possibly even winning, proportions – would still have rushed to vote Labour. For it was a party, in those days, savouring strongly of earnest, intelligent, working-class endeavour, as opposed to the 'public-school-cum-Oxbridge' breeding which clothed most Tory politicians; making them unrealistically remote to peasantry like us – who had been drilled all these years, after all, into seemingly permanent subservience to those with that mystical advantage of 'being commissioned'. (Surely, they were the only ones amongst us properly qualified for Conservatism?) I suppose that, like most of the others, I was nourishing an ever-growing suspicion of the English class system; so highlighted, I felt, in this kind of allocation of the jobs with ability to wield patronising power. Yet here, too, the Army was to smooth out my thoughts; converting them, before I knew it, into a much more proportioned attitude altogether. Not so very long after the War's end, you see, '107' suffered the sudden replacement of its Commanding Officer.

Those two, the one from the other, were certainly different. Almost as extravagantly so as the top and the bottom of the class system itself. Whilst facial features usually tell only part of the story, with them it told the lot. Major Cooke, who had seen us through all of the campaign from Middleton onwards, was one of those rare folk who can combine a benevolently effective variety of firmness with cheerfulness, whatever the situation. And he had a face to match; chubbily contoured, with health of colour and a mouth which had clearly been designed in the first place for slipping easily into smiling sympathy. Was he an Old Etonian (or Harrovian)? I have no idea, but it wouldn't have surprised me; he spoke fluently and educatedly, yet with nothing of that 'toffee-nosed', knife-edge veneer of an accent which had always seemed a sudden but essential acquisition for the one or two 'peasants' whose unusual elevation into the clouds of a commission I had witnessed over the years. *His* 'crowns', at any rate, rested as comfortably on his shoulders as if they were the natural birthmarks of his cradle days. In support of this distinct possibility, he had invariably played down the power they gave him.

And then, again – taking Cooke's place above me, now, as the overlord of what remained of my time in the Army – there was Major Ward. Nothing in the slightest rounded or sympathetic about *him*. That sallow-complexioned face was just as lean and spare as the rest of him; and, never mind the mouth, not a suggestion about his eyes, either, that a single smile had ever entered into any of their repertoires. Evidently a man self-made out of plenty of hard, serious effort. One who wasn't likely to short-sell an iota of the authority he must have envisaged as positively shining out from his particular pair of crowns. Could it be that muscle strain from the way he carried them so

Of Straw And Stripes

unrelaxedly, so preciously, might even have worsened the natural slope of his shoulders? A regular soldier if ever I saw one, risen (it would seem belabouredly) from the depths of 'other-rankdom', those insignia obviously represented the epitome to him of things of real importance.

Still, we had won the War in the cause of democratic freedoms, and the look on a man's face, or the entire mask of his personality for that matter, wasn't for objection just because of non-conformity. I doubt, indeed, whether I would have remembered either of them importantly, just as individuals. But it was the different attitude which each had towards 'managing' the men around me at '107', and the compared effect of it on us, which proved so lasting in value. If only I had been able to realise it at the time! I was being told, at a stroke, most of what later experiences in post-demob Britain would only gradually reinforce into certain belief.

And this was that effective motivation of people undoubtedly falls within the realm of Art rather than Science. Perhaps this is why outstanding managers are so hard to find; artists of real distinction, after all, being rare diamonds in any sphere. In his way, however, our Major Cooke must surely have been one of them. Instinctively, he seemed to sense that ready acceptance of his directions by our minds was almost as important as the enforced, 'knee-jerk' obedience of our bodies; whereas Ward was solely concerned with getting his orders carried out to the letter, never minding what we thought of them – or of him, either. Adjusting to this precipice of a drop to the rigidities of undiluted autocracy needed time; and – the Army being the most unlikely provider of it – I was, as you will soon learn, still insufficiently prepared at the juncture of that eventual 'incident', the one which would momentarily tarnish me with the suspicion that I might even be court-martialled for it! Most severely disciplined, at any rate. But this is side-stepping the preliminaries ...

Of course, Ward wasn't the only major change to our little community following the end of the War. With the disappearance of nearby battle conditions – when the achievement of simply staying alive had been our only regular 'up-beat' reassurance against the daily grind of the work – there was now the thought and feasibility of more normal relaxations. An occasional drink, for example; one no longer restricted to the over-brewed tang of NAAFI tea – something more sociably warming and stimulating than that.

Unfortunately, there wasn't to be much of it. Beer, that is. The incredible organisation of all kinds of supplies which had progressed, against all odds, during the campaign couldn't now, seemingly, extend to this extremity. And, in respect of the more plentiful supply of hard spirits, the Sergeants' and Officers' Messes only were its unvarying destinations. My restriction as yet to just a couple of 'stripes' leaving me still an outside spectator, I mentally labelled the places a periodic drunken den and very nearly a 'hostel for dipsomaniacs' respectively. Exaggerations, maybe, but our own comparative sobriety was certainly in contrast to reports from the inside of each of them.

In support of these, just before Cooke's transfer-out in fact, I recall the illustrative, light-hearted visit we had from him and two of his fellow-officers, at two in the morning; unexpectedly rousing us from our beds apparently for a kind of informal 'inspection' of the Unit's nocturnal readiness. None of the three of them displayed any obvious signs of 'wooziness': for that hour of day, indeed, they were all uncommonly calm, pleasant and dignified. Yet when they left, after only five or ten minutes, there were, I thought, undoubted whiffs of alcoholic fumes newly flavouring the atmosphere, as we desperately sought to recapture our sleep. It was a routine, I may say, with which they never troubled us ever again.

If anything showed up the gulf between the régimes, it was this episode. Despite the possibility of its having been an inebriated post-party joke, played on us at the spur of the moment, we dismissed it easily enough from our concerns; hardly recalling it at all, in fact, by reveille. Whereas a like juvenility under Ward would have roused unquenchable resentment, with even deeper undercurrents than before of our critical hangings, drawings and quarterings of him.

But I had to remember that this was no longer wartime. Worthwhile, effective underground 'resistance movements' had had their day: those within one's mind had become quite pointlessly petty. The moment that Major Cooke finally disappeared from view, abruptly and permanently, there was the dread realisation that we were now irrevocably saddled for ever more with nothing better than second-rate, in this immovable substitute for a 'proper' public-school-trained officer. So much for my previous prejudices!

Appropriate may it have been, nevertheless, that Major Ward's reign over us materialised at this particular stage of my story. If nothing else, it prevented a mere fizzling-out of this in gradual, nondescript, anonymous fashion, with none of the sheer exhilaration in which I was to revel when I eventually got free of the man and the rest of his Army for good. As it was, condensed to manageable proportions by that persistent concertina of mine, the period I spent under him now assumes the smatch, in the concert hall, of a symphony's last-movement turbulence; the three principal confrontations I had with him resounding in my ears as the selected emphases of the percussionist's gong, in forecast of the closing bars of the work.

Truth to tell, mind you, I must have been the only 'confronter' present at the start of the first of those reverberations, if indeed there was one there at all. In his ungracious way, Ward was actually trying to *give* me something! A third stripe, believe it or not! By this time, the original shape of '107' had split down most of its seams; and on this occasion, incredibly, it was the stitching around Tug Wilson which was loosening, for the turn which had now reached him, too, of a journey 'back to the future' in England. Thus, with the chevrons already on my arms looking apparently well-bedded to those who mattered, I learned that I was about to be thrust headlong into a full three-stripes-worth of a replacement job for him – as the new 'be-all-and-end-all' of the Unit's Orderly Room.

If I had needed a second opinion on the essentials of the man facing me, he supplied it unmistakingly when (obviously to his amazement) I tried to turn down the appointment. Affronted – anger, verging on fury: that was his flash-point display of temperament. It must have been his very first experience of anyone wanting to abdicate from even a whiff of promotion; and from then onwards, I think, this abstract variety of confrontation was in constant danger of seeping into the rest of the proceedings. But instinct was to avoid potential disaster; the look in his eyes being less daunting by far than the prospect of the Sergeants' Mess. For that, of course, was the bugbear. Nothing wrong with the job itself; as attractive and familiar, perhaps, as self-confidence could wish for. And the adventure of a third stripe, charismatic even now, after the 'end of the main story', was not to be sneezed at. No; it was the obligatory drunken soddenness of the place which was the overall impossibility. I would be the most peculiarly warped character ever to be seen in it. I didn't even smoke cigarettes, the tribal universality of those days, and – hush! – I was *still* a virgin! The first of these astonishing purities might be accepted and the second concealed, but I was teetotal as well; which last word in malformation of character would, I knew, prevent me ever surviving the place.

It was a situation which called for quickly invented advocacy; all of which was bound to be fictional, for casting stones at the moral tone of the Sergeants' culture would surely imply imminent boulders against the leisure philosophies of the officers. I desperately conjured up what I considered impassioned logic; that I wasn't really up to the added responsibility; didn't have the time left in my Service career for good job-continuity (in the Unit's best interests); and as much more of the same as I could manage to get out, before Ward cut me short. Alas, I was on the wrong tack altogether. None of this, I heard him barking, was my concern. *He* was the one who made the decisions; *he* the only one qualified to assess me; *he* the man in charge of all the Unit's needs! Before I knew it, I was outside again, clutching my undoubted 'sentence' of the new stripes in readiness for the stitching-on of them; and hopelessly resigned, as from now, to the change in my sleeping accommodation.

Now, I have never been absolutely sure. Was I ever, in fact, properly introduced to my new bed-space, the day that I first walked into the Mess through the front door of the building? I was so instantly immersed in the party-scene already under way that I can only imagine my belongings having conveniently been taken upstairs on my behalf. Certainly, the first recollection of bodily contact with the bed itself was when I woke up on it, in the middle of the night, with the vague sense that this must be what a drunken stupor was all about. Or was I on a bed at all? Much more like a revolving spit, on which – the sweat on my brow adding to the realism – I was being slow-roasted, like some prize porker for the next-day's main meal: it was the most horrible awakening that I have ever suffered. Thankfully, after rolling clumsily off on to my feet via the horizontal of the floor, I fell back again across the bed; at which stage the nausea and the dizziness began to leave me, and my coma to return. When daylight finally returned me to full consciousness, I was merely left with the impression of living death which I subsequently learned was called a 'hangover'. The whole procedure was most decidedly a further stage of the Army's finishing of my education.

For much of that day, it was difficult for me to believe that I had ever been capable of actual enjoyment; as opposed to this present painstaking recovery of the mere ability to exist. The ambience and excitements of the previous evening came back only in bits and pieces, most of which were inspired by the grins and winks and snide remarks of the other sergeants as they passed by me. At any rate, I cannot have disgraced myself in their eyes; not even, seemingly, by their need to drag my collapsed dead weight upstairs, as the combined consequence of all those stimulating little 'shorts' which they had successively placed in front of me. Having decided, for once, to join the herd (not wishing to be trampled underfoot in the course of a universal stampede), I had proceeded to sip pleasantly away at these gifts – under the innocence of an idea that quantity rather than strength could be the only danger. I now knew, at any rate, the quite titanic muscle possessed by that German gin with the nom-de-plume of *Steinhager*! Any sense of indignity from the thought of what my slumped drunken body must have looked like was reassuringly countered, amusingly, by reports from one or two of the girls at the party – the only ATS, incidentally, whom I had seen since England days. They had adjudged my eyes (while these still remained in a state of openness) to have been 'glittering' most seductively all night. (I vaguely remembered chatting merrily away with female company.) Who knows? My virginity might have gone out of the door in company with my teetotalism, had I not blacked out!

Whatever the attractions of English ATS girls, however, an undue number of the duties I found awaiting me as Orderly Room Sergeant seemed to centre around the sexual habits and life-styles of the district's German fräuleins. Together, of course, with those of a substantial percentage of '107's' hitherto sex-deprived male personnel. 'Condoms'? The name hadn't yet been thought up. 'French letters'! That was more like it; each one so much more important than the whole of that nation's alphabet put together. I found myself the duly appointed watchdog of their adequate provisioning, with power (well up my priority-list) for emergency requisitions whenever the stockpile seemed near to danger level – as often, with outgoings so persistently avaricious. This aspect of the routine was straightforward enough, however, and the chance of completely running out of the things usually remote; even if it carried fantasy consequences for me which almost reached 'incitement of mutiny in the ranks' proportions. But, always teetering on the edge, there remained that equal necessity for maintaining standards in the renewal supplies sent us for issue. And this was a different game altogether.

I could hardly be regarded an expert in the minutiae of such prophylactics, but there was a superabundance of unofficial 'inspectors' around in any event, each one of whom was. All the users of them, it seemed. Any pinhole or tiny laceration discovered in advance, or the slightest material weakness experienced 'on test', was brought unfailingly and post-haste to my notice with a desperate anxiety of concern – often passion which must more than have rivalled the romantic performances – surely more appropriate, I thought, to the threat of a third world war than the offshoot of leisure activities. At first, indeed, the strictly serious attitude of everyone involved was so incongruous as to seem funny in its own right. Side by side, after all, with the welter of bawdy, often revoltingly obscene, sexual jokes which had flowed constantly round me from Training Camp days onward.

In point of fact, this lightning-flash of amusement was quickly replaced by annoyance at the persistent hassle of it all. If I sometimes felt like yelling at them, 'Hop it, the lot of you! Think of your wives back home!', I had to remember that the Army's Top Brass, more sensibly pragmatic than me, had long since made their decision. While they could successfully train men to attack enemy machine-gun nests, any question of getting the same men to comply with a code of civilian-type morals was quite unreal in the extent of its absurdity – a completely impossible proposition, as opposed to the obvious and thoroughly realistic hygienic possibilities offered by the Campaign's supply lines; an accepted policy now traditionally as serious as any of the present pesterers of my Orderly Room. Possibly taking my recent part-entry into the Mess's alcohol culture as a pointer, and knowing, in any event, that I had no potential for solitary evangelism, I therefore played 'follow my leader' again and simply got on with it.

And so we come to the second stroke of the gong. By then, my sergeant-stripes were almost as much the bloodbrothers of my sleeves as those crowns had been of the shoulders of Major Cooke. Without in any way overpreening myself, I sensed that I had got to running the Orderly Room side of things as proficiently as that venerable gentleman had previously caressed the affairs of the whole Unit. I was on top of the job, with mounted confidence from the way I found myself dealing with all its mixed headaches and difficulties. Surprisingly smoothly! If I had been able to master the intricacies of those French letters, after all – and moans about their supply and strength alike were now matters of the past – I could surely conquer anything still to come. How was it, I wondered, that I had ever been jostled out of my stride by Edney? Where was *he* now? Departed evidently, quite stripeless, into some meaningless nothing. In my present state of euphoria, even Major Ward

Of Straw And Stripes

no longer really bothered me.

Of course, I was only thinking in earthly terms; earthly tasks, earthly problems – certainly not those of Heaven or Hell or any other such imponderable. And, lurking around when I was normally in no state for suspecting its arrival, there was always the danger of that witching hour of two in the morning – when *was* it that I last remembered sampling its fantasies? – which now exploded upon me the most unexpected of developments. That night, at any rate, after the telephone bell had, half-and-half, roughed me up out of the solidity of my sleep, I heard an abrupt grating into my ear of the order for immediate evacuation outdoors of the whole of '107', complete with spades and pickaxes for some completely unexplained purpose! A nocturnal job of intricate troop marshalling which, I had to assume, was contained somewhere or other within these three stripes of mine.

Now, on the face of it, the message was balderdash; credible only if I imagined myself still in the midst of active warfare, with the kind of battle-orders that had always been tailor-made for blind obedience, undistracted by trifling subtleties like reasons. Then, we would probably have been assuming – this early in the morning (a favourite surprise-time of his) – that Von Runstedt had simply started another of his 'Bulge' offensives, this time directly towards us. (Even if, in that event, the stipulated requirement might have been for as many weapons as possible rather than builders' tools?) As it was, such of my intellect as had yet surfaced from its original sleep wasn't coping at all well with the suddenness of such a weird conundrum. Were our wagons even stocked with pickaxes and the like? Wasn't it the Pioneer Corps who was? How many of us would it take to run around riving all the others, too, out of their beds? And with what morale-boosting slogan? The very most that my mind could manage was a vague recollection of the last time there had been one of these 'two-in-the-morning' confusions – that meaningless 'inspection' by Major Cooke and Company, and our slight suspicion, then, of merry party pranks. A pity this time round, I felt, that there hadn't been a similar personal appearance: I might have been able to get a second opinion from the assessment of Ward's alcoholic breath-level. No doubt swayed by the latter train of thought, and unable to make any other sense of what I thought I had heard, I finished up by simply resuming my sleep.

If I had ever imagined the slightest resemblance in personality between the successive men to preside over us as Commanding Officer,

Of Straw And Stripes

such fallacy was finally dispelled when the morning's daylight eventually and properly roused me. Yet my first residual instinct, on waking, must still have been to link them to some degree. In fashion with the aftermath of Cooke's nocturnal episode, I was in course of putting the present one similarly aside in my mind as a passing triviality, when, like a thunderclap and before breakfast, too, I was summoned to Major Ward's office; where he greeted me with a loudly bellowed demand for explanation of my disobedience!

I would like to believe that I had stalked confidently into the room, gazing with defiance straight at him, but, on an empty stomach, this is hardly likely to have been the case. The fierce aggression of his features generally was bad enough, without extending my greetings as far as his eyes. On the positive side of things, however, the deep flush which, unusually, was now correcting his usual pallor bolstered an impression of boisterous good health – until one sensed that the anger engendering it might just as easily extend at any time to an accompanying heart attack; such was the tension of the moment. On the other hand, there was no shade of uncertainty whatsoever about the invective with which I was now being battered. Quite a frontal machine-gun burst of it, you might say. No time, either (or the genius within me), for inventing any worthwhile shield of a tactful, fictional excuse which might still avoid the firing of those boulders against the Officers' Mess. So, what? It seemed my continuing existence was at stake. I decided on the highly dangerous policy of honesty, and dispatched one of the largest of the rocks straight in his direction!

And, unexpectedly, it achieved a remarkable transformation. Fortunately, I remembered the obligatory outward respect of any military peasant (albeit a striped one) to his military master. I was polite, if firm; logical, if accusatory in alcoholic terms; steadfast, if with a suitable garnishing of implied apology. But, even as the words were coming out of my mouth, I knew that they should have added up to a defence which was hopeless. In the Army, an order was an order, however ridiculous the sound of it. (In Training Camp mentality, to the extent of the hypothetical greasy pole for meaningless climbing.) Yet here was straightforwardness which our Major Ward must never before have experienced. Certainly, he seemed dumbfounded, and, far from continuing to harangue me – or from exploding into even wilder a tantrum – our 'session' drifted off, imperceptibly, into a thoroughly amicable discussion of Unit administrative affairs generally. Even

Ward's skin had resumed its normal neutrality by the time I eventually walked out of the room – in that state of calm which I would dearly like to have enjoyed when first presenting myself. The strangest aspect of the whole affair was that, whilst his instructions had plainly been serious enough, I never learned what the spades or the pickaxes (or both) had ever been scheduled to achieve. Nor why, if truly important, there had been no further telephone call to me at the time. Somehow, to this day, there is still a faint whiff of *Steinhager* about that early-morning fairy story . . .

Chapter 29

'Land of hope and glory,
When shall I be free?
Just when the demob numbers
Come round to forty-three.'

As you will suspect by now, the Army was never to convert me into a 'proper' soldier of any real conviction or ability. An assault course was still as much in the realm of my impossibilities when I came out as when I went in. Agility, stamina, strength of muscles, all the physical side of things which *is* the Army – not one of these attributes had newly migrated into my genes over all the years of my disguise beneath this veneer of khaki. Yet, in a strangely negative way, the Military did achieve for me the unlikely end-product of secret lyricist, and to Elgar at that! If I must have been one of an extremely select few to manage scribbling a diary entry during their landing-craft's transit of the Channel, I'm somewhat more confident of my complete uniqueness in having a signature tune at all for the impending ritual of the demobilisation camp!

If I needed one, it would serve as a ready reminder of how far down I was on that list of the hordes of release candidates; mid-forty categories being light-years behind the magical vanguard, long since allowed to escape, of 'number one'. And recalculation of the actual time-scale, by reference to the eventual arrival of autumn of the year 1946, is to have to resuffer the leaden crawl of the weeks and the months which still, even then, blocked the far exit of the tunnel of my Army life. At this stage, at any rate, I was at last able to find a black-and-white translation of '43' into its actual date on the calendar; almost a synchronisation with the end of the year itself. Only another three of those months to go now, after all!

Or, more realistically, twelve weeks, for each of these now seemed to expand into a whole month in its own right. Far from my relaxing

Of Straw And Stripes

into a 'nothing-can-now-go-wrong', smooth glide into the final days of my saga, there was at the back of me an obstinate sense that something could, indeed, still go very much wrong. I suppose that I was lapsing into an abstract version of that perpetual bugbear of mine, another 'doom scenario'. And – unlikely shadow of a comparison with a distant piano examination! – it was one which, again, duly came to pass, in the most un-abstract form of a written notification from RAOC Headquarters. Their proposal? To put back the release of certain 'age and service' groups, in relation to a few short-supply trades. Square in the middle of each of these targets for curtailment (as you will have guessed), I was evidently due for some undefinedly longer endurance of the Forces.

History now advises me that the extent of my reaction in terms of sheer misery, near despair, was somewhat out of proportion. But, then, doesn't hindsight so often simplify past problems and blockages with its patronising knowledge of what had been the uncertainties of their secrets? At the time, it was Fate pronouncing dourly against the whole of my long-term happiness. Now, I can see it as merely ensuring one final, farewell (you could say), confrontation with Ward before I departed for good. Anything less, I suppose, would have left my relationship with him quite illogically truncated (for I was never to give him a final handshake) an unresolved silence in place of the final chords of the symphony.

It was the memorandum's 'small print', of course, which sparked off the final eruption. I might have missed the detail of it altogether, had not the general contents been quite so unexpected. Democracy had managed to infiltrate the Army's Top Brass! (The War must well and truly be over.) An appeal procedure, indeed, against their present proposal! This was an offshoot I could barely credit; but, in course of the sudden rush to my head of desperate adrenalin, I quickly found myself before the Orderly Room's typewriter, rattling out a firm, considered defence so far as '107's' affairs were concerned.

Only afterwards did Ward's exaggerated sensitivities about my submission make any sense to me. Given that his desk was just its staging post on the way to GHQ, well beyond his parochial influence, he may have imagined that his personal authority at '107' was in some way being challenged; his general reputation, as well. He was the one saddled for ever more with replacing people like me – and never, he could have thought, with more than the luck of the dice on his side as to whom they sent in exchange. Delay, when offered, must always have been his best bet. ('The devil he knew'?)

I question whether knowing the inside of the man's mind would have altered a jot of my course of action; but there is no doubt that, under all the laws of repetition, I should by now have been able to recognise each nuance of his emotional extravaganzas, together with the likely ingredient to foment it. Yet the cannon-ball of this particular summons 'to the presence' was to land upon me with even sharper a shock than previously.

Whatever else it might have signified, the battleground on to which I stepped when I opened his door was well worthy of climaxing the whole of the fighting of the War itself. Missiles like 'Who do you think you are?', 'How dare you presume that?', and 'None of your business in the first place!' were soon bouncing around the room in the general direction of my head. Minutes passed before I can recollect an opportunity for contributing more than the odd word of my own into the maelstrom. Only when our Major Ward unexpectedly exhibited the human frailty of having to take breath in any substantial quantity did I have the chance for reasoned argument. And then, remembering our previous encounter, I again set out to be as straightforward, and as 'short and sweet', as my own rising temper and the resumption of his breath supply would in any event allow.

In point of fact, however, I was never in danger of replying in kind by simply trying to shout him down. My 'defence', such as it was, centred around one basic question; inviting him as it were to come straight back into the argument and recite the whole of his 'prosecution' again from the beginning, so that I might this time properly understand it! What had I done wrong? HQ hadn't restricted appeals to those on compassionate grounds. Mine (which wasn't) had merely stressed the strictly minimal disruption to '107' if the threatened few of us left as first time-scheduled. I had assumed that he would readily have been seconding this certainty of mine of our Unit's resilience. Did he, nevertheless, now propose to veto the procedures laid down by HQ? This was an additional poser popped in by me for good measure at the very last moment; and, in common with my previous experiences with him, breath, at this juncture, seemed to take rather longer than expected to regain tenancy of his lungs – before he resumed what had now, amazingly, changed to more than reasonable a meeting of minds.

It would have been nice to take the memory of these brushes with

Major Ward into civilian life, as *curriculum vitae* categories of 'steely determination and pugnaciousness' which I had never before suspected of my character. But why was it, then, that I never similarly confronted any of the little tyrants who later brooded over me in 'civvy-street' from time to time, often to the discomfort of my career prospects? Partly, it may have been because of the differing respect I held for the military and civilian promotion structures. I never hankered after a recommendation by Ward for further advancement, simply because I didn't relish the three stripes I already had; and any danger of losing them altogether was equally trivial, since I had never wanted the Corporal's stripes, either. Admittedly, demotion in the Civil Service was a well-nigh unknown feat of dexterity – a sheer impossibility of course for me, at first, re-entering down at the basement! – but even the smidgen of a career was unrealistic without a recommendation for one of their be-all-and-end-all 'promotion boards'. There was a kind of supreme, negative power always hovering around, the continuing absence of anything positive being truly the kiss of death. Talent was traditionally second to carefulness, the in-built ability for never making the slightest mistake of any kind. And a stormy interview rated high on the list of the very worst mistakes one could make.

That said, I fear it is gilding the lily, where I am concerned, to paint a comparison of Ward's fearsomeness quite so vividly. With longer exposure to him, there might even have developed a streak of boredom to the projection of his personality on me; for, as I have described, he was one of those individuals with a bark of very different quality from his bite. Indeed, during the latter stages of our sessions, he often finished up not obviously biting anything at all; not even chewing it. More a question of his rounding things off by sucking on an imaginary boiled sweet, the sugar of it dispersing all of his previous show of acidity.

What was it this time, I wonder? A mint humbug? All I knew was that my advocacy was soon on its way to those distant HQ Offices, suffering from only the most minor of flesh-wounds – the deletion of half of one of its sentences; a surface scratch which damaged nothing, I thought, of the rationale of the piece.

* * *

'10578753'! That will always be the number of all numbers for me. Etched on the discs I carried round my neck for five years, it is still as indelibly so on the cells of my brain as throughout the countless years which have since swirled by, ever so much more rapidly. But, running it a close second at the time, was that tantalising, provocative, infuriating code reference of '43'! In the beginning, just a theory, a position on a list; then the living breath of a date on a schedule; and, now, this regression to the shadow-world of unsolved enigmas. Would it ever in a day reveal its true identity? I could but wait.

As it turned out, the whole of the remainder of my time in Germany was clouded by the same kind of blind uncertainty with which I had been burdened all those years ago, just before my call-up at Richmond and afterwards, as well. For, though I naturally imagined that I would soon learn the outcome of my appeal, I never actually did! The weeks dragged themselves onward, each seeming more likely than the others for receiving the missing verdict; but this continuing dead silence might well result, I began to think, from not one of my written 'words in anger' having been properly scrutinised. Yet, obviously, there had to be new dates for '43' and its like. Surely these, if nothing else, were already overdue? Not even the softest of whispers ever in fact reaching us, the symmetry of those far-off days of 1942 and this, the near-finish of my Service history, was accordingly perfected by a state of common-or-garden muddle. I was only reassured, eventually, of the complete lack of damage to '43's' original identity by the excitement of its actual arrival at close quarters; sweeping me off – almost unexpectedly by then – into the sheer glories of demobilisation itself; entirely undeferred; entirely as first promised!

Chapter 30

The pulse of life having amazingly accelerated all of a sudden, I found myself, one moment, saying my goodbyes to Germany and, only the very next it seemed, with the welcoming gates of the Demobilisation Camp already facing me. Almost the only thing to stick in my mind about the journey back to England was the last yard or so of it; lumbering, kitbag-laden, along the ship's swaying gangway, accompanied by the final 'doom scenario' of its tossing me off into the water – agonisingly short of my goal! But a few steps more, and I was on dry land again, with all the returned confidence in the world of my being back this time for good.

There were so many similarities between the beginning and the end of my saga. The excitement blurring the outlines of this safari from Europe, just completed, almost matched the mental anxieties which had disguised the ancient, frosted transporting of my adolescence from South Shields to Richmond all those years ago. I still had vague recall of how roughly, and in such a wild state of mismeasurement, my original battledress had been slung at me. Yet, once the preliminary queuing was over, here I was grabbing the nearest civilian outfit on free issue, without a thought of first fitting myself into it. (Needless to say, I never subsequently managed the task!)

Not, mind you, that there was much resemblance between the Army battledress I was presently sporting and that original ragamuffin khaki of years back – ramming into us, at the time, its obvious, poverty-stricken inferiority to the standard dress of American and Canadian soldiers. The easy access to well-stocked 'ADOS Dump' stores in Europe had enabled half of my uniform to finish up completely un-British, with the other half made acceptable only by the restyling of German tailors, easily bribed by free Army-issue cigarettes or blocks of chocolate. Each of us had long ago acquired a Canadian beret, as well as collar-attached Canadian shirts and one of their matching khaki ties, whilst our best battledress blouse (such as the one I now wore) would miraculously have developed smart lapels; in imitation of a British commissioned officer – or, as a matter of course, of any old American 'other ranker'. In addition (unseen to the world but equally morale-boosting), our very underclothes had latterly turned just as thoroughly foreign. My trusty 'long-johns', for example – the staple covering of my body-skin for so many years of nights and days – were no longer with me; replaced, you might guess, by silk-texture Canadian vests and short (!) underpants. (Had we really been pre-eminent in winning the War? I was left with a vague impression of our having slipped to second-best in many things . . .)

I may say that, on the day, none of this was of interest to me. Obsessed with 'jilldie-ing' this return of mine to normality – ideally, meeting Training Camp requirements: should I not 'already have been home by now'? – I was mostly concerned with searching out the general exit of the establishment, pausing at only its most indispensable 'pit-stops' in the process. In point of fact, had the QM Stores not loomed up directly in front of me, I might well have deliberately avoided them, chancing the bits and pieces in my wardrobe back home as stop-gap substitutes for all this khaki. (A provisional logic most wisely thought up, as it happened, in view of my subsequent dire need of it.)

One signpost, however, which even my present state of irrepressible hustle didn't dare to ignore, motioned me to the queue at the office where military railway warrants were being authorised. Before too long, I had wormed my way through it to the requisitioning of the very last one for which I would ever qualify. Hurriedly checking that 'South Shields' was indeed correctly and decipherably endorsed on the precious slip of paper, I sensed, with a certain amount of residual unbelief, that I was at last fully equipped for proceeding on my way. More than that, I soon found myself lounging on an actual seat on an actual train; experiencing all of its huffing and puffing and rattling and quivering, as it started off on the way to my home town. Very much the same, steamy commotion as had accompanied me on that original trip; though, in reverse direction, sounding then so much more pessimistically ugly as for me to have wished the brute to go as slowly as possible. Today, I thought, it should be straining every puff it had in its belly to break the speed record for the route.

It didn't, of course. Nor, during the journey, was there the slightest evidence of its even trying. The driver must have thought the guard's van contained the coffin of some deceased member of the Royal Family, in course of transport to the start of the obligatory ceremonial funeral. This would explain the train being quite so restrained in character as this; sufficient, surely, for it to be part of the procession itself. Into the realm of more unquestionable reality, however, fell the spare time with which I was thus laden for reflective thought – the first lull in the action, as you might label it, of the whole day.

During the time that I sat there, imprisoned beside the window of that gently swaying railway carriage, the well-known, slightly shabby greens outside of the countryside of the North-East creeping all too gradually into view, I must have got through the making of most of my past 'goodbyes'. Part subconsciously, maybe, but none the less nostalgically for that. They had all been queuing up against my total blockage so far of sentiment – regret, or sadness, or even a mental thumbing of my nose – at finally leaving '107' behind; a part of history, now, that I would never revisit, except eventually like this, on the magic carpet of the written word.

The frozen state of my emotions, when jumping on to the Army truck which was to whisk me away in the direction of the German railway and thence vaguely towards a ship and England, had surprised even me a little. Not even a touch of that wistfulness which my final War diary entry had aroused? But that had been in the days when the Unit was still fully alive; that which had finished up around me being but the shell of it, with the majority of its original qualities, like the chubby benevolence of Taffy Evans, and the virile hustle and bustle of Tug Wilson, and even the cultured mystery which had symbolised the shaven pate of 'Edney', long since departed, long before me. Norman Rounce was still there, of course – but where did the spirit of 'Rex', the most important part of him, now repose? While Dickie Watts would undoubtedly bounce around '107' as before for a while yet, my Sergeant's stripes had arguably turned *him* into a remote memory already, months back. And my colleagues in the Mess itself? Nothing more, the lot of them, than recent acquisitions; not one, not even that guru of mine 'Q' Davies, having developed into a real friend. I must have realised that I was going out as I had come in – by myself; and still a loner.

In emphasis of it, this final, English stage of my round trip was only sparsely populated with fellow travellers; very few indeed, when compared with my original 'journey into conscription', as I now remembered it. Almost everyone then on board had been part of the

Of Straw And Stripes

same military pilgrimage to the Training Camp; whereas, here, I was one of only a tiny minority with remaining Service links, to go by the rarity of a uniform of any design. Such a great proportion of the 'demob' programme was, thus demonstrably, a thing of the past. Most certainly, at any rate, I was late in the day to consider myself a 'Johnnie coming marching home again'. Or to expect to hear anyone whomsoever cheering me back on that basis. In my new role of recreated civilian, I would have to accept, in fact, the somewhat lower category of an afterthought to the rest of them.

That said, I doubt whether, that afternoon, I had either capacity or instinct for prolonged dissection of any topic whatsoever. And of those jumbled images which did flicker through my brain, as the train chuffed its way ever closer to South Shields, there are none, of course, which now remain sharp and clear and precise. For that matter, they can't have been much sharper at the time, with the rocking nature of my travel doing its best to lull me to sleep. But, of all the years of the War, those spent at Borehamwood were the ones now knocking the most often at the door of my mind.

How far, indeed, had they receded within the relentless universe of Time! So much was now packed in front of them, almost to hide them altogether – Swaffham, Middleton, Normandy, Belgium, Holland, Germany; as well as all those intermediate 'to's and fro's'. This was an accumulation of distance more than capable of lending special enchantment to that old 'Grange' of a building. Yet, hadn't there been, at the time, a touch of actual magic to the very fabric of the whole place? And what could possibly have been more real than those ATS girls? Eddie, of course, most particularly! (Here, my mental sigh must have led to the twin cul-de-sacs of 'what-might-have been?', and 'what-should-have-been?' – uncomfortable recriminations very probably truncated only by a jolting of the carriage and the wide-awake return of the *current* version of reality.)

The order in which the rest of them popped in and out of my thoughts is by now the stuff of fantasy. But there is one thing of which I am absolutely sure. No-one could possibly have been AWOL from that impromptu inspection parade, even though, reassembled (here in my imagination) all of half a century later, it is obviously a much more systematic affair than before.

Mick Gilgallon strides up, as sturdily straight-shouldered and forthright as ever he was. He gazes (glass eye and all) at me –

unblinkingly and unwaveringly, and with that hypnotic Cheshire-cat grin of his still for putting me at my ease. On the other hand, Dick Watson, slightly late for the proceedings, lopes loose-jointedly into view, his smile, even more expansive than Mick's, diffusing into me his friendly aura of worldly-wise experience, just as before. The contrasting duo of Hubert Smith and Reg Kemish arrive with their continuing oppositions to the Army's normal requirement of 'stripes' to bellow and bawl; the first epitomising quiet, calm, civilised efficiency, and the other civilian culture even more untypical – fussily and artistically precise, the man who had been my first window on the world of London's musical life-forms. And then, of course, rushing in as a contradiction to all the rest of them, this lean dynamo of a 'two-striper'; none other than Arthur Pratt, the most voluble of them all, accompanied by his machine-gun, Birmingham translation of fast English patter. Possessed of what I have since found the rarest of treasures, enthusiasm so profuse as to overflow with advantage on to others. (Though may I flatter myself that my own may have overflowed on to him?)

As well as all these, there was one individual whom I had continued to remember in everything but name. That spare, studious, all-powerful yet benevolent dictator of an SQMS; the one who had operated as the 'director of postings' at The Grange. Could it be that he might eventually have been caught up in his own net? One of the final replacements for overseas, maybe, when 'reservoir' stocks were running dry? Come to that, where had some, or all, of the others finished up? (Only of Mick's discharge, after all, had I any knowledge.) Perhaps a few of them had even been destined for Normandy and the rest of it, like me? Useless to ask the question, of course. I think I knew, in my heart of hearts, that I would never see any of them again.

And, eventually, there was the clanking, the grating, the shuddering, and the hissing clouds of steam of our arrival at South Shields, to put all such nostalgia irrevocably into a history of the past. And to usher in both my present and my future.

Stepping down tentatively on to the concrete of the platform, I could so easily have been treading 'no-man's-land'. The deaths of my parents had turned into inevitabilities of the far past; my immediate family (the sense of whose unseen, background cohesion had sustained me throughout) was now fragmented; and, since I had left no friends behind me, back in 1942, there could be no reacquaintanceships of that sort for me to make. Yet, strangely, illogically, there was already the instinct in me to avoid any renewable close family ties. Self-interest – was it the hollow feeling in my stomach of a possible nothingness to which I was returning? – made me desperate for a really strong, initial finger-grip on this renewal of my civilian existence. The emphasis had to be on me. These stripes on my arms might soon be obsolete decorations, but demoting myself from them to just the subsidiary part again of the whole family was unthinkable.

Not that I needed to have worried. As I now took for granted, there was no-one to greet me at the station; but that sister of mine – bless her memory! – was nevertheless in wait for me at her newly acquired, self-contained flat; with a bed, more comfortable than any of the fattest-filled of straw palliasses in the world, freely on offer for as long as ever I might want it. At one time or another, Hilda had served as my sole link with the life back home; her letters proving very reasonable substitutes for those the others were receiving, no doubt from their wife or sweetheart or parents. And this, I suppose, was her effort at a final, more realistic paragraph; to serve as an essential 'kick-start' to the new, Immediate Present of my transition. A message almost as welcome as those first 'words from home' arriving for me in the days of Normandy. Very willingly did I accept, albeit on the honest basis of a short-term lease. It was a happy re-beginning of things for me.

As for that unending, rolling mystique of the Future which lay ahead, amongst its early unwritten chapters and out of proper context altogether, there was awaiting me the happy ending which rightly belongs to *this* book. After all my gypsy-like meanderings around such a large slice of Europe, I was soon to find that my destined girl-of-all-girls, Hilary, had been living all the while only 'up the road', you might say, at nearby Sunderland. And, having been happily married to her for so many years, now, as to make their number quite unbelievable, the strict conclusion of this section of my case-history seems almost as much so, when I constantly have to re-convince myself that she was not already part of my life, even then! But – all was to be well that ended well!

And, you may wonder, where did all those stripes of mine finish up – the Sergeant's, as well as the long-service ones? The answer is quite straightforward: they hang still, cleanly and primly clinging to my final battledress, in the main wardrobe of our house. The two 'Desert Rats', one to each sleeve, are safely (if, perhaps, unnaturally) cosseted in there, too. Mementos of that often horrendous era which I managed to survive. My own little private cenotaph to the past . . .